Essentials

616.8 HEB

of **Psychological Assessment** Series

Everything you need to know to administer, score, and interpret the major psychological tests.

I'd like to c

- ❏ WAIS®-IV
- ❏ WJ III™ C
- ❏ Cross-Bat
  (w/CD-R(
- ❏ Nonverba
- ❏ PAI® Asse
- ❏ CAS Asse
- ❏ MMPI-2™
- ❏ Myers-Bri
  978-0-470
- ❏ Rorschach
- ❏ Millon™ I
- ❏ TAT and (
- ❏ MMPI-A™
- ❏ NEPSY® /
- ❏ Neuropsy
- ❏ WJ III™ T
- ❏ Evidence-
- ❏ WRAML2
- ❏ WMS®-III
- ❏ Behaviora
- ❏ Forensic F
- ❏ Bayley Sca
- ❏ Career Int
- ❏ WPPSI™-I
- ❏ 16PF® Ass
- ❏ Assessme:
- ❏ Stanford-B
- ❏ WISC®-IV
  978-0-470
- ❏ KABC-II /
- ❏ WIAT®-II
- ❏ Processing
- ❏ School Ne
- ❏ Cognitive
  & Other F
- ❏ Assessme:
- ❏ Creativity
- ❏ WNV™ As
- ❏ DAS-II® As
- ❏ Executive I
- ❏ Conners Ra

Please complete the order form on the back.
To order by phone, call toll free 1-877-762-2974
To order online: www.wiley.com/essentials
To order by mail: refer to order form on next page

Essentials

of **Psychological Assessment** Series

ORDER FORM

Please send this order form with your payment (credit card or check) to:
John Wiley & Sons, Attn: J. Knott, 111 River Street, Hoboken, NJ 07030-5774

QUANTITY	TITLE	ISBN	PRICE

Shipping Charges:	Surface	2-Day	1-Day
First item	$5.00	$10.50	$17.50
Each additional item	$3.00	$3.00	$4.00

For orders greater than 15 items,
please contact Customer Care at 1-877-762-2974.

ORDER AMOUNT _____

SHIPPING CHARGES _____

SALES TAX _____

TOTAL ENCLOSED _____

NAME_____

AFFILIATION_____

ADDRESS_____

CITY/STATE/ZIP _____

TELEPHONE _____

EMAIL_____

❑ Please add me to your e-mailing list

PAYMENT METHOD:

❑ Check/Money Order ❑ Visa ❑ Mastercard ❑ AmEx

Card Number _____Exp. Date_____

Cardholder Name (Please print) _____

Signature _____

Make checks payable to **John Wiley & Sons.** Credit card orders invalid if not signed.
All orders subject to credit approval. • Prices subject to change.

To order by phone, call toll free 1-877-762-2974
To order online: www.wiley.com/essentials

WILEY

Essentials of
Neuropsychological Assessment
Second Edition

Essentials of Psychological Assessment Series

Series Editors, Alan S. Kaufman and Nadeen L. Kaufman

Essentials

of Neuropsychological
Assessment

Second Edition

Nancy Hebben

William Milberg

John Wiley & Sons, Inc.

Library of Congress Cataloging-in-Publication Data:
Hebben, Nancy.
  Essentials of neuropsychological assessment / Nancy Hebben and William Milberg. – 2nd ed.
      p.   cm. – (Essentials of psychological assessment series)
  Includes bibliographical references and index.
  ISBN 978-0-470-43747-6 (pbk.)
  1. Neuropsychological tests.   2. Neuropsychological tests–Evaluation.   3. Clinical neuropsychology. I. Milberg, William. II. Title.
  RC386.6.N48H43   2010
  616.8'0475—dc22
                                                                                2009013354

Printed in the United States of America

10   9   8   7   6   5   4   3   2   1

To our parents, who gave us so much;
To our children, Jan and Aron, who always surprise us;
And in loving memory of Elizabeth Hebben, who left us too soon.

Contents

Series Preface

In the *Essentials of Psychological Assessment* series, we have attempted to provide the reader with books that will deliver key practical information in the most efficient and accessible style. The series features instruments in a variety of domains, such as cognition, personality, education, and neuropsychology. For the experienced clinician, books in the series offer a concise, yet thorough way to master utilization of the continuously evolving supply of new and revised instruments, as well as a convenient method for keeping up to date on the tried-and-true measures. The novice will find here a prioritized assembly of all the information and techniques that must be at one's fingertips to begin the complicated process of individual psychological diagnosis.

Wherever feasible, visual shortcuts to highlight key points are utilized alongside systematic, step-by-step guidelines. Chapters are focused and succinct. Topics are targeted for an easy understanding of the essentials of administration, scoring, interpretation, and clinical application. Theory and research are continually woven into the fabric of each book, but always to enhance clinical inference, never to sidetrack or overwhelm. We have long been advocates of "intelligent" testing—the notion that a profile of test scores is meaningless unless it is brought to life by the clinical observations and astute detective work of knowledgeable examiners. Test profiles must be used to make a difference in the child's or adult's life, or why bother to test? We want this series to help our readers become the best intelligent testers they can be.

In this updated and expanded second edition of the *Essentials of Neuropsychological Assessment*, the authors have presented an overview of the assumptions, logic, knowledge base, and skills underlying the practice of neuropsychological assessment. This edition explores the rapidly changing technologies and concepts affecting the development and validation of neuropsychological test instruments, and includes expanded coverage of a number of newly available measures that are becoming popular in clinical practice. This book describes how clinical history, behavioral observations, and formal test results are used to make inferences about the contribution of normal and pathological brain functioning to psychological functioning. This volume also discusses how to report this information in a manner that will be useful to referring professionals and clients. Practical and conceptual issues related to neuropsychological assessment in geriatric, pediatric, forensic, and other specialized settings are reviewed, with practical advice offered for each. In each chapter the reader is given additional sources of information that can be used to deepen knowledge of these areas. The reader is also provided with a discussion of the professional development and training of clinical neuropsychologists as well as extensive information about resources for test materials, journals, and textbooks in the area. This book will be a welcome addition to the reading list of any graduate-level course in neuropsychological assessment as well as the bookshelves of practitioners looking for practical information on the procedures and logic of one of the fastest growing specialties in clinical psychology.

Alan S. Kaufman, PhD, and Nadeen L. Kaufman, EdD, Series Editors
Yale University School of Medicine

One

INTRODUCTION TO NEUROPSYCHOLOGICAL ASSESSMENT

OVERVIEW

From the perspective of contemporary psychology's identity as both a biological/neurobiological and social science, it may be hard to imagine that it was only in the 1970s that clinical neuropsychology began its emergence as a clearly defined discipline in private practice and medical settings. Although many of the techniques and concepts that form the basis of modern practice of neuropsychological assessment were established between the World Wars, it is probably not coincidental that clinical neuropsychology saw its emergence as a coherent discipline in parallel with the cognitive revolution in psychology (i.e., the change in focus from behaviorism to cognitivism) and the explosion of the technology of neuroimaging, both of which began in the mid-1970s. In the few decades since that critical period, clinical neuropsychology has matured into a discipline with a number of subspecialties that include pediatrics, geriatrics, rehabilitation, education, and forensics. Its further growth and professional development is supported by a rich network of university-based graduate programs and clinical sites providing pre- and postdoctoral training, boards offering advanced clinical certification, and the increasingly neuroscientific emphasis of basic research in academic psychology. To comprehend the remarkable rate of growth in this field, one needs only to read the foreword of the first general textbook on clinical neuropsychology (Reitan & Davison, 1974). Even in 1974, Reitan and Davison heralded the "large growth in substantive knowledge" in neuropsychology and neurosciences preceding the landmark event of the first American Psychological Association (APA) Symposium on Clinical Neuropsychology in 1970. Their text introduced the power of empirically based approaches to neuropsychological assessment to what was probably the first large postwar wave of clinicians who identified themselves as specialists in neuropsychology. It today seems to be a gentle irony that at the time of that writing, fewer than six journals focused on clinical or experimental neuropsychology and the related medical discipline of behavioral neurology. Now, nearly 40 years later, more than 100 journals deal with the brain or brain–behavior relationships, and there exist literally hundreds of texts and monographs to support university courses in both clinical and experimental neuropsychology and to summarize research findings for clinical and academic professionals.

HISTORY OF CLINICAL NEUROPSYCHOLOGY

In the early 1970s the professional identity of a neuropsychological specialty was just emerging. In 1967 the International Neuropsychological Society (INS) began its evolution from a few disparate, informal, and geographically scattered groups of psychologists interested in the relationship between brain and behavior into the first scholarly–professional society explicitly dedicated to neuropsychology. By 1973, around the time of the publication of Reitan and Davison's textbook, approximately 350 members of INS represented the United States, Canada, Great Britain, Norway, and a number of other nations. In 2002 INS, the principal scientific society of neuropsychology, had more than 3,000 members (Rourke & Murji, 2000), and by February 2008 INS boasted approximately 4,950 members.

In 1975 a group of clinically oriented neuropsychologists organized the National Academy of Neuropsychology (NAN), largely to help clinicians keep up with the growing number of techniques and findings directly related to clinical practice. As of January 1, 2009, NAN had 3,657 active members from 24 countries (T. Brooks, e-mail communication, January 5, 2009).

By 1980 neuropsychology had become sufficiently established as a specialized area of interest to organize its own division of the American Psychological Association (Division 40), and in 1996 APA officially recognized neuropsychology as a specialty area. Division 40 (Clinical Neuropsychology) consists of a wide variety of psychologists involved in both clinical practice and research and serves to represent neuropsychology within the larger association of psychologists in the United States. Division 40 had approximately 433 members in its charter year and as of this writing has 4,464 members. Although some clinicians are members of more than one group, memberships in INS, NAN, and Division 40 do not completely overlap. As a definitive sign of the establishment of neuropsychology as a recognized clinical specialty, the American Board of Clinical Neuropsychology (ABCN; Meier, 1998) was formed in 1981 and began to offer diplomate status in clinical neuropsychology in 1983, after coming under the auspices of the American Board of Professional Psychology (ABPP). In 1996 the American Academy of Clinical Neuropsychology (AACN) was founded with a principal mission of promoting excellence in clinical neuropsychology. This organization is for psychologists who have achieved board certification from ABCN (see Yeates & Bieliauskas, 2004, for a review of milestones for ABCN and AACN). As of May 2009, 701 clinical neuropsychologists in the United States, Canada, and Mexico held this board certification, signaling advanced practice competence (Greg Lamberty, e-mail communication, May 13, 2009). Clinical neuropsychology remains the second largest board-certified specialty within ABPP with nearly half as many specialists as clinical psychology. In 1982 the American Board of Professional Neuropsychology (ABN) was also established to award board certification for competence in clinical neuropsychology. As of January 2009, ABN had 230 orally examined diplomates with 17 new diplomates since January 2008 (M. Raymond, e-mail communication, January 21, 2009). Rapid Reference 1.1 provides a brief chronology of the development of clinical neuropsychology as a separate discipline.

Perhaps the emergence of clinical neuropsychology was inevitable, given the increasing centrality of biology and medicine in science itself and what has become an almost universal interest in the problems of neurobiology in such diverse scientific disciplines as physics (e.g., Penrose, 1997) and philosophy (e.g., Churchland, 1989). It is safe to say that a discipline considered only 35 or so years ago as esoteric and arcane as alchemy by many psychologists and physicians is now an established and respected part of the assessment, treatment planning, and

≡ *Rapid Reference 1.1*

Major Historical Events

- 1967 International Neuropsychological Society formed
- 1970 First American Psychological Association (APA) Symposium on Clinical Neuropsychology
- 1975 National Academy of Neuropsychology formed
- 1980 Division 40 (Clinical Neuropsychology) of APA created
- 1981 American Board of Clinical Neuropsychology formed
- 1982 American Board of Professional Neuropsychology formed
- 1983 ABCN offers diplomate status under ABPP
- 1996 APA recognizes clinical neuropsychology as a specialty area
- 1996 American Academy of Clinical Neuropsychology founded
- 1997 Houston Conference on Specialty Education and Training in Clinical Neuropsychology convened

rehabilitation of children and adults with histories of psychiatric, neurological, or developmental problems, or a combination of these.

Definition of Clinical Neuropsychology

Neuropsychology is usually broadly defined as the study of brain–behavior relationships. Of course, this definition does not capture the multiplicity of questions and approaches that have been used to explore how the central nervous system represents, organizes, and generates the infinite range of human capabilities and actions. Modern neuropsychology includes the study of the classic problems of psychology—attention, learning, perception, cognition, personality, and psychopathology—using techniques that include the methods of experimental psychology as well as the methodologies of test construction and psychometrics. Its scientific palate includes such state-of-the-art technologies as high-resolution structural and functional neuroimaging and other techniques such as computational modeling, and it is beginning to be integrated with genomics and other advanced biological technologies such as proteomics and metabalomics. This book presents some of the core concepts of the particular discipline of clinical neuropsychological assessment. According to a consortium of representatives of a number of professional neuropsychological organizations that convened in 1997 in Houston, Texas, clinical neuropsychology can be defined as "the application of assessment and intervention principles based on the scientific study of human behavior across the lifespan as it relates to normal and abnormal functioning of the central nervous system" (Hannay et al., 1998, p. 161). In practice, this translates into using standardized psychological tests, which are usually designed to assess various aspects of human cognition, ability, or skill, to provide information to a variety of clinical questions about the central nervous system and behavior. Less often, tests of personality or affective behavior have been adapted as neuropsychological instruments.

In practice, the question of "normal versus abnormal functioning of the central nervous system" (Hannay et al., 1998, p. 161) is posed in an extremely broad range of clinical situations that includes not only the assessment of the consequences of diseases and physical damage to the central nervous system, but also the consequences of psychiatric conditions in which central nervous system involvement is assumed but not well defined. In some cases, the central nervous system function in question may be abnormal because of a neurochemical rather than a structural abnormality, as might be the case in some metabolic disorders, or because of the presence of a prescription or street pharmacological agent. Neuropsychological assessment is also increasingly being used to assess variations in early development

DON'T FORGET

....

Neuropsychology is the study of brain–behavior relationships. Clinical neuropsychology is "the application of assessment and intervention principles based on the scientific study of human behavior across the lifespan as it relates to normal and abnormal functioning of the central nervous system" (Hannay et al., 1998, p. 161).

that may be a reflection of variations in the rate of normal maturational processes rather than definable pathology (at least currently). The latter has become so common as a source of clinical referrals for neuropsychological assessment that a new subspecialty known as educational or school neuropsychology has emerged and is becoming an increasingly important part of the role of school-based practitioners of psychology. To capture the breadth of these clinical questions, we use the term *brain dysfunction* in this book to represent the diverse conditions in which measurable variations in psychological abilities are assumed to be causally related to the operations of the central nervous system. This term is in itself somewhat narrow, because it is probably most accurate to construe neuropsychological test performance to be a reflection of brain "function" and not just the state of abnormality that is the focus of clinical referrals.

Historically, the tests used by neuropsychologists were usually not developed for the purpose of assessing brain dysfunction, and in many cases, they reflect clinical assessment traditions more than basic research in cognition or neuroscience. For example, the Wechsler Adult Intelligence Scale (WAIS; Wechsler, 1955) and its successors were developed as tests of intelligence, primarily to aid in the identification of mental retardation and to facilitate academic, military, or vocational assessment (Kaufman & Lichtenberger, 1999; Matarazzo, 1972). The Seashore Rhythm Test, a traditional component of the Halstead–Reitan Neuropsychological Test Battery (HRB), was part of a test of musical aptitude (Saetveit, Lewis, & Seashore, 1940). What all tests used by neuropsychologists have in common (or should have in common) is known reliability and validity as predictors of the presence of brain dysfunction. Minimum requirements for neuropsychological tests are sensitivity to the presence of brain dysfunction and the ability to distinguish correctly the presence of abnormal brain function from normal brain functioning. Over the years, these basic criteria for neuropsychological tests have grown to include the ability to predict the site and severity of brain dysfunction and, in some cases, the more controversial ability to predict the specific cause or etiology of that dysfunction. During the inception of the first formally validated neuropsychological tests, the sensitivity of neuropsychological instruments was gauged by their agreement with the clinical judgments of neurologists (Reitan &

Davison, 1974). As neuroimaging and other technologies have advanced, so has the expectation that neuropsychological tests will be sensitive to changes observable with increasingly sensitive and detailed views of brain structure and physiology. Today, it is not uncommon to see neuropsychological instruments used to detect the presence of brain dysfunction in both research and clinical settings. As we discuss in Chapter 5, this is a controversial development from which many practitioners distance themselves. Its existence, however, is a reflection of the respect these instruments have gained.

Some clinicians advocate using a fixed battery of tests to anchor and compare observations across different patient populations, whereas other clinicians advocate using a flexible battery of tests that are dictated by the specific referral question or unique presentation of the patient. Clinical neuropsychological assessment may employ clinical interview and behavioral observation techniques that have not necessarily been subject to the usual methodological standards of test construction but are usually considered indispensable in providing rich descriptions of a patient's behavior. In clinical settings, many neuropsychologists employ unique variations on standardized tests or procedures developed on the fly in an attempt to capture qualitative features specific to the patient in question. The advantages and disadvantages of these approaches are discussed later in this chapter.

Uses of Neuropsychological Assessment

One can identify at least seven different but related purposes or uses of neuropsychological assessment. These categories are derived from what are probably the most common clinical referral questions presented to neuropsychologists, as well as from the information presented in many neuropsychological reports. These categories of use can arise in a number of contexts, including medicine, law, education, and research. These categories are presented here in the order reflecting the logic in which clinical inferences are typically made.

1. *Describing strengths and weaknesses and identifying changes and disturbances in psychological functioning (cognition, behavior, emotion) in terms of presence/absence and severity.* Although the raison d'être of clinical neuropsychology may appear to be to predict the presence of brain dysfunction, the ability to describe function is far more important than this seemingly core purpose of neuropsychological tests. Neuropsychologists are usually expected to provide a description of a patient or client by identifying cognitive strengths and weaknesses and then by making the basic inference of whether the patient's current status represents a change

from some previous, usually not precisely defined, baseline or premorbid level of functioning and whether or not any changes rise to the level of dysfunction. Neuropsychological assessment may also be used to infer the presence of congenital or developmental abnormalities that are neuropathologically determined. When children are evaluated and there is little basis to estimate premorbid abilities, clinicians may attempt to infer change from expected developmental milestones and family background. The issues of strengths and weaknesses and the presence or absence of change and abnormality are addressed before any other inferences regarding brain function or recommendations for interventions may be considered. The neuropsychologist must try to infer what part of the current observations reflects the patient's "normal" allocation of intellectual functions versus what parts of the current observations show changes attributable to brain dysfunction. Accurate description and reference to correct normative standards for the individual are the most basic and critical purposes of neuropsychological assessment, and all determinations must be made in the context of the patient's history.

2. *Determining the biological (i.e., neuroanatomical, physiological) correlates of test results: detection, gradation, and localization of brain dysfunction.* After they have described the patient's behavior, neuropsychologists typically try to determine whether the pattern of test results, clinical behavior, and particular historical context of the observations can be attributed to abnormal brain function. Such abnormalities may be the presence of a structural brain lesion, a developmental disorder, or, in some cases, neurochemical lesion. Part of this determination is trying to ascertain which region of the brain is involved. In this era of increasingly sensitive noninvasive neuroimaging techniques, the clinical importance of this traditional function of neuropsychological assessment has somewhat diminished and, in some cases, has become almost vestigial. However, the ability to establish specific causal links between areas of the brain and psychological symptoms may take on fresh importance as new biotechnologies emerge for the treatment and rehabilitation of the consequences of brain abnormalities. For example, an understanding of lesion–behavioral relationships is important in determining treatment targets of transcranial magnetic stimulation (Pascal-Leone et al., 2002). As these technologies develop, it is possible that lesion localization will become integral to the process of rehabilitation planning (see Item 5).

3. *Determining whether changes or dysfunction is associated with neurological disease, psychiatric conditions, developmental disorders, or nonneurological conditions.* The next kind of inference that clinical neuropsychologists often try to make or are asked to make concerns the likely etiology or etiologies that produced the changes or dysfunction described. In the case of neurological disorder and known history, this can sometimes be done accurately. This is particularly true in cases in which the behavioral changes involve unusual and dramatic phenomena that have historically been related to the presence of lesions in specific parts of the brain and are usually caused by a highly limited set of etiologies. For example, nonfluent aphasia symptoms (e.g., hesitant, agrammatic speech) are most likely related to a limited set of diseases that, if present by history, can be considered causative of the observed changes in language. Many changes or apparent abnormalities in neuropsychological functions, however, may be caused by psychiatric, motivational, developmental, or cultural factors and may not be attributable to a specific neurological etiology even when present by history. Often, neuropsychological test findings are nonspecific to etiology and may be related to a host of factors, such as depression, anxiety, sleep deprivation, or even chronic pain. In these instances, the neuropsychologist must work as an investigator to review the test findings thoroughly in the context of the patient's history.

4. *Assessing changes over time and developing a prognosis.* One of the most useful applications of neuropsychological assessment is to track improvements and decrements in performance over time. This helps to determine the etiology and progression of a disease, to develop social or financial plans for a patient, and to track whether treatment or efforts toward rehabilitation are effective.

5. *Offering guidelines for rehabilitation, vocational, or educational planning, or a combination of these.* The ability to provide inferences regarding etiology and descriptive power has made neuropsychological assessment a popular tool in rehabilitation and educational planning. Therapists and teachers can often use a patient's profile of strengths and weaknesses and the manner in which they go about tasks to develop and optimize rehabilitation and educational programs. Knowledge of which problems or weaknesses are attributable to brain dysfunction and which are likely the result of nonneurological sources can help a therapist allocate time and resources toward the treatment priorities that are most likely to be effective.

6. *Providing guidelines and education for family and caregivers.* In a similar vein, neuropsychological data can help families and caregivers to understand the strengths and weaknesses of their loved ones and to cope with patients who may suffer from challenging limitations on independent functioning. Beleaguered family members are less likely to be angry with a patient's behavior when they understand that symptoms that appear to be related to motivation or personality are actually causally related to a disease state. An understanding of the prognosis of the illness can also be invaluable to families who must plan their use of finances and future care.

7. *Planning for discharge and treatment implementation.* Neuropsychological deficits can sometimes be insidious and difficult to describe, even for sophisticated clinicians. An understanding of a patient's capabilities can help the clinician assess the degree to which a patient is going to comply with treatment recommendations and medication use, as well as the extent to which the patient or the patient's family may need continued supervision after discharge.

Rapid Reference 1.2 provides a quick summary of the uses of neuropsychological assessment.

In the ensuing chapters of this book, we review the essential information about neuropsychological assessment techniques that clinicians need to help in the description, diagnosis, and treatment process of patients.

≡ *Rapid Reference 1.2*

Uses of Neuropsychological Assessment

- Describing strengths and weaknesses and identifying changes and dysfunction in psychological functioning
- Determining the biological correlates of test results
- Determining whether changes or dysfunction are associated with neurological disease, psychiatric conditions, developmental disorders, or nonneurological conditions
- Assessing changes over time and developing a prognosis
- Offering guidelines for rehabilitation, vocational, or educational planning
- Providing guidelines and education to family and caregivers
- Planning for discharge and treatment implementation

THEORETICAL AND RESEARCH FOUNDATIONS OF MODERN NEUROPSYCHOLOGICAL ASSESSMENT

Much of clinical psychology has drawn from the psychology of learning and cognition, developmental psychology, social psychology, and psychodynamic traditions for its scientific paradigms and language. Clinical neuropsychology adds to this mixture the paradigms of biology and medicine to grapple with the problems of human psychopathology.

The problems that are the focus of modern clinical neuropsychology have been described for centuries and have captured the imaginations of physicians and philosophers. A detailed history of neuropsychology is not within the focus of this book (see Benton & Adams, 2000; Meier, 1997), but an examination of several modern conceptual and investigative trends is important to help practitioners understand the source of many of the assumptions and practices currently in use.

Holism Versus Localization

Observations of behavioral changes that occur following injuries to the head can be found in the earliest written records of history, including translations of 5,000-year-old Egyptian medical documents (as described in Finger & Stein, 1982). The idea that thoughts, memories, and sensations somehow originate in the brain, however, did not gain wide acceptance until the beginning of the 17th century, although some still believed Aristotle's declarations regarding the heart's role in understanding human behavior and motivation (Finger & Stein, 1982). By the 19th century, there was little contention with the idea that the brain was the center of consciousness, memory, language, feelings, and passions, but there has never been complete agreement on how these basic categories of psychological function are actually accomplished. Although the levels of technology and sophistication have evolved dramatically over the centuries, the conceptualization of how the brain organizes its task as the organ of the mind boils down to two prevailing views that still guide the organization of research, theory, and clinical practice of neuropsychology.

Perhaps the most intuitively appealing and most clearly stated notion is that of a localized correspondence between structure and function. This idea suggests that different psychological functions are subserved by distinct and separate structures in the brain. The idea of localization found its clearest statement in the writings of the French physician and physiologist Franz Joseph Gall in the latter half of the 18th century. Gall (1835) argued that separate organs within the brain controlled such faculties as wisdom, poetic ability, religiousness, language, and memory. This position's appeal lies in its ability to account for the countless observations of variations in symptoms accompanying variations in brain lesions. Since Paul Broca (a dedicated follower of Gall) masterfully documented the association of damage to the left frontal cerebral hemisphere of humans with the loss of the capacity to speak, much of neuropsychological research has attempted to document correspondences between other psychological functions and focal brain lesions.

Much of today's research is guided by the doctrine of localizationism, in which the description and localization of function are a primary goal of neuropsychological assessment. This idea has found its most modern form in the relatively new subdivision of neuropsychology, sometimes called cognitive neuroscience, which uses neuroimaging techniques such as magnetic resonance imaging (MRI) and positron emission tomography (PET) to detect minute changes in blood flow to relatively circumscribed areas of the cerebral cortex. Much of the literature using this technology documents increasingly specific localization of blood-flow changes associated with increasingly specific experimental measures of cognition. The goal of much of this research is to create detailed charts of cognitive localization in the brain. The strongest form of localization theory appears in the work of Jerry Fodor (1983), who introduced the concept of *modularity*. Modularity refers to the idea that localization is a necessary consequence of the distinct processing requirements of the sensory systems and such higher order cognitive functions as language. Fodor argued that the physical requirements of processing information in different sensory modalities mandate distinctly adapted and localized neural mechanisms. He proposed that language, which requires the use of specific, automatically accessed rules, also requires specific and localized neural mechanisms.

Localizationism is not the only conceptualization of how the brain is organized. As Pierre-Marie Flourens (1824), Hughlings Jackson (1894), Kurt Goldstein (1939), and Alexander Luria (1966) argued, the localization or correlation of symptoms or behavior with lesions (or even documented changes in blood flow) does not necessarily prove that the function of that behavior is localized in the observed brain structure. Although these writers acknowledged that lesions might have effects that differ as a function of location, they believed that brain function itself always involved multiple structures working together. This position is often associated with Kurt Goldstein's term for this principle: *holism*. The following example illustrates the central principle of holism: Although a loose screw might be responsible for a malfunction that prevents an automobile engine from starting, it would be erroneous to localize the function of locomotion in the screw itself. A symptom may arise because an important component of a larger network of functions is disrupted or because only the most complicated and susceptible or weak "function" of many functions subserved by the same area is disrupted. Imagine concluding that piano playing (a relatively complex motor skill) was localized in the fingers, but that scratching (a relatively simple motor skill) was not because a sprain disrupted one but not the other. This was essentially Hughlings Jackson's argument regarding Paul Broca's and others' localization of expressive language (a relatively complex cognitive skill) to a specific part of the frontal lobes, when evidence showed that patients with lesions in Broca's area could articulate words in an emotional or even musical context.

In 1929 Karl Lashley published research showing that highly focal ablations of brain tissue had only mild and temporary effects on the recovery of maze learning in rats (Lashley, 1929). As a result, he concluded that the brain followed the principle of mass action and that various brain structures had the potential to take over the same function. His conclusion was a major influence on Ward Halstead's creation of the first psychometrically sound neuropsychological test battery and forms the basis of many of the instruments and standards for test construction used today. For example, the HRB, a widely known and used approach to neuropsychological assessment, is largely based on nonlocalizationist assumptions (Reitan & Wolfson, 1996).

One of the most sophisticated approaches applied to the study of brain–behavior relationships is the development of computer models, constructed out of building blocks that function and interact very much like neurons that imitate cognitive function and dysfunction. There has been remarkable success in making computer models that mimic various aspects of cognition and changes in cognition following brain lesions.

Many of these models do not use the assumptions of modularity or localization of function; instead, they are constructed using assumptions of mass action and equipotentiality (see Anderson, 1995). In the literature of functional neuroimaging, a view is also emerging that most functions should be conceptualized as distributed among neural networks (Damasio, 1995). Some researchers also make arguments against strict localizationism based on the fact that many functions substantially return after brain injury. Such recovery may indicate that other parts of the brain are doing the job of the damaged tissue (Finger & Stein, 1982).

The localizationist view is currently the most popular way of conceptualizing the results of neuropsychological tests. It is common to make the inference that a change in test performance (or pattern in performance across tests) is an indication that some function (presumably measured by the impaired test performance) is localized in a specific region of the brain. Even the HRB has been adapted to this tradition. However, the clinician should be cautioned (or at least aware) that such direct inferences might be simplistic and inaccurate. Test performance is not necessarily an indication that a function is localized in a specific part of the brain. Moreover, predictions that may be accurate in one context (e.g., during the acute phase of a lesion) may not be accurate in another (e.g., several years after a lesion occurs, in children, or even in older adults). As Luria, Damasio, Finger, and Stein have argued, neuropsychological test performance and symptoms may reflect the disruption of an organized, distributed network of structures that participate in the function in question. The symptoms of brain dysfunction may reflect the disruption of a system rather than a single localized function in a specific circum-scribed part of the brain.

Empiricism Versus Cognitivism in Test Construction

Much of the variation in today's approaches to neuropsychological assessment is layered on the foundation of two issues: how behavior should be conceptualized (empiricism or functionalism) and how brain organization should be conceptual-ized (cognitivism).

Most of the neuropsychological assessment techniques used currently are derived from the psychological–philosophical tradition of empiricism/ functionalism. This means that tests are constructed using the ideas that predic-tion of performance is primary and that test content and psychological meaning are secondary. In contrast, tests from the cognitive tradition are constructed pri-marily to measure specific psychological, usually intellectual or perceptual func-tions; clinical prediction is a secondary or derived goal. A detailed discussion of these issues would be too digressive for this text, but neuropsychologists should have some general understanding of the basic interpretative and methodologi-cal assumptions that organize contemporary approaches to neuropsychological assessment.

Where do all the tests and measures that are used by neuropsychologists come from? A fair discussion of this seemingly simple question could easily consume this volume and would likely lead to a full-fledged barroom brawl if presented to more than two neuropsychologists at a time. It is raised here just to make the point that clinical neuropsychology derives its techniques in much the same way as do other clinical disciplines. In many cases, tests are used because they work or were thought to work based on previous observations. The term *empiricism,* the idea that knowledge is derived from direct experience, refers to this approach to creating tests. The empirical (or *functional*) approach is perhaps the most easily defended and the one most identified with the nonlocalizationist approach to neuropsychology. Ward Halstead and his most famous student, Ralph Reitan, adopt (sometimes implicitly) the view that much of the brain follows the principle of mass action; thus, the primary consideration in selecting neuropsychological instruments is their observed sensitivity in detecting brain impairment. After a set of optimal measures is derived, they are used to test a variety of populations; in many cases, the primary goal is the detection of changes associated with brain pathology or dysfunction.

This process represented the primary trend in American neuropsychology well into the 1970s. Today, because localizationism has become the mainstream view of brain function, many of the tests that come from the Halstead–Reitan tradition are used to predict or detect the presence of focal lesions. In most of these cases, empiricism nevertheless rules: The tests themselves (and how they are derived or created) are not as important as their ability to predict the presence of brain dysfunction or their empirically demonstrated validity.

Independently constructed theories of cognitive function or dysfunction, which include sensitivity to brain dysfunction as an important but secondary consideration, provide another source of neuropsychological tests. Many modern tests were created in this way. For example, the Boston Diagnostic Aphasia Exam (Goodglass & Kaplan, 1983) and the California Verbal Learning Test (Delis, Kramer, Kaplan, & Ober, 1987) were created primarily using prevailing theories of language and memory, respectively, and in both cases were created to measure specific aspects of function known to be affected by brain dysfunction. In these cases, the tests' construct validity or theoretical interpretation was as important as their sensitivity to the presence of brain dysfunction. Literature documenting the sensitivity of the tests' tasks to the presence of brain lesions came primarily after their creation. In both cases, the assumption was made (either explicitly or implicitly) that the psychological functions measured were cognitive domains that could be affected independently by brain dysfunction. Further, it was assumed that the functions associated with these tests could be localized.

An understanding of these historical distinctions is helpful in understanding the strengths and weaknesses of neuropsychological tests. Some tests are excellent detectors of brain dysfunction but may be difficult to use as tools for describing abilities or as sources of real-life recommendations. Other tests do not demonstrate sensitivity to brain dysfunction as clearly but may provide clear, descriptive measures of a psychological domain; these measures can then be used to make recommendations for rehabilitation or treatment planning. Ideally, tests should be sensitive to the presence of brain dysfunction and theoretically coherent while also being functionally descriptive and ecologically valid (Sbordone,

1996; Sbordone & Guilmette, 1999; Sbordone, Saul, & Purisch, 2007); however, because of their historical origins, in practice many tests are compromised or limited to one of these two goals.

Ecological Validity: Representiveness, Generalizability, and the Future of Neuropsychological Test Development

Burgess and colleagues (2006) provide an incisive analysis of the consequences of neuropsychology's history of adaptation of assessment instruments from what they term *conceptual and experimental frameworks far removed from those currently in favor.* Using the example of tests of executive function, they argue that neuropsychological tests that focus on constructs that denote basic cognitive functions and that happen to be sensitive to the presence of brain dysfunction are not necessarily informative of how patients will perform in actual situations. They argue that the majority of assessment instruments currently in use by neuropsychologists were developed without regard for how well they predict "observable" adaptive behavior. Adapting concepts from Brunswick's (1956) classic treatise on the development of experimental procedures to test perceptual processes, Burgess et al. (2006) suggest the next generation of neuropsychological assessment instruments should be developed to be both "representative" of actual real-world "functions" and be "generalizable" or predictive of the performance of those functions across a range of situations. Although these criteria could be applied to any domain assessed by neuropsychological instruments, including intelligence and memory tests, Burgess et al.'s (2006) discussion focuses on tests of "executive functions" (examples of which are presented in Chapter 4 of this volume). They point out that the Wisconsin Card Sort Test (WCST), one of the most widely used measures of executive function, was not originally developed as a neuropsychological measure and was preceded by a number of sorting-based measures that were in fact developed around observations of the effects of brain damage (e.g., Weigl, 1927). The WCST, however, became an almost instant benchmark of "frontal lobe function" based on a single study of Brenda Milner (1963), who showed that patients with dorsolateral frontal lobe lesions had greater difficulty with it than patients with orbitofrontal or nonfrontal lesions. Although the WCST may involve "set shifting" and "working memory," data that would allow a clinician to "really know what situations in everyday life require the abilities that the WCST measures" (Burgess et al., 2006) are virtually nonexistent. They advise the next generation of neuropsychological tests should be "function led" rather than purely "construct led." These tests should meet the usual standards of reliability, but validity should be defined by both sensitivity to brain dysfunction and generalizability to real-world function.

THE MAJOR NEUROPSYCHOLOGICAL ASSESSMENT APPROACHES: THEIR HISTORY, DEVELOPMENT, STRENGTHS, AND WEAKNESSES

In this section we briefly review the background of the major testing approaches used in contemporary neuropsychology practice. Rapid Reference 1.3 provides publication information for the HRB, the Luria–Nebraska Neuropsychological Battery (LNNB), and the Boston Process Approach (BPA).

Halstead–Reitan Neuropsychological Test Battery

The discipline of using psychological tests to assess systematically the effects of brain dysfunction originated in the midwestern United States in the late 1930s and early 1940s. In the years between the two World Wars, clinical neurologists in Great Britain (e.g., Hughlings Jackson and the appropriately named Henry Head and W. R. Brain) and Europe (e.g., Constantin von Monakow, Kurt Goldstein, and Rezsö Balint) had already created an extensive history of the effects of brain damage on language, attention, vision, and personality. Ward Halstead, however,

≡ Rapid Reference 1.3

Publication Information for the Three Major Approaches to Neuropsychological Assessment

HRB

Reitan, R. M., & Wolfson, D. (1993). *The Halstead–Reitan Neuropsychological Test Battery: Theory and clinical interpretation*. Tucson, AZ: Neuropsychology Press.

LNNB

Golden, C. J., Purisch, A. D., & Hammeke, T. A. (1985). *Manual for the Luria–Nebraska Neuropsychological Battery: Forms I and II*. Los Angeles: Western Psychological Services.

BPA

Kaplan, E. (1988). A process approach to neuropsychological assessment. In T. Boll & B. K. Bryant (Eds.), *Clinical neuropsychology and brain function: Research, measurement and practice* (pp. 125–167). Washington, DC: American Psychological Association.

worked in relative isolation from these observations and developments. Although his ideas were influenced by Karl Lashley's concepts of mass action and equipotentiality, Halstead started with a relatively blank slate, putting together after much trial and error a battery of psychological tests that, taken together, could be used by clinical neurologists and neurosurgeons to distinguish patients considered to have brain dysfunction from patients with no known history of brain abnormality. After trying and rejecting hundreds of tests that did not perform the basic job of discriminating normal adults from adults with brain dysfunction, he put together a battery of tests originally developed for a variety of purposes. For example, his battery included the Seguin–Goddard Form Board, a test that originated in the mid-19th century as a measure of so-called feeble-mindedness (Seguin, 1907), the Seashore Rhythm Test from the Seashore Test of Musical Aptitude (Saetveit, Lewis, & Seashore, 1940), and modifications of other tests (e.g., Boston University Speech Sound Perception Test) as well as tests that he originated, such as the Finger Oscillation or Finger Tapping Test (Halstead, 1947), and the most original, the Category Test (Halstead, 1947). From these tests, he constructed an index of impairment that could be used to predict the presence of brain dysfunction. In the early 1950s, his former graduate student, Ralph Reitan, continuing in this perfect example of the empiricist tradition, modified and systematized Halstead's original battery to include observations of left- versus right-sided motor performance, a sensory-perceptual examination, and an aphasia screening examination (Reitan, 1955). He also developed a set of test norms for the battery after administering the battery to patients with known focal and diffuse brain dysfunction and to a group of normal control subjects. In addition, he developed indexes of brain impairment, permitting localization and inferred causality. The resulting fixed battery of tests, widely known as the Halstead–Reitan Neuropsychological Test Battery or the Halstead-Reitan Battery (HRB), stimulated a remarkable body of research as Halstead's original methods were applied to different patient populations, such as children and patients with epilepsy psychiatric illness.

The HRB is clearly empiricist with a clearly nonlocalizationist origin. The fixed battery approach pioneered by Halstead and Reitan has the advantage of providing a standard set of measures by which different patients can be compared. After the measures are established, it is easy to extend the scope of the battery to new populations and to collect extensive norms. Although the advantage of stability and comparability is clearly the strength of a fixed battery approach, this particular battery has found itself decreasing in popularity in recent years for a number of reasons. In 2006, a practice survey revealed that only 7% of practitioners used a standardized or fixed battery approach such as the HRB or the LNNB (Sweet et al., 2006). This represents a decline from 18% in 1989. The practical problem with the purely empiricist approach is that it does not necessarily lead to the most efficient or interpretable measures. The HRB is extremely long and tedious for some patients, leading to reports of noncompliance and discomfort, particularly in older and more impaired patients. In today's environment of limited or capped payment of medical expenses, batteries of this size are difficult to justify economically. In addition, it is sometimes difficult to describe what the constituent tests are measuring other than the obvious intuitive characteristics of the tasks. In many cases, the relevance of task performance is difficult to tie to real-life situations.

Although not strictly antilocalizationist, the research tradition of the HRB has allowed for the prediction of focal lesions only as they emerge from the variables available in the battery. This has led to the development of a variety of prediction formulae and decision rules that have been offered to predict the presence of focal lesions. These formulas, which are difficult to interpret, sometimes appear to be random comparisons of tasks (e.g., Parsons, Vega, & Burn, 1969) or do not generalize beyond the populations in which they were validated. In recent years, as more cognitively based approaches have emerged, some psychologists have attempted to relate the tests and findings of the HRB to the cognitive domains of language, memory and other functions (Reitan & Wolfson, 1996), although such tasks as the Aphasia Screening Test and even the venerable Category Test seem anachronistic in view of the evolution of the concepts of language and executive functions these tests were designed to assess. Still, the wealth of referent validating data, the fact that the battery may be administered by a technician, and the convenience of receiving training in this approach have made the HRB a model for other approaches.

Luria–Nebraska Neuropsychological Battery

Alexander R. Luria, a Russian neuropsychologist, was a contemporary of Ward Halstead. Although Luria worked at roughly the same time as Halstead, he took a different approach from his American colleague to the development of techniques for assessing the effects of brain dysfunction. Luria published in the Soviet Union, where scientists felt great pressure to relate research to the Pavlovian concepts of conditioning and inhibition. He and his mentor, Leon Vygotsky, were staunch cognitivists who concerned themselves with the formulation of rich descriptions of the development and structure of human mental functions. Luria's model of brain organization was a direct reflection of the concept that human mental faculties were composed of elementary intellectual building blocks; these components could be used to solve the problems of action and thought in a variety of manners. Cognition was a dynamic process that varied as function of development, the demands of a particular problem situation, and, in the case of Luria's neuropsychology clinics, of the presence of brain dysfunction.

Luria described his approach in some detail in his landmark book, *Higher Cortical Functions,* published in English in 1966. He described hundreds of tasks that could be used in a seemingly infinite array of patterns to characterize the details of the effects of brain dysfunction in each particular case. This approach was acknowledged as brilliant and insightful but was seen as forbiddingly complex and impractical for the average clinician, who would not have the mentorship available to develop the skills needed to apply these methods reliably. In addition, the standard set by the Halstead–Reitan approach made many clinicians suspect that Luria's inherently variable methodology could not be subjected to conventional means of assessing reliability and validity.

Although Luria's conception of brain organization and his approach to the development of cognitive theory were remarkable in that they foreshadowed much of what characterizes modern cognitive neuropsychology and experimental psychology research, his approach to assessment would have remained an exotic curiosity if not for a Danish student, Anne-Lise Christensen, who after apprenticing herself to Luria, introduced to the United States a detailed description of Luria's test techniques, titled "Luria's Neuropsychological Investigation," (Christensen, 1974) that included a set of materials (stimulus cards, photographs, etc.) to which Luria alludes in *Higher Cortical Functions*. Charles Golden, a Nebraska-based neuropsychologist who was an expert in the Halstead–Reitan approach, used these materials along with Thomas Hammeke and Arnold Purisch to develop a new battery of tests. Golden hoped both to take advantage of Luria's knack for developing tasks that seemed to reveal the details of basic brain functions and to retain the rigorous empirical tradition of the Halstead–Reitan Battery.

The publication of the LNNB (Golden, Hammeke, & Purisch, 1978) represented a controversial landmark in the development of neuropsychological test methods. Golden's method, which combines items that can discriminate between subjects with brain dysfunction and normal subjects into scales named after various cognitive or functional domains such as reading and writing, was severely criticized for not representing the concepts advocated by Luria. Luria, for example, described a variety of variations of how a seemingly simple function such as writing can break down depending on the specific underlying brain lesion or system that was disrupted. Luria mentioned basic orthography (the development of letters and words as holistically represented symbols), the association of sound with letter and word, and so forth as potential components of writing that may be affected independently as a reflection of the type and localization of a lesion.

According to Golden's critics, combining the tasks that Luria used to develop a description of variations in a function into a single scale subverts Luria's goal of finding the correct descriptive recipe for every variation in performance. The LNNB has also been criticized for its lack of sensitivity to certain problems such as language. Although the LNNB never gained the popularity of the HRB, it developed a loyal following that appreciated its relative brevity and the increasing base of empirical findings to support its validity as a neuropsychological instrument. Although many psychologists would argue that the LNNB represents a failed attempt to make Luria's methods more accessible and reliable, most would admit that it provides some hope that more efficient, empirically based approaches to assessment can be developed.

Boston Process Approach

While the HRB was establishing itself as the benchmark method for assessing brain dysfunction, a critical mass of investigators in the Boston area had begun to work on the problems of brain–behavior relationships. Researchers and clinicians interested in language, memory, perception, and other classic psychological issues coalesced under the charismatic leadership of Norman Geschwind, one of the great behavioral neurologists of the 20th century, and Harold Goodglass, a clinical psychologist who brought the study of aphasia into the realm of psychology. In Boston, American psychology's then-new focus on cognition had begun to revolutionize studies of the brain. Geschwind and Goodglass came from different disciplines, but both researchers approached the task of studying the brain as a process of analysis and reduction to basic elements. Influenced by German neurology, theoretical linguistics, and cognitive psychology, this work used an experimental approach different from that of the Halstead–Reitan tradition. Davis Howes, Jean Gleason, Edgar Zurif, and Sheila Blumstein joined Dr. Goodglass's efforts to adapt the methods of psychophysics, linguistics, and developmental psychology to revolutionize the study of aphasia. At the same time, Nelson Butters's and Laird Cermak's studies of memory and amnesia helped bring the subject of brain dysfunction to the attention of mainstream experimental psychology.

It was in this atmosphere that Edith Kaplan, a graduate student of developmental psychologist Heinz Werner, came to work. Dr. Kaplan, an assistant to Dr. Goodglass, brought to what was then known as the Boston Veterans Administration Hospital an acute eye for observing patients' behavior and Heinz Werner's lesson that different cognitive processes could be used by different individuals to solve the same problem. Werner taught that cognitive development was characterized by changes in the means by which children solved problems. Encouraged by the sympathies of other clinicians and researchers with whom she worked, Dr. Kaplan applied Werner's ideas to patients who had undergone a newly developed neurosurgical treatment for epilepsy involving the cutting of the corpus callosum, the major neural bridge between the two cerebral hemispheres. She noticed that the patients solved a puzzle construction task called Block Design from the WAIS differently when the task was placed to the right of the patient from when the task was placed to the left of the patient. Over the next 20 years, Kaplan compiled hundreds of such observations, which she imparted to students and other psychologists through supervision and seminars. In 1991 she published a complete modification of the WAIS—Revised (WAIS-R) in the WAIS—Revised Neuropsychological Instrument (WAIS-R NI), reflecting her adaptations and observational recommendations (Kaplan, Fein, Morris, & Delis, 1991). The BPA, as these methods were dubbed in 1986 (Milberg, Hebben, & Kaplan, 2009), has at its core the idea that task performance is more important than the task itself. In practice, although most patients would receive a core battery of tests including the WAIS, the Wechsler Memory Scale, the Rey–Osterrieth Complex Figure, and other tests, Dr. Kaplan would use what would be considered a *flexible battery approach*. This approach adds measures from a long list of tests borrowed from various domains to reflect referral questions and to follow up on the observations made with the initial battery given. At present, 76% of clinical neuropsychologists report using a flexible core battery (i.e., variable core depending on type of patient group) and 18% report using a totally flexible approach (i.e., variable tests depending on the individual case; Sweet et al., 2006).

Initially, the BPA was criticized for not having supporting norms or sufficiently detailed standard methods to assess the psychometric properties of reliability and validity. A growing body of research in the past 20 years, however, supports Kaplan's observations (e.g., Bihrle, Bellugi, Delis, & Marks, 1989; Freedman et al., 1994; Joy, Fein, Kaplan, & Morris, 2001; Wecker, Kramer, Wisniewski, Delis, & Kaplan, 2000). In addition, some researchers have attempted to quantify the BPA (Poreh, 2000, 2006). Nevertheless, the BPA never sparked the explosion of research that the HRB did and still suffers from relatively limited normative information. The WAIS-R NI (Kaplan et al., 1991) was one of the few examples of tests published with some standard information about reliability and standard errors of measurement. Even this landmark test, however, does not provide reliability and validity information for the hundreds of observations that Kaplan and her students used for making clinical inferences. Despite these significant limitations, the approach has gained increasing popularity in recent years because it provides clinicians with much greater descriptive power than either the Halstead–Reitan or Luria–Nebraska batteries. Even the recently released WAIS—Fourth Edition (WAIS-IV) now includes some process approach variables for which base rate data are available. To many it is seen as a modern version of the methods taught by Luria, using conventional, familiar neuropsychological instruments and techniques that are more readily learned and adapted.

Interestingly, the BPA has also spawned a number of conventional tests for which the structures were derived from Kaplan's and her students' observations of patients' test behavior but without relying on those same observations for scoring or interpretation. A now well-established example of this is the Delis–Kaplan Executive Function test (D-KEFS; Delis, Kaplan, & Kramer, 2001), which takes the approach of breaking down such commonly used tests as the Trail Making Test, into multiple tasks, each of which is designed to be differentially sensitive to the various component "processes" that comprise the original measure.

Rapid Reference 1.4 provides a summary of the principal advantages and disadvantages of the major approaches to neuropsychological assessment.

≡ Rapid Reference 1.4

Advantages/Disadvantages of Major Approaches to Neuropsychological Assessment

Halstead-Reitan Battery

Advantages
- Empirically designed battery with nonlocalizationist origins
- Wealth of validating data
- Reliability and comparability across different patient groups
- Ability to be administered by a technician

Disadvantages
- Length and inefficiency
- Complex measures; difficulty knowing which functions are being measured
- Difficulty of economic justification, often because of length
- Declining in popularity

Luria-Nebraska Battery

Advantages
- Empirically designed battery based on Luria's measures
- Single scales for various functional or cognitive domains
- Relative brevity of administration time
- Increasing base of empirical findings

Disadvantages

- Not an accurate reflection of Luria's method
- Not as popular as Halstead–Reitan Battery
- Single scales inconsistent with Luria's view of individual variation
- Declining in popularity

Boston Process Approach

Advantages

- Frequent use of adaptations of validated measures
- Flexibility in matching tests to referral question
- Great descriptive power in the clinical setting
- As an example of flexible battery, the most commonly used approach

Disadvantages

- Produces a relatively limited set of normative data for qualitative findings
- Depends on observational skills for its use
- Requires specific training

Other Approaches and Contributions

In addition to the HRB, LNNB, and the BPA, a number of laboratories have made significant contributions to test practices, providing tests and clinically available data that have proved useful in a number of settings. In many cases, these laboratories have produced a wealth of supportive data and have made substantial contributions to both experimental and clinical research.

Because of the limits of space in this text, we have painted some of these remaining contributors to clinical neuropsychology with relatively broad strokes, grouping together the work of those who otherwise deserve individual mention:

- *Contributions from Canada.* A number of major contributors to clinical assessment resources have been located in Canada. These contributors include the laboratory of Brenda Milner, who conducted hundreds of studies of the neurosurgery patients at the Montreal Neurological Institute. She and her colleagues and students, including Doreen Kimura and Sandra Witelson, were responsible for producing highly sophisticated tests of executive and motor functions and memory (e.g., Design Fluency Test, Dichotic Listening, and Dihaptic Perception Test).

- *Contributions from Europe.* A number of countries, including France (e.g., Henri Hecaen), Italy (Ennio DeRenzi et al.), Norway (Halgrim Klove), and Germany (Klaus Poeck), have supported acclaimed laboratories in neuropsychology, contributing important tests of language, memory, and visual functions (e.g., Token Test and the Grooved Pegboard Test), as well as scoring schemes for apraxia (e.g., Poeck, 1986).

- *Contributions from Britain.* Great Britain has supported several internationally famous neuropsychology laboratories. The laboratory of Elizabeth Warrington, for example, has been responsible for several generations of major contributors to clinical and experimental neuropsychology. The group of psychologists working at the Rivermead Rehabilitation Hospital published a number of well-normed tests of functions that are designed to represent real-life situations (e.g., Warrington Recognition Memory Test and the Rivermead Behavioural Memory Test), including a battery of tests to assess memory and attention. These tests, which reflect contemporary ideas derived from cognitive neuropsychology, are highly adaptable to the purposes described earlier in the section titled "Uses of Neuropsychological Assessment." They deserve to be considered by any practicing neuropsychologist and may become (in terms of popularity) the HRB of the future.

- *Contributions of Arthur Benton.* The Arthur Benton Laboratory in Iowa City, Iowa, deserves special mention (Benton, Sivan, deS Hamsher, Varney, & Spreen, 1994). Dr. Benton pioneered the development of highly specific descriptive tests of cognitive functions (e.g., Line Orientation and the Benton Visual Retention Test). It is not clear why these tests have not gained more popularity, other than the sheer force of data supporting the HRB, which appeared contemporaneously with many of Benton's tests. He designed and normed memory and visual functions tests that are still useful in special clinical testing situations.

🦫 TEST YOURSELF 🦫

....

1. The majority of tests used by neuropsychologists were specifically developed for the purpose of assessing brain dysfunction.

   True or False?

2. Tests such as the Boston Diagnostic Aphasia Exam and the California Verbal Learning Test were constructed with sensitivity to brain dysfunction as the primary consideration.

   True or False?

3. **Which neuropsychological test battery is the best example of test development based on an empirical approach?**
   (a) Luria–Nebraska Neuropsychological Battery
   (b) Halstead–Reitan Battery
   (c) Boston Process Approach Battery
   (d) Luria Neuropsychological Investigation

4. **What is a clinical neuropsychologist?**
   (a) A psychologist board certified in clinical neuropsychology by the American Board of Professional Psychology or the American Board of Professional Neuropsychology
   (b) A psychologist with a doctorate in clinical neuropsychology
   (c) A psychologist licensed as a neuropsychologist in his or her state
   (d) All of the above

5. **Holism theory suggests that different psychological functions are subserved by distinct and separate structures in the brain.**
   True or False?

6. **Localization theory holds that brain lesions may have effects that differ as a function of location, but that the brain involves multiple structures working together.**
   True or False?

7. **Ideally, neuropsychological tests should be sensitive to the presence of brain dysfunction and have ecological validity.**
   True or False?

Answers: 1. False; 2. False; 3. b; 4. d; 5. False; 6. False; 7. True

Two

THE DISCIPLINE OF NEUROPSYCHOLOGICAL ASSESSMENT

OVERVIEW

Before we discuss some of the specific skills required for the collection and interpretation of neuropsychological test data, we should consider the knowledge, training, and experience that provide the professional skills necessary for the practice of neuropsychology. It was not so long ago that the skills necessary for competence as a neuropsychologist were acquired on the job—few graduate programs or predoctoral internships provided formal skills in this area. Many members of the generation of neuropsychologists trained shortly after World War II were largely self-taught or were guided by mentors who directed them toward texts and medical school courses helpful to the development of what were effectively apprenticeship roles. A traditional path was to obtain a doctoral degree in clinical psychology and then to receive specialty training in neuropsychology. Because of the lack of specific guidelines on training in neuropsychology, those choosing to call themselves clinical neuropsychologists had widely disparate backgrounds and experience. Many were simply psychologists who administered neuropsychological tests, others were psychologists who had taken a weekend workshop in neuropsychological assessment, others were clinical psychologists with specialized training in neuropsychology, and a minority were psychologists, board-certified in clinical neuropsychology following credential review and examination. As we shall see in this chapter, the growth of neuropsychology and academic psychological neuroscience as scientific disciplines has been paralleled by the development of clinical neuropsychology as a profession. Today, there is a clear-cut path of education, pre- and postdoctoral clinical experience, and formal credentialing that marks the maturation of a true clinical specialty.

EDUCATION AND KNOWLEDGE BASE

In 1987 a joint task force sanctioned by the International Neuropsychological Society (INS) and Division 40 of the American Psychological Association (APA) published the first formal guidelines on the education, accreditation, and credentialing of neuropsychologists (Adams & Rourke, 1992), setting some basic standards for training in clinical neuropsychology. The committee concluded that doctoral training in neuropsychology should prepare students for "health service delivery, basic clinical research, teaching and consultation" relevant to neuropsychology. Such graduate study should include a core of generic clinical and general psychology courses accompanied by "specialized training in the neurosciences as well as basic human and animal neuropsychology" along with "specific training in clinical neuropsychology."

The standards in effect today, though, were developed in September 1997 in Houston, Texas, by a delegation of 40 neuropsychologists representing Division 40 and the National Academy of Neuropsychology (NAN), as well as directors of training programs in neuropsychology at the doctoral, internship, and postdoctoral levels (Hannay et al., 1998). The consensus report of the Houston Conference, as this meeting is known, mandates that education and training in clinical neuropsychology follow the scientist–practitioner model (Belar & Perry, 1992). The scientist–practitioner model, which was adopted in 1949 at the Boulder, Colorado, conference on doctoral education and training in clinical psychology, specified that clinical psychologists should be trained first as scientists and second as practicing professionals. As applied to neuropsychology, this model dictates that education and training in clinical neuropsychology integrate all aspects of general neuropsychology. Professional education and training would begin with doctoral education and continue through internship and postdoctoral residency education and training. The Houston Conference defined a clinical neuropsychologist as a "professional psychologist trained in the science of brain–behavior relationships. The clinical neuropsychologist specializes in the application of assessment and intervention principles based on the scientific study of human behavior across the lifespan as it relates to normal and abnormal functioning of the central nervous system" (Hannay et al., 161).

The Houston Conference envisioned that education and training in the specialty field of clinical neuropsychology would be necessary for individuals who engage in clinical neuropsychology and those who supervise clinical neuropsychologists, as well as those who call themselves clinical neuropsychologists. According to this delegation, education and training in the specialty of clinical neuropsychology is also essential for psychologists involved in the education and training of others in the specialty of clinical neuropsychology.

In keeping with the earlier 1987 standards, the Houston Conference recommended a particular knowledge base necessary for clinical neuropsychologists: a generic psychology core, a generic clinical core, a specific neuropsychology core, and a specific core for the study of brain–behavior relationships. This knowledge base is acquired through doctoral courses and other didactic methods. The generic psychology core comprises courses drawn from a general psychology curriculum, including courses in statistics, research design, and methodology; learning, cognition and perception; the biological basis of behavior; social psychology and personality; life span development; history; and cultural and individual differences. For practicing neuropsychologists, a working knowledge of these areas is not a mere academic exercise. Clinical decision making in both clinical psychology and neuropsychology requires an understanding of basic statistical and psychometric concepts, the norming and standardization of tests, and the use of normative data in making clinical judgments.

It could be argued that neuropsychological assessment is a direct application of cognitive psychology, because knowledge of modern concepts of such functions as attention, memory, and language are necessary to interpret and explain correctly the content of most neuropsychological instruments. For example, an understanding that memory may be dissociated into processes important for the encoding, storage, and retrieval of information and that these functions may be related to different brain systems, guides the interpretation of such clinical measures as the Wechsler Memory Scale—Fourth Edition. A course in the biological basis of behavior is requisite for understanding the biological or physiological functions that may be disrupted by brain dysfunction; such a course provides considerable information on the neuroanatomical connections between various cortical and subcortical structures. Knowing that the frontal lobes are intimately connected with these cortical and subcortical structures, for example, is critical to understanding the far-reaching effects of lesions in this area. An understanding of personality, social behavior, and life span development also provides essential information that clinical neuropsychologists use to understand test performance and to make recommendations that take into account the overall context of behavior presented by a patient. What may appear to be deficits on a neuropsychological test for a young adult, for example, may be a reflection of normal development for a child on one hand or normal aging for an elderly adult on the other. Coursework in cultural and individual differences is a prerequisite for understanding test findings as they apply to a particular patient because tests may contain cultural biases.

The Houston Conference also recommended a core of courses typically offered as part of a clinical psychology program, including psychopathology, personality theory, psychometrics theory, interview and assessment techniques, intervention, and ethics. This recommendation reflects the view that clinical neuropsychology should be regarded either as a subspecialty within clinical psychology or as a separate specialization having requirements similar to those of clinical psychology. The clinical neuropsychologist must understand all the manifestations and variations of personality and psychopathology, as well as how these issues can affect test performance and human adjustment. The clinical neuropsychologist must have skill in interviewing techniques and assessment procedures, a sound foundation in test theory, and a good basic understanding of professional ethics.

Neuropsychological test performance can be affected by many nonneurological factors, and neurological disease may mimic nonneurological conditions. For example, high levels of anxiety and depression can impair test performance in the absence of neurological disease, and patients with brainstem and basal ganglia lesions may have symptoms that mimic depression. Because neuropsychological test performance is not affected only by neurological conditions, the clinical neuropsychologist must always make neuropsychological judgments in the context of clinical judgments about psychopathology and psychological issues.

In addition to more general clinical coursework, a clinical neuropsychologist requires knowledge in several particular specialized areas. The Houston Conference recommended that the specialty curriculum include topics that provide foundations for the study of brain–behavior relationships. These topics include functional neuroanatomy, neurological and related disorders, nonneurological conditions affecting central nervous system functions, functional neuroimaging, neurochemistry, and neuropsychology of behavior. A working knowledge of neuroanatomy, neuropathology, and neurosciences provides a brain–behavior framework for the judgments that a clinical neuropsychologist makes. Specialty training in clinical neuropsychology might also include coursework on the neuropsychology of perceptual, cognitive, and executive functions, as well as research design and methods specific to the study of brain–behavior relationships.

Additionally, the Houston Conference recommended that clinical neuropsychology programs include courses specific to the discipline of neuropsychology, including specialized neuropsychological assessment and intervention techniques, research design and analysis in neuropsychology, professional issues and ethics in neuropsychology, and practical implications of neuropsychological conditions. Unique to neuropsychology, these courses expand on basic education and training in clinical psychology and provide a knowledge base for the specialty of clinical neuropsychology.

The Houston Conference also mandated that clinical neuropsychologists acquire skills in basic areas germane to neuropsychology through the aforementioned core coursework in graduate school and through other didactic training. In the area of assessment, the Houston Conference stated that clinical neuropsychologists should possess skills in information gathering, history taking, test selection, test administration, interpretation and diagnosis, treatment planning, report writing, feedback, and recognition of multicultural issues. In the area of treatment and intervention, the necessary skills included identification of intervention targets; specification of intervention needs; formulation, implementation, and monitoring of intervention plans; outcome assessment; and recognition of multicultural issues. In the area of consultation, the Houston Conference named important skill areas such as effective basic communication, determination and clarification of referral issues, knowledge of referral sources regarding neuropsychological services, communication of evaluation results, and education of patients and families regarding services and disorders. In the area of research, important skills to acquire were selection of research topics; review of the scientific literature; design, execution, and monitoring of research; outcome evaluation; and communication of results. In the areas of teaching and supervision, the Houston Conference recommended that skills be acquired through methods of effective teaching, planning, and design of courses and curricula; use of effective educational technologies; and use of effective supervision methods.

In 1987 the Joint Committee suggested that training in clinical neuropsychology include an internship devoting at least 50% of 1-year, full-time training experience to neuropsychology and at least 20% of the training to general clinical training. Perhaps feeling that this recommendation was too narrow, the Houston Conference proposed that the percentage of time devoted to clinical neuropsychology "should be determined by the training needs of the individual intern" (Hannay et al., 1998, p. 163). It also recommended that the internship be completed in an APA- or Canadian Psychological Association (CPA)-approved professional psychology training program. This means that graduate training in neuropsychology should also occur in an APA- or CPA-approved program in clinical or counseling psychology. Students can gain experience through attendance at neurobehavioral rounds, neurology rounds, and neuropsychological case conferences, as well as through hands-on testing and supervision.

Recognizing that the skills needed for independent practice in neuropsychology could not typically be acquired through only a 1-year internship, the Houston Conference suggested that specialty training be completed with a 2-year postdoctoral residency in neuropsychology. They recommended that accreditation of such programs be based on the presence of a board-certified clinical neuropsychologist, that the program be held at one or more training sites, that on-site supervision be provided, that access be available to clinical services and training programs in medical specialties and allied professions, and that interactions with other residents be required. The Houston Conference indicated that a "significant percentage of time" should be spent in clinical service, research, and education. Preferably, the neuropsychologist should train in a medical setting and gain exposure to a wide variety of patients with neurological and psychiatric disorders.

These training experiences are necessary to attain the advanced skills required for advanced understanding of brain–behavior relationships, as well as for independent neuropsychological evaluation and treatment. By virtue of their education, training, and experience, graduates of residency training must be both capable of scholarly activity and eligible for licensure or certification in the independent practice of psychology. In addition, upon completion of training, the neuropsychologist should be eligible for board certification in clinical neuropsychology by the American Board of Professional Psychology.

Recognizing that education and training do not end with the completion of a postdoctoral residency, the Houston Conference indicated that the clinical neuropsychologist would be expected to engage in continuing education "to enhance or maintain the already established competence of clinical neuropsychologists by updating previously acquired knowledge and skills or by acquiring new knowledge or skills" (Hannay et al., 1998, pp. 164–165). They cautioned that continuing education by itself is not sufficient to retrain as a clinical neuropsychologist or to acquire the skills necessary to educate and then "identify oneself as a clinical neuropsychologist" (Hannay et al., 1998, p. 165). Rapid Reference 2.1 provides a summary of the Houston Conference guidelines for specialty education and training in the field of clinical neuropsychology.

≣ *Rapid Reference 2.1*

The Houston Conference: Guidelines for Specialty Education and Training

- Knowledge Base
  - Generic psychology core
  - Generic clinical core
  - Foundations for the study of brain–behavior relationships
  - Foundations for the practice of clinical neuropsychology
- Skills
  - Assessment: Information gathering, history taking, selecting and administering tests, interpreting data, making a diagnosis, treatment planning, report writing, providing feedback, and recognizing multicultural issues
  - Treatment and interventions: Identifying intervention targets, specifying intervention needs, formulating, implementing, and monitoring intervention plans, assessing outcomes, and recognizing multicultural issues
  - Consultation: Communicating effectively, determining and clarifying referral issues, knowing referral sources, communicating results and recommendations, and educating parents and families
  - Research: Selecting research topics; reviewing literature; designing, executing, and monitoring research; evaluating outcomes; and communicating results

- Teaching and supervision: Methods of effective teaching, planning and designing courses and curricula, using effective educational technologies and supervision methods
- Doctoral education in clinical neuropsychology at regionally accredited university
- Internship training in clinical neuropsychology in APA- or CPA-accredited program
- Residency education and training in clinical neuropsychology for equivalent of two years full-time
- Continuing education in clinical neuropsychology

Source: Hannay et al. (1998).

DEFINITION OF A CLINICAL NEUROPSYCHOLOGIST

With recognition of the specialty of clinical neuropsychology by the APA and the CPA, defining who is a clinical neuropsychologist has taken on increased importance. The Houston Conference has set out the preceding specific guidelines for that purpose. In May 2001 NAN also approved an official position on the definition of a clinical neuropsychologist (Weinstein, 2001). NAN takes the position that:

A clinical neuropsychologist is a professional with special expertise in the applied science of brain–behavior relationships. Clinical neuropsychologists use this knowledge in the assessment, diagnosis, treatment, and/or rehabilitation of patients across the lifespan with neurological, medical, neurodevelopmental and psychiatric conditions, as well as other cognitive and learning disorders. The clinical neuropsychologist uses psychological, neurological, cognitive, behavioral, and physiological principles, techniques and tests to evaluate patients' neurocognitive, behavioral, and emotional strengths and weaknesses and their relationship to normal and abnormal central nervous system functioning. The clinical neuropsychologist uses this information and information provided by other medical/healthcare providers to identify and diagnose neurobehavioral disorders, and plan and implement intervention strategies. Both the American Psychological Association and the Canadian Psychological Association recognize the specialty of clinical neuropsychology. Clinical neuropsychologists are independent practitioners (healthcare providers) of clinical neuropsychology and psychology. (www.nanonline.org, 2001)

According to NAN's official position, the minimum educational and training criteria for a clinical neuropsychologist include state licensure as a provider or practitioner in psychology or clinical neuropsychology, a doctoral degree in psychology from an accredited university training program, an internship in a clinically relevant area of professional psychology, and 2 years (with at least 1 year at a postdoctoral level) of full-time specialty training "in the study and practice of clinical neuropsychology and related neurosciences" with supervision by a clinical neuropsychologist. NAN also recommends that clinical neuropsychologists undergo board certification through written and oral examinations, peer review, and formal verification of credentials to demonstrate "further evidence of advanced training, supervision, and applied fund of knowledge in clinical neuropsychology."

NAN's definition is similar to the definition of a clinical neuropsychologist adopted as the official position of the Division of Clinical Neuropsychology (Division 40) of the APA on August 12, 1988 (Division 40, 1989) and included in the policy statement of the Houston Conference on Specialty Education and Training in Clinical Neuropsychology:

> A Clinical Neuropsychologist is a professional psychologist who applies principles of assessment and intervention based upon the scientific study of human behavior as it relates to normal and abnormal functioning of the central nervous system. The Clinical Neuropsychologist is a doctoral-level psychology provider of diagnostic and intervention services who has demonstrated competence in the application of such principles for human welfare following:
>
> A. Successful completion of systematic didactic and experiential training in neuropsychology and neuroscience at a regionally accredited university;
>
> B. Two or more years of appropriate supervised training applying neuropsychological services in a clinical setting;
>
> C. Licensing and certification to provide psychological services to the public by the laws of the state or province in which he or she practices;
>
> D. Review by one's peers as a test of these competencies.
>
> Attainment of the ABCN/ABPP [American Board of Clinical Neuropsychology (ABCN)/American Board of Professional Psychology (ABPP)] Diploma in Clinical Neuropsychology is the clearest evidence of competence as a Clinical Neuropsychologist, assuring that all of these criteria have been met (Division 40, 1989, p. 22).

This definition is similar to the definition of the specialty of clinical neuropsychology that was approved by the APA Council of Representatives in 1996, when clinical neuropsychology was designated as a specialty area in psychology. The definition was then reapproved in 2003. This definition states, "Clinical neuropsychology is a specialty that applies principles of assessment and intervention based upon the scientific study of human behavior as it relates to normal and abnormal functioning of the central nervous system. The specialty is dedicated to enhancing the understanding of brain-behavior relationships and the application of such knowledge to human problems." (www.div40.org/def.html).

The American Academy of Clinical Neuropsychology (AACN) developed and published its first set of practice guidelines for clinical neuropsychologists (Board of Directors, AACN, 2007). Those guidelines defined clinical neuropsychology simply as: "an applied science that examines the impact of both normal and abnormal brain functioning on a broad range of cognitive, emotional, and behavioral functions" (Board of Directors, AACN, 2007, p. 211). They distinguished neuropsychological evaluations and consultations from psychological evaluations and consultations by specifying that such evaluations consist of "the use of objective neuropsychological tests, systematic behavioral observations, and interpretation of the findings based on knowledge of the neuropsychological manifestations of brain-related conditions" and "where appropriate, these evaluations consider neuroimaging and other neurodiagnostic studies and inform neuropsychologically oriented rehabilitation interventions" (Board of Directors, AACN, 2007, p. 212).

TRAINING, EXPERTISE, AND CREDENTIALS

Most programs that offer specialty training for clinical neuropsychology students are those for a Ph.D. or Psy.D. in clinical psychology. These programs provide students with the opportunity to specialize in clinical neuropsychology in the context of general clinical training. A few have been specifically accredited as clinical neuropsychology programs. Some neuropsychologists come from degree programs other than neuropsychology, obtaining the necessary specific coursework outside their degree programs.

Although the latter was a more common training route for the first postwar generation of neuropsychologists, most students do not choose this route today because these students have difficulty obtaining internship and practicum training. Training

CAUTION

Remember: The term *neuropsychologist* is not well regulated. Most states do not prohibit licensed psychologists from performing so-called neuropsychological evaluations and calling themselves neuropsychologists regardless of their specific training.

programs that obtain APA accreditation must usually take students from clinical psychology, counseling psychology, or clinical neuropsychology programs, making it difficult (if not impossible) for students without clinical degrees to gain admission. It is difficult to estimate precisely how many doctoral students graduate with specialties in clinical neuropsychology from accredited programs each year. Division 40 of the APA maintains on its Web site (www.div40.org/training/index.html) a list of 32 accredited programs offering doctoral training in clinical neuropsychology that admit between 93 and 121 new students each year. This is likely an underestimate because this list does not include all doctoral programs that offer some or all of the recommended coursework in neuropsychology. The list of training programs also contains 44 internship offerings and 82 postdoctoral programs. Division 40 lists the name of the training program and its directors, as well as contact information. The list also specifies additional program details, such as the number of positions available, names of the faculty and their interests, credit-earning coursework, and whether faculty are board certified. Contact information for predoctoral internship training programs in clinical neuropsychology is also available from the Association for Internship Training in Clinical Neuropsychology at www.utmem.edu/AITCN, and similar information concerning postdoctoral training in clinical neuropsychology is available from the Association of Postdoctoral Programs in Clinical Neuropsychology at www.appcn.org. Another resource for internship and postdoctoral training programs is the Association of Psychology Postdoctoral and Internship Centers at www.appic.org.

Neuropsychological assessment requires that practitioners be able to evaluate and recognize behavioral, personality, and psychiatric consequences of neurological disorders and attribute correctly behavioral or cognitive symptoms to neurological versus nonneurological causes, or a combination of these. Training in clinical psychology programs provides many prerequisites for developing such skills. Furthermore, many doctoral programs offering specialty training in clinical neuropsychology are parts of universities that have programs in medicine or strong affiliations with independent local medical schools; such associations ensure that necessary coursework and practicum experiences are available.

Doctoral programs in clinical psychology with a specialty in neuropsychology or doctoral programs in clinical neuropsychology typically require 5 years for completion. Internships usually occur in the fourth or fifth year, most often in general hospital or medical center settings. These settings allow access to a broad range of patient populations and should offer experience with patients with a wide variety of neurological and psychiatric disorders.

Practitioners in neuropsychology must usually obtain state licensure in psychology. With the exception of Louisiana, most states do not offer specific licensure in neuropsychology, leaving the representation of professional expertise in neuropsychology to the ethical judgment of the psychologist—that is, psychologists obtain a license to practice psychology and then are expected to limit their practice to those areas in which competence has been gained through professional education and training derived through an organized training program and supervised professional experience. Technically, one could argue that the only professionals who can call themselves clinical neuropsychologists are those with one or more of these qualifications: a doctoral degree in clinical neuropsychology, licensure as a clinical neuropsychologist, or board certification in clinical neuropsychology. However, the only credential that currently demonstrates recognized competence in neuropsychology is the achievement of board certification or diplomate status through peer review and examination.

Today, diplomate status certifying competence to practice neuropsychology is offered by the American Board of Clinical Neuropsychology (ABCN) and by the American Board of Professional Neuropsychology (ABN). Both governing bodies do so on the basis of a review of credentials, work samples, and some form of examination, often leading to confusion among practitioners and the public. Some significant differences exist between the procedures for obtaining diplomate status from these two boards.

ABCN offers its diplomate status under the auspices of the American Board of Professional Psychology (ABPP). ABPP has its own general standards and criteria for all diplomates that are implied in the ABCN degree. These standards include completion of basic and more advanced coursework in psychology, supervised training and receipt of a doctorate in psychology, and the equivalent of 3 years of experience and licensure for independent practice in psychology in the psychologist's state or province. ABCN currently requires training that conforms to the guidelines of the Houston Conference (see Rapid Reference 2.1). This means coursework relevant to the specialty of neuropsychology in the areas of basic neurosciences, neuroanatomy, neuropathology, clinical neurology, and neuropsychological assessment and intervention, in addition to a generic psychology core and more clinically based courses such as psychopathology and

DON'T FORGET

Diplomate status certifying competence to practice neuropsychology is offered through examination only by the American Board of Professional Neuropsychology or by the American Board of Clinical Neuropsychology under the auspices of the American Board of Professional Psychology.

psychological assessment and intervention. ABCN also requires a doctoral degree in psychology and licensure or certification in psychology. The current ABCN degree also requires supervised predoctoral and postdoctoral experience in clinical neuropsychology. There is no formal supervision requirement for individuals who obtained their doctorate before 1981, but 4,800 hours of postdoctoral experience is required. For those who completed their doctorate between 1981 and 1989, the supervision requirement is 1,600 hours at the pre- or postdoctoral levels. For those who obtained their doctorate after 1989, the supervision requirement is 2 years of clinical neuropsychological training, of which 1 year may be predoctoral. For both groups, supervision must be performed by a clinical neuropsychologist. After successful completion of the credential review, the applicant must pass a stringent 100-item, multiple-choice written examination to demonstrate his or her breadth and depth of knowledge in clinical neuropsychology; if successful on the examination, the applicant is invited to submit two work samples for review. These samples must include the original clinical report and raw test data, as well as a summary sheet of test scores that contains normative information. ABCN uses specific criteria to evaluate the work samples; if two of three reviewers approve the samples, then ABCN invites the candidate to sit for an oral examination covering fact finding, work samples, and ethics and professional responsibility. The pass rate for the work samples was 75% in 1998; pass rates for the written and oral examinations are usually in the 60% to 70% range (Ivnik, Haaland, & Bieliauskas, 2000). ABCN no longer tracks pass rates, but in 2008 52 psychologists passed the written exam and 45 passed the oral exams. Armstrong, Beebe, Hilsabeck, and Kirkwood (2008) offer guidance on applying and obtaining board certification in their recently published book, *Board Certification in Clinical Neuropsychology: A Guide to Becoming ABPP/ABCN Certified Without Sacrificing Your Sanity*. Another practical guidebook available for individuals seeking certification from the ABPP is *Becoming Board Certified by the American Board of Professional Psychology* (Nezu, Finch, & Simon, 2009).

Board certification in clinical neuropsychology by ABPP is a credential designating competence to practice; additionally, "The APA recognizes the significant service to the profession and to the public that is rendered by the American Board of Professional Psychology" (APA Association Rules, Section 130–2). Board certification in clinical neuropsychology by ABPP is comparable to board certification in various medical specialty areas by the American Board of Medical Specialties, the only specialty certification organization recognized by the American Medical Association. Board certification in clinical neuropsychology by ABPP is a recognized credential denoting competence for work in many arenas (e.g., the courtroom and HMOs). The credential confers preference in faculty positions in psychology training programs and increased pay in the armed services; it also ensures licensure reciprocity in many states (Ivnik et al., 2000).

ABN also requires that the applicant have a doctoral degree in psychology and current licensure or certification to practice psychology in a state, province, or territory. In addition, ABN requires professional experience in neuropsychology for a minimum of 5 years, of which 1 year may be a supervised neuropsychological internship. The applicant must also have been engaged in providing neuropsychological services for a minimum of 500 hours per year during the previous 5 years. In addition, ABN requires involvement in continuing education in neuropsychology either by taking or teaching APA- or CPA-approved continuing education courses. As part of the standard application process, ABN requires passing a multiple-choice examination and written response to a clinical scenario and submission of two work samples (one of which may be a scholarly article published in a peer-reviewed journal) for review by a panel of examiners. After successful completion of the work sample review, the applicant is invited to an oral examination covering the areas of core knowledge, work samples, and ethics. The pass rate for second submission of work samples was 80% in 1999 and 2000; pass rates for the oral examination in the same time period averaged 95% (personal communication, J. Blasé, June, 2001). Board certification in clinical neuropsychology by ABN indicates an advanced level of competency as a clinical neuropsychologist.

ABCN and ABN differ in their requirements for board certification, but both require the production of work samples and oral examination. Most important, both boards are different from the so-called vanity boards that require only submission of an application and payment of a fee for board certification. These vanity boards do not require a demonstration of competence through peer review or examination.

ORGANIZATIONS

Clinical neuropsychologists have several major organizations available for affiliation, including the International Neuropsychological Society (INS), the National Academy of Neuropsychology (NAN), and Division 40 (Clinical Neuropsychology) of the APA. The purpose of the INS is to promote research, service, and education in neuropsychology and to encourage and enhance the worldwide exchange of

DON'T FORGET

The major organizations for clinical neuropsychologists are

- International Neuropsychological Society (INS)
- National Academy of Neuropsychologists (NAN)
- Division 40 of the American Psychological Association (APA)
- American Academy of Clinical Neuropsychology (AACN)

information about brain–behavior relationships among scientific disciplines involved in brain–behavior research. INS meets twice each year; the annual meeting is in February and takes place in the United States or Canada, and the midyear meeting usually occurs in July and is most often in a European country. The membership directory for INS lists more than 3,000 members from all over the world—from Argentina to Yugoslavia—with most members from the United States.

As of this writing, NAN had 3,657 members. The objectives of NAN include preserving and advancing knowledge of the assessment and remediation of neurological impairments by psychological means; fostering the development of neuropsychology as a discipline, science, and profession; and joining with other professional groups to exchange information in pursuit of the advancement and development of neuropsychology. NAN has held annual meetings each fall (October or November) since 1981.

In addition, neuropsychologist members can join Division 40 of the APA, the Division of Clinical Neuropsychology. According to APA bylaws, Division 40 was developed "to enhance the understanding of brain–behavior relationships and the application of such knowledge to human problems" (www.div40.org/APA_Division_40_Bylaws_2005.pdf). Division 40 seeks to advance "clinical neuropsychological practice, scientific research, and professional education in the public interest." Each summer at the annual meeting of the APA, Division 40 presents scientific symposia in the area of clinical neuropsychology for education, training, and the promotion of the exchange of scientific research.

NEUROPSYCHOLOGICAL RESOURCES

Books

Many books on clinical neuropsychology can serve as reference books or resources for the clinical neuropsychologist. Rapid Reference 2.2 provides a sampling of essential works for the clinical neuropsychologist. For a more comprehensive list, please see the annotated bibliography at the end of this book.

Journals

Enhancement of one's knowledge base requires keeping current with the latest scientific research. Numerous journals are available for that purpose. Rapid Reference 2.3 lists journals important for the continuing education of the clinical neuropsychologist. For a more comprehensive list, please see the annotated bibliography at the end of this book.

≋ *Rapid Reference 2.2*

Sample of Clinical Neuropsychology Sourcebooks

- Baron, I. S. (2004). *Neuropsychological evaluation of the child.* New York: Oxford University Press.
- Grant, I, G., & Adams, K. M. (2009). *Neuropsychological assessment of neuropsychiatric & neuromedical disorders.* New York: Oxford University Press.
- Heaton, R. K., Miller, S. W., Taylor, M. J., & Grant, I. (2004). *Revised comprehensive norms for an expanded Halstead–Reitan Battery: Demographically adjusted neuropsychological norms for African American and Caucasian adults.* Lutz, FL: Psychological Assessment Resources.
- Heilman, K. M. (2003). *Clinical neuropsychology* (4th ed.). New York: Oxford University Press.
- Jarvis, P. E., & Barth, J. T. (1994). *The Halstead–Reitan Neuropsychological Battery: A guide to interpretation and clinical applications.* Odessa, FL: Psychological Assessment Resources.
- Larrabee, G. J. (Ed.). (2005). *Forensic neuropsychology: A scientific approach.* New York: Oxford University Press.
- Lezak, M. D., Howieson, D. B., & Loring, D. W., with Hannay, H. J., & Fischer, J. S. (2004). *Neuropsychological assessment* (4th ed.). New York: Oxford University Press.
- Loring, D. W. (Ed.). (1999). *INS dictionary of neuropsychology.* New York: Oxford University Press.
- Mitrushina, M. N., Boone, K. B., Razani, J., & D'Elia, L. F. (2005). *Handbook of normative data for neuropsychological assessment* (2nd ed.). New York: Oxford University Press.
- Strauss, E., Sherman, E. M. S., & Spreen, O. (2006). *A compendium of neuropsychological tests: Administration, norms, and commentary* (3rd ed.). New York: Oxford University Press.

≋ *Rapid Reference 2.3*

Sample of Relevant Journals

- *Applied Neuropsychology*
- *Archives of Clinical Neuropsychology*
- *Archives of Neurology*
- *Brain*

- *Child Neuropsychology*
- *The Clinical Neuropsychologist*
- *Cognitive Neuropsychology*
- *Cortex*
- *Journal of Cognitive Neuroscience*
- *Journal of International Neuropsychological Society*
- *Neurocase*
- *Neuropsychologia*
- *Neuropsychological Rehabilitation*
- *Neuropsychology*
- *Neuropsychology Review*
- *Psychological Assessment*

TEST YOURSELF

1. **A clinical neuropsychologist is any psychologist who administers neuropsychological tests.**
   True or False?

2. **The knowledge base for a clinical neuropsychologist should include**
   (a) statistics and methodology.
   (b) neuropsychological assessment techniques.
   (c) psychopathology.
   (d) functional neuroanatomy.
   (e) all of the above.

3. **ABCN and ABN differ in their requirements for board certification, but both require the production of work samples and oral examination.**
   True or False?

4. **Licensure in clinical neuropsychology is widely available and is the single best credential available to clinical neuropsychologists.**
   True or False?

5. **The Houston Conference did not consider which of the following necessary in the education and training of a neuropsychologist?**
   (a) Doctoral degree in neuropsychology from a regionally accredited institution
   (b) Internship training in clinical neuropsychology
   (c) Core coursework in psychometric theory
   (d) Residency training in clinical neuropsychology

Answers: 1. False; 2. e; 3. True; 4. False; 5. a

Three

ESSENTIALS OF THE INTERVIEW AND CLINICAL HISTORY

OVERVIEW

A detailed reconstruction of a patient's medical, social, cultural, intellectual, and emotional past is an integral piece of the puzzle of neuropsychological assessment. Most of the clinical issues assessed by the neuropsychologist occur in the fabric of many years of development and experience. In some instances, an individual's life may be changed in only a few moments by a brain injury or stroke. In other cases, the changes in neuropsychological functions wrought by diseases of the central nervous system may unfold over months or years or may be a reflection of abnormalities in the process of development itself. A disease of the central nervous system may affect a mature adult differently than a developing adolescent, who may in turn be affected differently than a preverbal child. The patient's history and clinical interview provide the data essential to an understanding of the characteristics and time course of a patient's current problem; they may also provide critical clues as to diagnosis and prognosis. The history and clinical interview also supply information about psychological or medical conditions that can affect cognitive and emotional functioning and therefore can affect test performance. Finally, the patient's educational, social, and developmental history informs the clinician about what the patient was like before the illness or injury, so that current and past function can be compared. In many cases, history may be as important (or more) as formal test results as a source of answers to the questions described in Chapter 1. In addition to the clinical history, astute observations of a patient's behavior before, during, and after a test session not only provide important clues to aid in the interpretation of neuropsychological test results but may even supersede those results in drawing conclusions about core clinical referral issues.

CAUTION

....

Neuropsychological test results cannot be interpreted in a vacuum. Neuropsychological test results can only be interpreted within a historical context.

To understand these statements, we must examine the basic logic of neuropsychological test interpretation. Neuropsychological tests are psychological tests that have been shown to be sensitive, but not necessarily specific, to the presence of functional compromise in the central nervous system. In other words, although below normal performance on these tests may be the result of brain dysfunction (i.e., the test is sensitive to the presence of brain dysfunction), below normal performance may also result from factors other than brain dysfunction (i.e., abnormal test performance is not specific to brain dysfunction). Thus, it is only within the context of a patient's history that an accurate reading of the data and then a diagnosis can be made. To allow for a correct interpretation of the test results, the neuropsychologist must follow a particular series of steps in analyzing the data.

First, historical information and behavioral observations are obtained through clinical interview; record review; and, when necessary, reports of significant others. Then a battery of tests is selected and administered to a patient to obtain a sample of behavior. The tests are scored and the results tallied. Next, the scores obtained from the patient are compared with normative data consisting of test scores of adults or children who are similar in age, education, and (if possible and relevant) cultural background. Typically, such normative test data are obtained from samples of adults or children who have either some documented history of brain damage or dysfunction or who are considered normal (with no documented history of brain damage or dysfunction). In most (but not all) cases, tests are scored for correct responses so that high scores reflect better performances than low scores. If the patient's scores on an individual measure or on multiple measures are lower than would be expected for a normal person of that age or education and are within the range of the scores of patients with brain dysfunction, then the neuropsychologist must decide whether the presence of brain dysfunction can be inferred for that patient. Can this fundamental neuropsychological inference be made simply because the patient has obtained an abnormal score? (The concepts of *normal* and *abnormal* are discussed further in Chapter 5.) The short answer to the question is no. The ability to make such an inference under the circumstances described is difficult and in most cases cannot be made on the basis of the test scores alone. The process of making clinical neuropsychological judgments involves the integration of details of the patient's past and current life circumstances with empirical test data.

THE ROLE OF HISTORY

The ability of a neuropsychological test (or any clinical test for that matter) to predict or decide the clinical category to which a patient belongs can be divided into two quantifiable criteria: *sensitivity* and *specificity*. Sensitivity is the probability that the test detects or classifies a condition that is actually present. Specificity is the probability that the test correctly detects or classifies a normal performance. Tests that are specific minimize the number of normal performances that are classified as abnormal. Tests that are sensitive classify a patient as belonging to a particular group.

Consider making the decision that an individual test score belongs to a healthy person (HP) or a person with brain dysfunction (BD). Sensitivity is the proportion of individuals with BD that the test will correctly identify as having BD, whereas specificity is the proportion of individuals who are HP and are correctly identified as HP. Values for sensitivity and specificity may vary between 0% and 100%. A test may be sensitive but not specific; that is, a test may correctly identify individuals with BD as having BD but may also misclassify HP individuals as having BD. A test may also be specific but not sensitive; that is, the test may have a low rate of misclassifying HP individuals as having BD but may also have a low rate of correctly classifying patients with BD as having BD. Well-designed tests usually try to maximize both criteria, allowing trade-offs to reflect the consequences of making an incorrect decision.

The ability of a test to be sensitive and specific is greatly affected by the proportion of actual individuals in the clinical and nonclinical categories. When a condition is rare, tests tend to be less specific (i.e., they tend to classify more individuals into the clinical group) than when the condition is more common. When a condition is common, a test (assuming it is less than perfectly sensitive) tends to miss the occurrence of the condition. We return to the topic of base rates and diagnostic accuracy in some detail in Chapter 5, but as a general rule, the patient's history provides information that allows a clinician to estimate the likelihood that a given individual is part of a particular diagnostic category. This knowledge in turn helps to determine the likelihood that the individual will show deficits on neuropsychological tests. Part of this estimation process includes determining the cognitive, behavioral, and personality characteristics that might predate any illnesses and that might contribute to the appearance of measurable performance deficits on neuropsychological tests. This determination is made by eliciting a patient's history; it is critical to the interpretation of neuropsychological tests because many neuropsychological tests are typically affected by both neuropsychological and nonneuropsychological factors, such as effort or motivation and mood. Performance on any test of cognitive ability (i.e., most neuropsychological tests) is affected by the level of cognitive or premorbid abilities as well as the illnesses or conditions that predate the neurological injury or illness. The social and cultural background of a patient can also affect performance on neuropsychological tests. Likewise, performance is affected by various lifestyle characteristics such as nutrition and sleep and by a variety of nonneurological medical conditions, such as chronic pain or medication effects. Performance can also be affected by personality characteristics such as attitude, motivation, and self-esteem.

If a neuropsychological condition is judged to be unlikely from a patient's history, this affects how test results are interpreted or used. Conversely, if a condition is judged to be common from history, this also affects how test results are interpreted or used. For example, an individual with a history of consistently poor academic performance and a vocational history consisting primarily of unskilled labor-based positions might be expected to achieve lower than normal scores on neuropsychological tests that are sensitive to the same factors related to academic performance; such tests include intelligence, vocabulary, and achievement tests. This individual is more likely to show what appear to be neuropsychological deficits than an individual with a history of excellent academic performance and a vocational history consisting of managerial or professional positions. Judgments about the effect of illnesses on brain function would need to be made more conservatively about the former patient than the latter. Ideally these judgments are made adjusted to normative data reflecting these two individuals' differing premorbid achievement levels. We revisit this issue in our discussion of test validity in Chapter 5.

HISTORY GATHERING

History is generally gathered from record review and clinical interviews. The sources for record review are many and varied. When possible, records pertaining to medical history, psychiatric history, family history, education, and vocation should be obtained. Interview information can also come from a variety of sources, including the patient and his or her spouse, parents, siblings, teachers, caregivers, or some combination of these individuals. Because a thorough review of a patient's history is an important part of the assessment process, every effort should be made to obtain relevant history from multiple sources and not from patient report alone, especially when patient report appears unreliable. Information obtained from significant others and records can corroborate the information obtained from the patient and can supplement those areas that are unfamiliar or unknown to the patient.

The most reliable sources of medical history are usually hospital or treating physician records. In many cases, however, historical information must

DON'T FORGET
....
A neuropsychologist's analysis and interpretation of the test results are limited by the history obtained.

be gathered from the patient or an informant. The clinician needs to be cognizant of the reliability of these data's sources and must temper any predictions or clinical judgments on the basis of the judged accuracy of the source. Self-report about the conditions causing unconsciousness, for example, may be particularly unreliable and should always be corroborated carefully. If self-report is the only source of information, the patient's motivation for presenting himself or herself as sick or well must also be considered. Patients and other interested informants may distort medical history to promote a particular perceived outcome of the examination. For example, a patient who is trying to avoid institutionalization or some other loss of independence may not reveal pertinent facts about falls, cardiac disease, or functional problems. Patients involved in litigation may sometimes embellish the facts surrounding the event at issue in the legal proceeding and may not report other illnesses or conditions that could have caused their problems. It is the neuropsychologist's responsibility to judge the accuracy and reliability of any source of medical history and, when possible and necessary, to corroborate the information.

CONTENT OF IMPORTANT HISTORICAL INFORMATION

Multiple items must be addressed in record review and clinical interview, varying from the mundane, such as demographic information, to the personal, such as psychiatric history. Every effort should be made to address each of these areas when they are relevant to a particular patient. Within each of the areas to be addressed, multiple questions arise that require answers. Rapid Reference 3.1 provides a summary of the categories of items that should be addressed in record review and clinical interview.

Basic Demographic Information

The questions here focus on name, age, date of birth, race, sex, address, phone number, and handedness. This information forms the basis for scoring of tests according to the correct demographic group and is important for billing purposes as well. An acute confusional state or dementia might be suspected if an adolescent or adult patient is unable to supply this information.

Description of the Current Illness or Presenting Problem

It is important to obtain a detailed account of the patient's current symptoms and complaints, their pervasiveness and severity, and their effect on day-to-day living.

≡ Rapid Reference 3.1

Important Items to Be Addressed in Record Review and Clinical Interview

- Basic demographic data
- Description of current illness or presenting problem
- Medical history
- Psychiatric history
- Educational history
- Vocational history
- Birth history and early development
- Family background and history
- Current situation
- Legal history
- Military history

The clinician is interested in the subjective characteristics of the illness and the length of time the patient has been affected by the illness. The clinician should find out when the illness or symptoms began and what provoked the disorder. It is also important to discover any variation in symptoms over time and what medications, treatments, and diagnostic tests the patient has received for the problems. The patient may have already been diagnosed, and the current evaluator should also know that information, as well as the functional impact that the illness or injury has had on the patient's life. Rapid Reference 3.2 provides an outline of the areas of focus when delineating the history of the presenting problem.

In many evaluations the referral question may center on an injury incurred as a result of an accident. In this instance, it is important to gather information about the accident. In addition to the patient's self-report, records that are particularly helpful include police records of the accident, records from emergency medical technicians or ambulance personnel, emergency room records, and nursing notes following the initial trauma. It also becomes important to gather postinjury records to track the course of the injury. Again, this comes from interviews with the patient (when possible) and from review of medical records (also when possible). The medical records that need to be examined include reports from independent medical examinations, reports of neurosurgical and neurological examinations and interventions, neuroradiological reports, hospital discharge summaries, and

Rapid Reference 3.2

History of Presenting Problem

- A description of current symptoms and complaints
- The severity of symptoms
- The pervasiveness and duration of symptoms
- Time of onset
- Treatments and their success
- Medications and doses
- Prior evaluations

Rapid Reference 3.3

Relevant Injury and Postinjury Records

- Police records of the accident
- Emergency medical technician and ambulance reports
- Emergency room records
- Reports of independent medical examinations
- Neurological, neurosurgical, and neuroradiological records
- Hospital records
- Physician records
- Psychological and neuropsychological assessment records, including raw test data

summaries of the examining and treating physicians, as well as previous psychological and neuropsychological assessment records, including the raw data or recording sheets for tests. Rapid Reference 3.3 summarizes the relevant injury and postinjury records that the neuropsychologist should try to obtain and review for evaluating an injury and its effects.

Medical History

This section focuses on the presence of major illnesses, accidental injuries, exposure to toxins, and episodes of loss of consciousness. Of interest are conditions that have some likelihood of affecting neuropsychological test results (e.g., brain injury, epilepsy, stroke, and so on) but may include other conditions that present some functional limitation on the individual (e.g., asthma, colitis, and chronic obstructive pulmonary disease). Details are needed in these same categories for current illness, including time of onset, pervasiveness and severity of symptoms, past and current treatments, and the progression of symptoms. In addition, data must be gathered concerning current and past health care providers and past and current medications and doses. Also of interest here are lifestyle variables that can affect physical health such as the use of drugs or alcohol, consumption of caffeine, quality of sleep, and history of nicotine use. Examination of medical history must examine instances of closed head injury; episodes of loss of consciousness, seizures, or epilepsy; cerebrovascular accidents; and other cerebrovascular conditions, such as aneurysm, congenital abnormalities, and so on. Each of these disorders carries a potential risk of long-standing permanent changes in cognitive functioning. Also important are a history of cardiac disease, hypertension, diabetes, and chronic obstructive pulmonary disease, because these disorders are risk factors for ischemic changes in the brain. Infectious diseases, such as encephalitis, meningitis, and brain abscesses; degenerative diseases such as multiple sclerosis, Parkinson's disease, and so on; and metabolic disorders such as hypothyroidism, hyperthyroidism, liver disease, and pituitary disease can also affect cognitive function. Examination of medical history must also consider a history of toxic encephalopathies; congenital or developmental diseases or disorders, such as Sturge–Weber, tuberous sclerosis, Williams syndrome, and Klinefelter's syndrome; and pervasive developmental disorders along with dementing disorder such as Alzheimer's disease and Pick's disease. Rapid Reference 3.4 provides a brief list of the many areas of medical history relevant to neuropsychological assessment.

Medical history is also concerned with the details of a patient's alcohol or drug use. Information concerning the drug or drugs of choice, the extent of a patient's use, and known health consequences needs to be obtained. Substance abuse history should focus on estimates of frequency and amount of use, presence of current or past blackouts, and history of alcohol- and drug-related treatment and legal involvement. Because of the social stigma associated with substance abuse, this information may be particularly inaccurate when provided by the patient, especially without adequate time for rapport and trust to be developed between patient and examiner. For this reason, it is important to document the source and circumstances in which substance abuse information was obtained.

It is also important to know a patient's past and present history of medication use. What medication a patient has been prescribed or is currently taking is

≡ *Rapid Reference 3.4*

Medical History Relevant to Neuropsychological Assessment

- Closed head injury
- Episodes of loss of consciousness
- Epilepsy or seizures
- Cerebrovascular accidents and other cerebrovascular abnormalities (e.g., aneurysm)
- Cardiac disease, hypertension, diabetes, chronic obstructive pulmonary disease
- Infectious diseases (e.g., encephalitis, meningitis, brain abscess)
- Degenerative diseases (e.g., multiple sclerosis, Parkinson's disease)
- Metabolic disorders (e.g., hyperthyroidism, hypothyroidism, liver disease)
- Toxic encephalopathy
- Congenital or developmental diseases or disorders (e.g., Sturge–Weber, tuberous sclerosis, pervasive developmental disorder)
- Dementing disorders (e.g., Alzheimer's disease, Pick's disease)
- Physical handicaps
- Alcohol or drug use
- Current and past medications and doses
- Past and current health care providers

important because the side effects of medications can include CNS changes and compromises.

Psychiatric History

Many psychiatric illnesses and their associated symptoms can negatively affect neuropsychological test performance and function. While gathering history, a neuropsychologist must therefore review past and present psychological and psychiatric symptoms and diagnoses. Details are needed in these same categories for current and past medical illness, including time of onset and the pervasiveness and severity of symptoms. In addition to obtaining information about diagnosis, the clinician should gather details about its effect on daily functioning. Information pertaining to number and length of psychiatric hospitalizations, counseling, and

≡ Rapid Reference 3.5

Psychiatric History Relevant to Neuropsychological Assessment

- Current symptoms and complaints
- Onset and course of symptoms
- Pervasiveness and severity
- Findings from past and present evaluations
- Hospitalizations
- Past suicide attempts
- Past and present treatment
- Effect of symptoms on day-to-day living

psychotherapy, as well as past and current medications and doses and history of electroconvulsive therapy are also relevant to this category. Additionally, information about past suicide attempts, including the means and subsequent medical consequences (e.g., hypoxia, loss of consciousness) can provide data about possible sources of neuropsychological dysfunction. Rapid Reference 3.5 provides an outline of the areas of focus when obtaining history concerning psychiatric history.

Particular attention should be paid to several classes of disorders because of their association with disorganized thinking, depressive or vegetative symptoms, and anxiety, all of which can disrupt performance on neuropsychological tests in the absence of objective neurological dysfunction. Attention also should be paid to psychiatric disorders that involve somatization or long-standing personality characteristics that may result in motivational issues or poor cooperation. Of particular importance are psychotic disorders, including schizophrenia; affective disorders, such as major depression and bipolar disorder; anxiety disorders, including posttraumatic stress disorder and obsessive–compulsive disorder; somatoform disorders, including conversion disorder and pain disorder; and personality disorders, such as borderline personality disorder or obsessive–compulsive personality disorder. Rapid Reference 3.6 provides a list of the psychiatric conditions relevant to neuropsychological assessment.

Educational History

Educational history is one of several variables that is used to determine premorbid IQ and serves as a baseline against which to compare neuropsychological test

≡ Rapid Reference 3.6

Psychiatric Conditions Relevant to Neuropsychological Assessment

- Schizophrenia and other psychotic disorders, such as schizoaffective disorder and delusional disorder
- Affective disorders, such as major depression and bipolar disorder
- Anxiety disorders, such as generalized anxiety disorder, posttraumatic stress disorder, and obsessive–compulsive disorder
- Somatoform disorders, such as somatization disorder, pain disorder, and conversion disorder
- Personality disorders, such as borderline personality disorder and obsessive–compulsive personality disorder

results. The information obtained in this category must go beyond simply learning the highest grade attained by the patient. Other important details that should be established include the schools the patient attended, the course or program of study and its difficulty level (e.g., vocational vs. college preparatory), pattern of attendance, and grade-point average. Information should also be obtained concerning academic strengths and weaknesses, as well as whether the patient has a history of learning disability and special education placements. Other important data include whether the patient has a history of attention-deficit/hyperactivity disorder (ADHD) or behavioral problems in school resulting in detention, suspension, or expulsion. Rapid Reference 3.7 summarizes the areas on which to focus when obtaining historical information about educational history.

Depending on the age of the subject and the reason for referral, educational history may be gathered through a patient's self-report or by the report of an informant such as a parent. Sometimes, however, the clinician should obtain school records and not rely on the patient's self-report or on the report of an informant. In these instances, school transcripts can clarify the patient's academic performance and may contain other important information such as standardized test scores. For children, school records will usually contain special education plans and reports from psychoeducational evaluations. Such records should almost always (if possible) be obtained if the patient is of school (including college) age. In addition to increasing the accuracy of information over self- or informant report, the school records for children and young adults can provide detailed information about the cognitive strengths and weaknesses that may be the focus of

≡ *Rapid Reference 3.7*

Relevant Educational History

- Highest grade attended
- Schools attended
- Academic strengths and weaknesses
- Course type and difficulty
- Grade point average
- History of learning disability
- History of attention-deficit/hyperactivity disorder
- Special education placements
- Transcripts of grades
- Standardized test scores
- Reports from psychoeducational evaluations

the neuropsychological referral in this age group. It is usually less critical (and often difficult) to obtain educational records for older adults; however, when available, school records may be helpful to determine whether an adult has a long-standing learning disability rather than a problem of new onset that is contributing to their current level of performance.

Vocational History

The historical information relevant to vocation includes the dates and types of occupational positions held, the reasons for leaving a job, job stability, level of attainment, and performance evaluations. By gathering this information, the neuropsychologist can learn much about the consistency of a patient's employment, his or her level of responsibility within a company, and the complexity of a patient's job. Information concerning the areas on which to focus when obtaining historical information about vocational history is provided in Rapid Reference 3.8.

This vocational information has in turn some predictive relationship to premorbid IQ. In particular, in adults born before World War II, vocational history may be a more accurate correlate of premorbid IQ than educational level. Many adults born before World War II did not finish high school, and few earned college degrees. A large number completed only 6 or 8 years of education (Matarazzo, 1972) but not necessarily because of limitations in cognitive ability. During and

≡ *Rapid Reference 3.8*

Relevant Vocational History

- Dates and types of occupational positions held
- Reasons for leaving a job
- Job stability
- Highest level of attainment
- Job complexity and level of responsibility and independence
- Performance evaluations

after the Great Depression in the 1930s, children were pressured to work and contribute to the economic survival of their families. Many of these adults who left school early went on to have successful vocational histories and relatively high socioeconomic status, thus making academic achievement a poor predictor of occupational success. In these circumstances, vocational history would more accurately predict a higher level of premorbid ability than years of education. After World War II, laws requiring students to be enrolled in school until their 16th birthday, a growing expectation that students would complete high school, and open enrollment policies for colleges have made education a critical predictor of premorbid ability for individuals born after World War II. The clinician must examine such cultural factors when making judgments about the accuracy and weight given to the different indicators of premorbid ability.

Birth History and Early Development

In some instances, the source of cognitive difficulties occurs early in life and is related to birth or postnatal trauma; thus, historical information concerning birth and early development is helpful in differential diagnosis. It is important to know about pre-, peri-, and postnatal difficulties. Information should be gathered about prenatal care and complications during pregnancy, labor, and delivery. In addition, age of attainment of early developmental milestones can assist the neuropsychologist in viewing a problem as long-standing versus new. Did the patient learn to walk and talk on time, or were there unusual delays? Did the patient develop at the same rate as his or her siblings? Information also should be obtained about childhood illnesses or injuries, their treatment, and the child's recovery, as well as

≡ *Rapid Reference 3.9*

Relevant Birth and Early Development History

- Pregnancy
  - Complications (e.g., anemia, toxemia, maternal diabetes, infections, toxic exposure)
  - Cigarette, alcohol, or drug exposure during pregnancy
  - Length of pregnancy
  - Mother's age at birth
- Birth
  - Length of labor
  - Complications (e.g., cesarean section, forceps, fetal distress, breech, nuchal cord, seizures)
  - Apgar scores
  - Birth weight
  - Neonatal problems
- Early development
  - Age of attainment of milestones
  - Complications (e.g., colic, apnea, failure to thrive, poor feeding)
  - Childhood illnesses and injuries (e.g., ear infections, asthma, scarlet fever, meningitis, febrile seizures, head injuries, allergies)
  - Behavior problems

information pertaining to behavioral disorders in childhood. Rapid Reference 3.9 provides an overview of the birth and early developmental history relevant to a neuropsychological assessment.

When evaluating a child, the neuropsychologist can usually acquire this information from parents or medical records. Many adults will not know specific details about their birth, such as weight at birth, or about their early development, but they may be aware of unusual occurrences or abnormalities and be able to share that information.

Family Background and History

Family history information is also important for analyzing the data obtained in a neuropsychological assessment and, in some cases, this may mean obtaining actual

≡ Rapid Reference 3.10

Relevant Family Background

- Age and health status or cause of death of parents, siblings, and children
- Educational achievement of parents, siblings, and children
- Occupational achievement of parents, siblings, and children
- Psychiatric history of parents, siblings, and children
- Medical and neurological history of parents, siblings, and children
- Cultural background

medical and school records to corroborate the report of family members. Records of family background include information about the age and health status (or cause of death) of parents, siblings, and children. Also relevant is historical information about the educational and occupational achievement, psychiatric history, and medical and neurological history of parents, siblings, and children. Many disorders may be genetically based (e.g., ADHD, learning disability) or associated with sociodemographic factors (e.g., poverty, maltreatment, or abuse); therefore, family history must be collected to ensure a comprehensive evaluation. Cultural background is also relevant because it may influence family values and development. Rapid Reference 3.10 summarizes the family history and background information of concern to a neuropsychological assessment.

Current Situation

It is also important to collect details about a patient's current situation. Knowledge of a patient's work, home, and social routines, including a description of a typical day, recreational activities, hobbies, and exercise programs, can provide a wealth of information about a patient's capabilities. Knowledge about current life stresses, including the recent death or illness of a significant other, distressed interpersonal relationships, recent job changes, and financial worries, can inform the examiner about pressures that may be hindering a patient's daily functioning or contributing to emotional upset. In addition, knowledge about a patient's home life is important. Does this child live with his or her parents and siblings, or is the child in a foster home? Is this adult patient married or divorced? Is this patient's spouse healthy, caring, and financially secure? Is this patient satisfied with his or her current relationship, including in the area of

≡ Rapid Reference 3.11

Relevant Current Situation

- Living arrangements
- Work, home, and social routines, including recreational activities, hobbies, and exercise programs
- Current stresses, including family crises, history of abuse, distressed interpersonal relationships, job changes or problems, and financial concerns
- Marital status and marital history

sexual intimacy? Is there a history of abuse? Rapid Reference 3.11 provides a summary of the areas to be explored when obtaining information about a patient's current living situation.

Legal History

Historical information about a patient's involvement with the legal system may also reveal important facts that affect the interpretation of the test data. In forensic cases, a history of frequent litigation may be an important point to consider. In the case of a patient with a behavioral disorder, the severity may be indicated by a history of criminal involvement. Again, because of the social stigma associated with criminal background, the clinician must be cautious about relying on only a single source for this information.

Military History

Obviously this category is not relevant in many cases. For those patients who have served in the military, however, historical information concerning dates of service, assignments, combat status, rank achieved, and discharge status may provide data consistent with or at odds with nonmilitary history and the presenting complaint. Also relevant may be the type and degree of any injury sustained while in the military.

THE CLINICAL INTERVIEW

In addition to giving the neuropsychologist the opportunity to gather information about a patient's medical and social history, the clinical interview is an important source of other information relevant to the interpretation of neuropsychological tests. Like a test measure, the interview provides a sample of behavior from which certain generalizations or inferences may be made. In this way, the clinical interview is one of the best sources of information regarding a patient's affect and mood, insight, and motivation for testing. The interview contributes critical samples of behavior relevant to attention, language, and memory functions. The interview may provide information about the organization, focus, and detail of the patient's thinking, as well as the subjective aspects of his or her presenting problem. From an interview the neuropsychologist may learn that formal testing is impossible. For example, the clinician may learn in the interview that the patient is simply too delusional, confused, or delirious to produce reliable or valid test results. The clinical interview also provides the examiner with an opportunity to explain the testing procedure and to decrease the patient's anxiety.

Interviewing is a skill that develops with practice, experience, and the supervision of a competent teacher. Although this textbook does not allow for a complete course in interviewing, we do discuss the basics of a clinical neuropsychological interview. No hard and fast rules for interviewing exist. Assuming a proper setting and a cooperative patient, the factors that make an interview more productive include establishing rapport, facilitating communication, and using questions effectively.

The interview and assessment should be conducted in a quiet area, free of as many distractions related to noise, visible activity, and environment as possible. Controlling distractions also means discouraging any intrusions or modifications to the environment that make the testing situation substantially different from the environment in which the tests were standardized. The presence of a third-party observer, which includes another neuropsychologist, audiotaping, videotaping, and using one-way mirrors, during an evaluation creates a potential confounding factor in the interpretation of test findings. Observers can interfere with testing by serving as a distraction or by altering performance by way of social facilitation effects (McCaffrey, Fisher, Gold, & Lynch, 1996). Observing behavior can influence and change behavior in ways that cannot be known. In addition, having an observer present during testing is inconsistent with testing standards, which demand a distraction-free testing environment (American Educational Research Association, American Psychological Association, & National Council on Measurement in Education, 1999). It is also at odds with testing manuals (e.g., Wechsler Adult Intelligence Scale—III, Wechsler Memory Scale—IV, and Wechsler Intelligence Scale for Children-IV) stating that no observers should be present in the testing room because it is necessary to minimize any potential distractions (Wechsler, 1997, 2003, 2009). The presence of a third-party observer during an evaluation also potentially decreases the neuropsychologist's ability to rely on normative data.

Neuropsychological tests were standardized in one-on-one conditions with only the examiner and the examinee present. To ensure reliable use of the normative data, administration of neuropsychological tests requires that the same standard set of procedures be followed. In 2000 the National Academy of Neuropsychology (2000a) set forth an official statement concerning the presence of third-party observers during neuropsychological testing, as did the American Academy of Clinical Neuropsychology in 2001. In some instances with young children it may be necessary to have a parent in the room initially to obtain the child's cooperation. In these cases, the clinician should try to begin with nonformal observational measures, and after the child is comfortable and after his or her parent leaves, standardized tests can be administered.

It is unethical to audiotape or videotape an interview or encounter with a patient without explicit permission. In addition, audiotaping and videotaping interviews may pose a risk to the integrity of the information obtained. According to McCaffrey et al. (1996), data suggest that replacing the presence of third-party observers with audiotape or videotape "may not be immune to the effects of social facilitation" (p. 446) because audiotaping and videotaping an interview and test session introduce the same risk of confounding the data (Constantinou, Ashendorf, & McCaffrey, 2002, 2005).

DON'T FORGET

Third-party observation and videotaping of interviews and testing sessions create potential sources of interference and diminish the examiner's ability to rely on normative data. Standardized tests should not be administered if third-party observers are present.

The setting also plays a role in the interview. A quiet, pleasant office with a testing table and a comfortable chair is preferable for many patients, but in some cases, it may be necessary to test the patient at bedside or while the patient is seated in a wheelchair. In other cases, the neuropsychologist may have little control over the environment, such as when the evaluation must be conducted in the attorney's room in a prison. The neuropsychologist's office should be a professional space. Although it should not be cluttered with too many distracting personal mementos or trophies, it also should not be sterile or void of personal touches. The testing table and any wall hangings should be arranged so that distractions are limited. If possible, the testing table should not allow the patient an opportunity to gaze out the window or be distracted by activities outdoors. Likewise, personal items in the office should be placed out of the patient's view during the test session. Interruptions must be eliminated or kept to a minimum. Phones should be switched to voicemail and a *do not disturb* sign should be placed on the door. Offices should be fairly soundproof. A white-noise machine can sometimes add a screen of noise to permit privacy if necessary. Neuropsychological test interpretation is based on the assumption that a patient's performance has been optimized. Any environmental factors that may affect a patient's optimal performance need to be noted and considered in the interpretation of the test results.

Initially, the interviewer should take some time to make the patient comfortable by attempting to establish rapport. Good rapport is necessary for the purposes of interview because a negative or hostile relationship makes interviewing difficult. The establishment of rapport with the patient is a matter of personal style and varies tremendously from clinician to clinician. Some clinicians spend time engaging the client in casual conversation, whereas others may begin testing immediately. Although engaging the patient in so-called small talk sometimes helps the process of establishing rapport, casual conversation usually should be kept to a minimum to maintain professional boundaries. In the beginning, however, conversation about innocuous events may help to break the ice and allow a patient time to adjust to the situation. Interviewer behaviors that can damage rapport include sarcasm, flippant remarks, and boasts about the interviewer's competence. Other behaviors that can damage rapport include allowing mail or notes to become a distraction and lecturing a patient about mistakes that could have been avoided. Copious note taking that distracts the interviewer from paying attention to the patient is strongly discouraged.

At the beginning of the interview, the neuropsychologist needs to discuss the limits of confidentiality and deal with the issue of informed consent. The neuropsychologist also needs to establish that the patient understands the reason for the evaluation and the basic features of the test session; this informs the patient of what is about to occur, how long the testing takes, and what the patient can expect. It also gives the interviewer a chance to alleviate any anxiety a patient may have about the evaluation, and it gives the patient time to become comfortable with the examiner before commencing the actual testing, which can be threatening to some patients. Many interviewers begin by asking patients to explain why they are being tested and to describe the problems they may be having. In addition to providing some clues about the potential cause of a patient's complaints and a basis for formulating recommendations addressing perceived problems, these relatively open-ended questions provide the patient with the opportunity to construct an organized narrative with some internal logic and connections. The clinician can then use this opportunity to observe whether the patient can tell the story of the illness or injury with a beginning, middle, and end. The clinician can observe whether a patient is focused, digressive, or tangential and whether his or her language is characterized by appropriate grammar, vocabulary, and prosody.

The clinician can also note whether the patient seems appropriately concerned about the impact of his or her problems or whether the patient even recognizes that he or she has a problem. The clinician can observe whether the patient appears inappropriately sad, elated, anxious, or indifferent. With experience, clinicians can learn to recognize whether the patient is able to plan responses, recall the details from the recent and remote past, and focus responses on relevant details.

In terms of communication, the interviewer should follow several guidelines. The interviewer must be sure to talk to the patient in a language that he or she understands and avoid clinical jargon and words outside a patient's background. It is also important to avoid using words that carry one meaning to the clinician and quite another to a layperson. Whereas a clinician might use the word *retarded* to mean an individual with an IQ below 70 and adaptive deficits, the layperson may see this term as pejorative. Effective communication also requires an effective use of silences. Silences must be judged for their meaning within an interview. The interviewer need not feel compelled to fill in silences just to hear him- or herself talk. During silences, patients may be gathering their thoughts or collecting themselves; they may need a brief break before continuing. Effective listening includes hearing silences as part of the communication process.

In an interview, the types of questions used guide the types of responses that are received. Open-ended questions often are more productive than questions calling for briefly worded responses. Open-ended questions do not allow a patient to respond with a simple *yes* or *no*. They allow a patient the opportunity to define what is important and to respond in ways that are more revealing than an affirmation or denial. For example, instead of asking: "Did you find that you were more forgetful after your accident?" it is preferable to ask: "How was your life different after your accident?" or "How did you function differently after your accident?" Open-ended questions also permit informal observation of the patient's language ability. Does the patient have difficulty expressing her or his thoughts, or are there word-finding difficulties in spontaneous speech? Is there a stutter or unusual pauses? Is phrase length normal? Ultimately, if specifics are needed, then open-ended questions can be followed by more precise questions.

When a patient seems to be having difficulty explaining something, the interviewer can aid with comments or questions asking the patient to expand on an issue or requesting the patient to describe a particular aspect of an issue: for instance, how he or she was feeling when the illness or injury manifested itself. Just as is in the testing situation, the interviewer can ask a patient to be more specific when talking about an issue or ask the patient to provide an example of a particular problem or complaint. Questions can also be used to clarify information or to rephrase a patient's statement to be sure that the interviewer has understood a response. Of course, when rapport has been sufficiently established, direct questions may be more useful in allowing a patient to get to the point more quickly.

The interviewer and patient communicate nonverbally as well as verbally during an interview. Both the patient and the interviewer communicate with each other through facial expressions, tone of voice, eye contact, body placement, and gestures. The interviewer should be aware that while he or she is observing the patient's nonverbal behaviors, the patient also might well be reading the interviewer's nonverbal communications.

BEHAVIORAL OBSERVATIONS

Although no norms are available to consult regarding interviews, the observations made during an interview can supplement formal test results, providing examples of behavior that may epitomize the problems determined by standardized measures. In some cases, the observations made in the course of the interview may alter the interpretations of test results. For example, if a patient was observed to have word-finding difficulty, characterized by word-finding pauses, circumlocutions, and even word errors, that patient would be expected to perform poorly on IQ tests requiring expressive language ability and on tests of verbal memory. In other cases, the observations made in the course of the interview may suggest nonneurological explanations for test results (e.g., anxiety, thought disorder). For example, if a patient is exceedingly anxious during testing, slowing or tremulousness may disrupt his or her performance.

> **DON'T FORGET**
>
> The means to collect data include
> • Record review
> • Clinical interview
> • Behavioral observation
> • Questionnaires
> • Neuropsychological evaluation

Behavioral observations during interview and testing provide a wealth of information to the context in which the test data will be interpreted. Behavioral observations allow the examiner an informal assessment of motivation and attention. It is important to recognize, however, that observing a patient cooperate with the interview does not mean observing that the patient is giving optimal effort. They also permit the examiner to see a patient's limitations in a nontest situation and allow the patient to demonstrate his or her symptoms. Behavioral observations may also give the examiner a chance to glimpse personality characteristics that could influence test performance, suggesting alternative explanations from brain dysfunction for the test results.

Behavioral observations center on issues such as the patient's appearance, the patient's level of alertness and arousal, and the patient's level of orientation and cooperation. Behavioral observations need to be made concerning use of language, sensorimotor functioning, and interpersonal skills. In addition, behavioral observations focus on a patient's mood, reality testing, and thought control, as well as on issues such as learning and memory, insight, and judgment. The following is a list of issues that can be addressed through observations made in the course of a clinical interview:

1. The interview showcases a patient's level of alertness and arousal and his or her susceptibility to distraction. Is the patient oriented to person, place, and date? The need for frequent repetition and reminders to perform a task, the need for frequent refocusing, responses to stray noises or movement, a sleepy or (on the contrary) hypervigilant appearance may indicate limits in attentional ability that would undermine test performance. These factors may also be indicators of the presence of some forms of brain dysfunction or psychiatric conditions. Also important here is activity, including energy level, motor findings, and speed.

2. The interview gives the interviewer a chance to observe how cooperative a patient is going to be with an evaluation. Indirectly, this can guide interpretations about the likelihood that test results are a reliable and valid reflection of optimal level of functioning. Although not as accurate as tests of compliance and motivation, it is additional data that can be assimilated into the whole clinical picture.

3. The interview provides an opportunity to observe the patient's level of hygiene and standard of dress. Attention must be paid to a patient's appearance, including manner of dress, level of grooming, gait and posture, mannerisms, and physical abnormalities. Is the patient appropriately groomed or disheveled and malodorous? A disregard for minimal standards of hygiene and neatness should be noted because it may be related to brain dysfunction and various psychiatric conditions.

4. The interchange that is part of a clinical interview allows ample opportunity to observe a patient's spontaneous speech in a situation requiring open-ended discourse. Use and comprehension of conversational vocabulary, word-finding difficulties, appropriateness of syntax, and prosody of speech production are all showcased for the examiner in this way. Rapid Reference 3.12 provides a list of the important behavioral observations that can be made during the interview and neuropsychological testing.

≡ *Rapid Reference 3.12*

Important Behavioral Observations During the Clinical Interview

- Level of arousal and alertness, including energy level, motor findings such as hyperactivity, and speed
- Appearance, including manner of dress, level of grooming, gait and posture, mannerisms, and physical abnormalities
- Level of cooperation, including motivation and effort
- Discourse abilities, including ability to understand and produce conversational speech
- Sensorimotor functioning, including eyesight, hearing, muscle strength, and the use of aids such as glasses, hearing aids, canes, and so forth
- Appropriateness of social skills and level of anxiety
- Speech, including rate, tone, prosody, articulation, fluency, and word choice
- Emotionality, including affect, mood, and appropriateness
- Thought content and processes, including organization and reality testing
- Memory, including retrieval of recent and remote events

5. The interview allows the neuropsychologist a chance to observe sensorimotor functioning and any abnormalities that may interfere with test performance. Does the patient wear glasses or contacts? Does the patient have difficulty hearing? Does the patient wear a hearing aid? Are there motor abnormalities? Does the patient walk with a cane? Is there evidence of ataxia, spasticity, or muscle weakness? The presence of sensorimotor abnormalities may contribute to the neuropsychologist's understanding of a brain disorder and may signal limitations in test interpretation because of interfering factors.

6. The interview provides an optimal opportunity to gather information about a patient's social skills and level of anxiety. Can the patient establish a comfortable interpersonal interaction with the examiner? Is the patient's behavior socially and age appropriate as evidenced by posture, eye contact, mannerisms, and so forth? Behavior that is excessively shy or excessively forward and familiar may be a correlate of some forms of brain dysfunction or different psychiatric conditions.

The patient's behavior in the interview situation may parallel his or her behavior outside the interview situation, thus contributing to an understanding of a patient's behavior in real-life social situations.

7. The interview allows the neuropsychologist to examine a patient's emotionality, including affect, mood, and appropriateness. Depression and anxiety are two nonneurological sources for disruption in neuropsychological test performance. Emotional lability and inappropriateness can also sometimes reflect a reaction to loss as a result of brain dysfunction or organic changes directly related to a brain insult.

8. The clinical interview gives the clinician a chance to gauge a patient's level of insight into his or her deficits and their causes. What is the patient's reaction to the nature and severity of deficits? Is the patient denying any illness, suggesting a possible anosognosia? Is the patient exaggerating symptoms, suggesting a cry for attention? Does the patient fail to appreciate the significance of physical limitations, suggesting impaired judgment?

9. The interview provides the examiner with an opportunity to observe the coherence of the patient's expository or narrative language, evidence of how well the patient's thoughts are organized. Is the patient prone to give irrelevant details when telling a story, suggesting circumstantiality? Can the patient stick to a particular train of thought, or is the patient tangential? Is the patient's thinking disorganized, reflecting a possible thought disorder or perhaps impaired reality testing?

10. The interview also allows an informal evaluation of memory abilities. In an interview a patient demonstrates his or her ability to recall the details of recent and increasingly remote autobiographical events. Does the patient have difficulty remembering events from yesterday versus a long time ago? Can the patient recall the details of events but not their order or the time frame of autobiographical events? Observations here can provide a basis for hypotheses about what results formal memory testing will provide, and the data can then be examined for consistency.

In Chapter 7, we discuss how to present the information from clinical interview, record review, and behavioral observations in a report and how to integrate it with the results from neuropsychological assessment.

TEST YOURSELF

1. **Neuropsychological test results can be interpreted adequately against a backdrop of demographic data alone.**

   True or False?

2. **Specificity is the proportion of individuals with brain dysfunction that a test will correctly identify as having brain dysfunction, whereas sensitivity is the proportion of individuals who are healthy, who are correctly identified as healthy.**

   True or False?

3. **Determination of the cognitive, behavioral, and personality characteristics that might predate any illnesses and that might contribute to the appearance of measurable performance deficits is critical to the interpretation of neuropsychological tests because many neuropsychological tests are typically affected by both neuropsychological and non-neuropsychological factors, such as motivation and affect.**

   True or False?

4. **Which of the following features is one of the most important features regarding the physical arrangements of an interview or test session?**

   (a) Privacy

   (b) Reclining chair or couch

   (c) Taking detailed notes

   (d) Videotaping

5. **What is the best practice regarding the use of clinical jargon in an interview?**

   (a) It should be used often, especially with bright patients.

   (b) It should be minimized.

   (c) It must never be used.

   (d) It doesn't matter if it is used or not.

6. **Videotaping eliminates the potential sources of distraction created by third-party observation in a testing situation.**

   True or False?

Answers:

1. False; 2. False; 3. True; 4. a; 5. b; 6. False

Four

ESSENTIALS OF TEST SELECTION, ADMINISTRATION, AND SCORING

OVERVIEW

This chapter covers the basic conditions and logistics of the neuropsychological examination. Some of the advice dispensed in this chapter may seem the paragon of common sense to an experienced clinician. Expertise with such issues as optimizing test performance, monitoring of clinical test behavior, recording data, using standard procedures of test administration, and understanding the logic of test selection, however, can mean the difference between obtaining valid, clinically useful test results and malpractice. Even experienced clinicians can be taken by surprise by malingering or by patients with somatization disorders or conversion reactions if these phenomena are not part of their typical practice.

OPTIMIZING PERFORMANCE

In most cases the interpretation of neuropsychological tests is based on the central assumption that the performance measured by those tests represents the best effort of the patient delivered under conditions as close to optimal as possible. The exclusion of nonneurological causes is the first logical step in making the decision that a lower than expected test score or the presence of an unusual behavioral symptom is related to dysfunction of the central nervous system. This task may be undermined if the patient is unusually anxious, too hot or cold, or subjected to unusual or unpredictable sights or sounds. For example, it would not be unusual for an otherwise normal adult to perform poorly on a test of attention if during the test, voices can be heard arguing or (as sometimes is the case on a busy hospital ward) other patients are being examined, trays are being dropped, announcements are blaring from the overhead paging system, and so forth. Patients who are extremely anxious, ruminative, or distracted by internal thoughts may perform poorly on a number of neuropsychological tests, especially those requiring intense or sustained attention. Although these factors may be significant in predicting cognitive performance in other situations, they often preclude drawing inferences about brain function. Most patients who are referred for neuropsychological testing want to do their best, particularly if they understand the reasons for the testing and their effort's possible benefits to their treatment, job, or school performance.

Some patients, however, do not give their best effort when tested. This may be because they do not understand the reason for the assessment, have been referred involuntarily, or are involved in a situation in which they may gain or be rewarded for poor performance. It is the task of the neuropsychologist to arrange the testing conditions so that a patient can take advantage of the opportunity to work to potential. In this chapter, we discuss issues concerning the optimization of a patient's performance and motivation, as well as the steps required for administration and scoring in neuropsychological assessment.

> # DON'T FORGET
>
> It is the obligation of the examiner to arrange the testing conditions so that the patient can take advantage of the opportunity to work to potential.

Appropriate Testing Conditions

Optimally, neuropsychological testing should be undertaken in conditions that are reasonably quiet, with no foot traffic or distracting views. In most cases, this environment is an examination room that has sufficient artificial light (without glare and reflection), is kept at a comfortable temperature, and has adequate ventilation. It is usually best to seat the patient facing away from windows and doors from which activity can be seen and to prevent glare. When this is not possible, it may be necessary to keep shades drawn and doors closed, particularly if much visible activity is outside the room. The seating plan should also take into account wall spaces containing distracting pictures. If the external environment is noisy, it may be necessary to use a white-noise generator or to take steps to soundproof walls and doors. Many clients are not affected by external distractions, but even healthy adults may find themselves turning toward unusual sounds and conversation that divert their attention, particularly when they are anxious about being tested.

The office should appear welcoming and friendly. It probably should be conservatively decorated, however, reflecting the standards of the community in which the clinician works. As discussed in Chapter 3, the office should be a professional space with minimal personal mementos but should not be sterile and devoid of

≣ *Rapid Reference 4.1*

Appropriate Testing Conditions

- Quiet, nondistracting environment
- Well-lit room surfaces without glare
- Welcoming and friendly (but not overdone) room with comfortable seating
- Test materials organized and at hand, but out of sight, if possible, while not in use

all personal touches. Comfortable seating should be available to both examiner and patient. When administering the tests, most examiners prefer that patients sit opposite them at a sufficiently large table or desk. In some instances, however, because of particular test materials that require a viewing stand, the examiner may sit at the end of a rectangular table while the patient sits on the side. The examiner should also arrange the room so that test materials are close at hand and available for easy access. However, to limit possible distractions, test materials should not be presented before they are necessary. Organization and readiness of test materials permit a smooth transition from one test to the next, thereby decreasing the overall time in testing. Knowing your materials and being practiced in a particular test also keeps the test session flowing, leaving less time for the patient to become bored or lose interest. In addition, a familiarity with administration rules and scoring allows the examiner to administer tests in an automatic fashion so that more time can be devoted to observing a patient's behavior. Rapid Reference 4.1 summarizes the features important for appropriate testing conditions.

Testing must often be done in less than optimal conditions under which the examiner has little control over environment. For example, a hospitalized patient may have to be tested at bedside on a hospital ward, or an incarcerated individual may have to be tested in whatever space is available at the prison. In these instances, the examiner should orchestrate whatever details possible to ensure the best possible testing environment. The examiner should also keep a record of the conditions under which testing took place and include the information in the test report, particularly when the conditions may have had a direct impact on the performance of a particular task.

Establishing Rapport

To optimize the patient's performance, the examiner should try to gain the cooperation and trust of the person being tested. As discussed in the previous chapter, the way an examiner establishes rapport is a matter of personal style. You should introduce yourself to the patient and acknowledge adults by their titles and surnames. This maintains the formality of the professional situation and communicates your respect for the patient. Some casual conversation may be necessary to break the ice initially, but one of the first issues addressed should be an explanation of the purpose of the testing and a discussion of how the session will progress. Issues of confidentiality should be discussed with adults. All patients, both children and adults, need to know that the tasks they will be doing range from easy to hard and that their job is to do their best.

Patients should be encouraged to try on all test items and, in some cases, to take a chance by guessing while the examiner remains supportive and encouraging. To avoid giving information about the correctness or incorrectness of an answer, praise should be given for effort, not for the answer itself. To avoid discouraging the patient early, the examiner should start with simpler tasks, and as tasks become more difficult, acknowledge that an item may have been difficult but that no one gets all the answers right. Also, praise should be given judiciously instead of for every answer; this also helps the patient avoid becoming discouraged.

CAUTION

Maintain a professional environment and respect for adult patients by addressing them by their titles and surnames.

Structure of the Test Session

The scheduling of a test session depends on the referral question, the nature of the tests being used, and the focus and stamina of the patient. In general, test sessions are limited by the severity of patients' presenting problems, their general health, and their age. In some instances, shorter test sessions are necessary to achieve reliable samples of optimal cognitive ability. For patients whose symptomatology includes distractibility and for patients whose energy level has been compromised by nonneurological health conditions, it may be unwise to attempt testing in only 1 day if the goal is to obtain the patient's best performance across many tasks. On the other hand, if the goal is to assess cognition and mental stamina over the course of a day, then administering the tests in a 1-day session would be more appropriate than dividing up the tasks over several sessions. Other patients who may be unable to work consistently well in one session include older adults, very young children, and patients who suffer from physical pain that is exacerbated by long periods of sitting.

In general, the clinician should try to complete the interview and testing in 1 day. This increases the likelihood that the tests are given under similar circumstances. When test sessions are given on different days, differences in sleep, illness, anxiety, and other situational factors may confound the results and make them difficult to interpret.

DON'T FORGET

It is generally preferable to complete the testing session in 1 day to eliminate potential confounds.

For example, if in the first session a patient is in a good mood and does well on an intelligence test but at the time of a second session does poorly on memory because the patient is sleepy due to a problem with insomnia, the examiner is limited in the ability to conclude that a deficit in memory is the result of brain dysfunction. When it does become necessary to test on different days, the examiner must always make sure that multiple-part tests are given in a single session when validity is dependent on the test being administered in a given time frame; information about circumstances that could affect test performance should also be investigated. The latter is usually done by finding out whether any events that may be influencing the results have occurred in the interval between test sessions. Also, if symptom validity tests (SVTs) are necessary in the assessment, then different SVTs should be administered at each session.

The length of a test session varies according to the examiner's skill, the test battery chosen, and patient characteristics. An examiner who knows the tests well and is organized can connect tasks with smooth transitions that facilitate an efficient test session. The more tests administered, the longer the time required for testing. Some patients work quickly, whereas others work slowly. Some patients need encouragement and multiple follow-up questions, whereas others work efficiently from start to finish.

When tests are given in a single session, the patient should be offered a reasonable number of breaks and time for lunch. Some patients may need few breaks, and others may need many. Breaks should be taken only between, not during, tests or subtests. Any signs of fatigue or variations in efforts should be noted. If a brief break with a moment for a small snack is not enough to restore the patient to sufficient levels of concentration and cooperation to return to testing, then the session may need to be terminated and rescheduled.

Balancing Test Order

Most clinicians who give fixed batteries of tests administer these tests in a fixed order for the majority of patients. In addition, some tasks such as the Wechsler intelligence tests have an inherently fixed order of administration. Even clinicians who give flexible batteries that can vary from patient to patient nevertheless tend to give the tests they choose in a specific order, sometimes by design; for example, the clinician starts with orientation tasks and less threatening tasks and does memory assessment early in the session before fatigue becomes a real possibility. Often, however, the order of tests reflects a longstanding tradition that has never been critically examined by the clinician. In many instances, it may not matter when some tests are administered; for example, it does not appear to matter where in the test battery the Letter–Number Sequencing subtest from the Wechsler Adult Intelligence Scale—Third Edition (WAIS-III) or Wechsler Memory Scale—Third Edition (WMS-III) is administered. Tulsky and Zhu (2000) administered the Letter–Number Sequencing subtest at three times during a test session and found no evidence of fatigue or ordering effects. The examiner may decide to plan test order on the basis of the particular needs of a patient, and to keep the patient interested, the clinician may consider counterbalancing tests by varying the tests' subjects and difficulty levels. Keep in mind, however, that there are some tests that need to be given completely before other tasks to avoid confounding the results. For example, some test manuals for visual tasks direct the examiner to avoid administering other visual tasks before and during the administration of that particular task. A failure to adhere to this regulation may make interpretation of the results difficult.

OPTIMIZING MOTIVATION AND ALERTNESS

Most patients referred for neuropsychological testing are motivated to expend sufficient effort to produce reliable test results. Usually, patients' desire to obtain information relevant to their health care or their academic or vocational performance serves as an impetus to attend to instructions and complete the examination. To increase the likelihood of adequate motivation, the examiner should spend some time before beginning formal testing explicitly asking the patient whether he or she understands the reasons for examination and offering an opportunity to ask questions about the session. Many clinicians use a standard introductory speech explaining that:

> The purpose of the testing is to assess a wide variety and range of skills and abilities. Because the tests are designed to test such a wide range of abilities, some of the questions will appear very simple, and some may appear very difficult and frustrating. You are not expected to solve every problem or answer every question correctly. The most important thing is to try your best.

Despite such procedures, some patient populations may not be motivated to perform optimally for the examination. Young children may not be able to expend consistently good effort. Patients who are medically ill or physically uncomfortable may find it extremely unpleasant to expend mental effort over long periods of time. Elderly patients and patients with psychiatric illnesses or histories of congenitally impaired intellectual abilities often are found to be inadequately motivated or uncooperative with long neuropsychological examinations. High school and college students seeking accommodations or medication for attention-deficit/hyperactivity disorder (ADHD) or learning disabilities may perform poorly to ensure a particular outcome. Finally, patients who are tested as part of a forensic examination are frequently reported as not expending optimal effort on neuropsychological examinations. Although poor motivation may be manifested by overt signs of distractibility, excessive slowness or carelessness, direct questions about the usefulness or meaning of the tests, or even expressions of contempt for the testing or for the examiner, it is frequently difficult, if not impossible, to determine through simple observation whether patients are applying adequate effort to the tasks at hand. Some circumstances cause certain patients to be actually motivated to perform poorly. These patients do indeed obtain unexpectedly low scores on tests and produce errors that either are extremely rare or are not characteristic of patients with objective evidence of brain pathology. The examiner should never assume that the patient is motivated to expend optimal effort and should be alert to the fact that motivation can vary during the course of an examination. A patient's motivation must be monitored and assessed for the duration of the session. When it is suspected that a patient may have motivation to perform poorly, it is a good idea to administer formal tests of effort or symptom validity. These tests, which are relatively new to the tool chest of the neuropsychologist, have been validated by comparing the performances of patients with known brain damage to those of subjects who have been asked to simulate the behavior of patients with brain damage. Many tests of symptom validity have been validated by comparing patients who have brain injuries and are involved in litigation to similarly injured patients who are not involved in litigation. In a typical test, the performance of simulators is shown to be more impaired than that of patients with various documented brain injuries. These tests are sensitive to effort but insensitive to brain damage. We return to a discussion of the issue of effort and malingering in Chapter 6.

Patients who repeatedly question the reason for the examination may do so because they are extremely anxious about their performance. This behavior may be most prevalent in patients who are in a confusional state or delirium or suffering from other significant cognitive limitations accompanied by mood swings or agitation. Patients suffering from affective or anxiety disorders may also be distracted.

In these cases, a reasonable effort must be made to allay any anxieties and make the patient comfortable. No universal rules delineate how to deal with these situations, but excessive anxiety can significantly compromise the reliability of the examination and should not be ignored. Frequently, an acknowledgment of the patient's anxiety helps to initiate a discussion of the issue. The patient can be assured that some of the tasks are easy and some hard, but that he or she is not expected to get all the answers right; the patient's best effort is the most important issue. The examiner should acknowledge the patient's reaction and explain that test items may be difficult.

The clinician needs to balance the efficiency and time constraints of the overall examination with the need to ensure a reliable and valid performance. At some point, it may not be possible to help a patient focus on the examination or give a reasonable and consistent level of effort. Under these circumstances, the clinician may choose to terminate the session because the examination is unlikely to produce data that can reliably support clinical neuropsychological inferences. If such a decision is made, the clinician should carefully document and report the behaviors that led to this decision.

BEHAVIORAL OBSERVATIONS

The state of the patient's motivation and degree of effort are just a few of the many inferences that are made on the basis of observable behavior during the course of a clinical session. Observations about a patient's dress, hygiene, posture, language, and behavior may be used to modify or support the results of clinical neuropsychological tests. Rapid Reference 4.2 provides a list of the behavioral observations important in an assessment.

≡ Rapid Reference 4.2

Behavioral Observations

- Appearance (dress, hygiene, posture)
- Arousal and alertness
- Attitude toward examiner
- Attitude toward tests
- Level of cooperation, effort, and attention
- Work habits
- Speech and language
- Behavior (motivation, anxiety, affective state)

The clinician should observe many factors about a patient during the evaluation. One of these factors is the patient's appearance. Is the patient appropriately dressed? Is the patient well-groomed? A formerly tidy individual who presents in a disheveled, malodorous state may be communicating information about his ability for self-care. The examiner should observe a patient's level of cooperation, effort, and attention to the testing. Does the patient listen when test directions are given, or do the test directions require repetition? Does the patient give up easily or refuse to quit a task? Does the patient appear interested and invested in testing?

The examiner should also observe how easily a patient adapts to the testing situation and the patient's adjustment or attitude toward the examiner and the tests. Does the patient appear highly anxious and frightened or relaxed and comfortable? Does the patient engage in nervous laughter or stammering? Is the patient overly eager or noncompliant? Does the patient frequently check on the accuracy of the responses? How does the patient react to successes or failures? What is the patient's attitude toward self? Is the patient confident, boastful, or self-derogatory?

The clinician must also make observations about the patient's work habits during testing. Does he or she work too quickly, sacrificing accuracy for speed, or does the patient work slowly and deliberately? What about the patient's behavior? Is he or she calm or overactive, fidgety and distractible? Does the patient lack self-control? Observations also must focus on level of arousal and alertness. Is the patient sleepy or hyperaroused? Is the patient oriented to person, place, and date, or does he or she appear confused?

Another area that may be used to supplement formal testing is careful use of observations regarding speech and language. The examiner should develop a sensitivity to normal variations in speech rate, word finding latencies (i.e., how long someone takes to find an average vocabulary word or to initiate a sentence), use of pronouns versus specifying nouns (e.g., *he* vs. *John; I read it* vs. *I read the book*), use of circumlocutions (e.g., *the paper thing with the words* vs. *the book*). Again, no norms exist for evaluating such naturalistic observations, but extreme deviations from the examiner's experience with typical native speakers of English may serve as clues to the presence of language difficulties. In addition, the examiner should note whether the patient's language is fluent and normal in rate and volume, and whether there is a loss of words conveying grammatical structure (i.e., articles, conjunctions, prepositions), word endings (e.g., *ed, ing,* pluralization), or normal word order. In addition to rate and volume, the examiner should mark other prosodic elements of the patient's speech, such as overall pitch and whether changes in pitch and volume are used appropriately to punctuate clauses and sentence endings. Observations about language should focus on whether a patient's speech is fluent versus nonfluent or exact versus imprecise. Observations should also be made about the content and responsiveness of a patient's speech. Is the patient's language bizarre or immature? Is the patient unable to stop talking or unusually reticent?

As noted in the previous chapter, behavioral observations are a primary source of information about the patient's motivation, anxiety level, and affective state. The clinician should note the amount of motor activity and fidgeting displayed by the patient in addition to deviations in eye contact and posture. Does the patient move around excessively in the seat, play with his or her hands, or inappropriately pick up and handle small objects that might be in reach on the examination table? Does the patient seem unusually still or quiet with a fixed posture and little movement? Does the patient's facial expression show observable variation? Are these expressions appropriate in direction and degree to the affect associated with the situation? Does the patient cry when discussing something only slightly negative or frequently laugh in situations that are not humorous? Do the patient's facial muscles seem stiff and fixed? The examiner should also note signs of asymmetry in facial muscles when observing the patient's speech or emotional expression because some neurological conditions produce asymmetries during one and not the other.

Observations must also concentrate on motor behavior during testing. Is the patient awkward or graceful? Coordinated or uncoordinated? Does the patient consistently use one hand for writing and drawing tasks and the other hand to aid in tasks that require bilateral hand movements? Is the patient constantly moving or abnormally still? Does the patient react too quickly or too slowly? In addition, behavioral observations must be made concerning sensorimotor functioning. Does the patient use a cane to assist with ambulation? Does the patient have a hearing aid or wear glasses? Sensorimotor abnormalities may compromise test performance and also help delineate brain dysfunction.

The clinician must carefully consider a patient's cultural and social background when making clinical judgments based on testing behavior, but at the same time must be careful not to be biased by misleading stereotypes of the patient's particular cohort or community. The neuropsychologist must try to decide whether behaviors observed during a session represent a change for the individual patient or whether these behaviors are appropriate for the age or cultural cohort. For example, in most Western cultures a certain amount of eye contact is anticipated during a typical conversation. Although it is hard to quantify what constitutes so-called normal eye contact, most adults find themselves uncomfortable carrying on a conversation with someone who rarely looks at them during the interaction or who studiously avoids eye contact. A patient who looks at the floor or away from the examiner for the majority of the examination may be displaying behavior indicative of extreme social anxiety or pervasive developmental disorder. This may not be the case in all cultures, however. In some cultures, excessive eye contact is considered rude, particularly when a patient interacts with an older adult in a professional role. It is not possible to apply accurately the internal norms of social behavior for every culture. As a clinician, the neuropsychologist should try to document any behavior that seems unusual or rare within his or her own typical experience, and then decide whether

DON'T FORGET
....
Take a person's culture into account when making clinical judgments about testing behavior.

this information is relevant to clinical decision making. In many cases, unusual deviations from implicit social norms and the examiner's own expectations are also deviations from the expectations of the patient's own culture. If these behaviors represent a change for the patient, they may be clues to the status of the patient's cognitive and emotional behavior and ultimately may help the clinician to make inferences about the status of brain function.

The details and interpretation of all the possible categories of behavioral observations relevant to neuropsychology are beyond the scope of this book, but as a rule, the clinician should observe and note both typical and unusual behaviors during testing, even when the meaning of these observations is not completely clear.

RECORD KEEPING AND NOTE TAKING

The rules for keeping records and note taking are relatively straightforward: The clinician should keep a written record of any material used to support the answer to a clinical referral question. This material includes notes about patient history from record review or interview, behavioral observations, test responses, and test result data. It is not necessary to keep every scrap of paper associated with the examination (e.g., an appointment slip), but the clinician should keep sufficient records to document anything stated in a written or oral report. In essence, the examiner's notes should allow the testing session to be reconstructed from the record at a later time. This habit is important because the clinician may forget important information in the time between collecting and reporting the data or may confuse information

CAUTION
....
Keep sufficient records to document in a written or oral report anything said by a patient.

from two similar patients. The examination offers potential for collecting an enormous amount of data. The significance of a behavioral observation or piece of historical data might not be clear until reviewed as a whole when the examination is complete.

The clinician should be careful to write clearly, using consistent common abbreviations, especially when collecting data used to derive formal test scores. Rapid Reference 4.3 provides a list of common abbreviations that can be used

≡ Rapid Reference 4.3

Common Abbreviations to Standardize Record Keeping

@	at
a/t	anything
CPT	correct past time
Cld	could
e/o	everyone
F	failed item
IDK or DK	I don't know
IDR	I don't remember
ll	looks like
OT	overtime
P	passed item
PC	pointed correctly
Prmt	prompt
PX	pointed incorrectly
Q or ?	examiner queried the response or questioned
R	item repeated
N	nothing
NR	no response
SHN	shake head no
Shld	should
s/t	something
w/	with
w/o	without
Wld	would
X	times

in record keeping. The examiner should record responses legibly and immediately in the appropriate places on a test form or test booklet. Illegible writing can lead to scoring errors. Behavioral observations, including the patient's style of response and spontaneous remarks, can be noted in the margins of test forms or on a separate sheet of paper. Many tests used in contemporary neuropsychological assessment like the WMS and the WAIS require scoring narrative responses

DON'T FORGET

Record a patient's or client's responses verbatim.

using fairly detailed and complex criteria. It is virtually impossible to score the responses to such tests without verbatim notes. Responses should be scored as they are given, so the examiner must be familiar with scoring criteria and be careful to avoid disclosing scores to the examinee. The use of a clipboard held at an angle or a test manual to block the patient's view can help prevent the patient from seeing a score and becoming discouraged or overly confident.

Without verbatim records, it becomes impossible to check the accuracy and reliability of the examiner's testing and scoring. Even highly skilled clinicians make errors in scoring. Without sufficient documentation of results through notes and response entries, it becomes impossible to determine whether a scoring error is the source of a discrepancy between different measures of a similar function or between measures administered by different clinicians at different times. An inaccurate test score undermines a valid analysis of neuropsychological data and may significantly affect the health and life of the patient.

Clinicians should be skilled in note taking so that they do not appear so immersed in their notes that they are unable to observe the patient or appear disinterested in the patient. Note taking is only one of the examiner's many responsibilities during an examination. Carefully recording responses must coexist with administering the test, keeping test materials ready, observing the patient's behavior, and scoring the patient's responses. Clinicians should not bury their heads in their notes, their clipboards, or test manuals.

In recent years, raw data and clinical records have become an important part of the forensic arena and civil litigation. In these cases, neuropsychological data may have important legal or economic implications for both client and examiner. Ethical standards of the American Psychological Association (APA; 2002) require that clinical records be stored in a secure location where patient confidentiality can be maintained. In practice, this means keeping records in a locked filing cabinet that is accessible only to authorized individuals. Similarly, computer files must be stored in a way that does not allow unauthorized individuals access to sensitive patient information. In the course of patient care, it sometimes is necessary to release raw data to other individuals. No records or reports can be released without specific permission from the patient or client. In practice, test reports are sent to the referring professional and may upon specific request (where appropriate) be sent to the patient or client. Current APA ethical guidelines indicate that raw test data can be released "pursuant to a client/patient release" to the client or patient "or other persons identified in the release," or if there is a specific legal mandate (e.g., in the case of a court proceeding) to do so. Raw test data is specifically defined in Standard 9.04, which specifies that only if there is likelihood of "substantial harm or misrepresentation of the data or the test" can the psychologist refrain from releasing the data. Test publishing companies, however, have exerted trade secret rights to exempt psychologists from releasing raw test data to those who do not have the proper credentials to purchase such test data. In the current set of ethical principles, raw test data is distinguished from test materials, which are to be kept secure by psychologists.

TEST PROCEDURE AND STANDARDS

Published reliability, validity, and normative data for neuropsychological tests are based on the tests having been administered using a set of repeatable standard procedures and conditions. If you wish to use test norms with confidence, then you must follow standard procedures. Following standard procedures means using the exact wording in the test manual, using the specific materials included with a test, following specific time limits and scoring rules, and using only standard inquiries. Even minor violations of the recommended standardized procedures published in the test manual can potentially reduce a test's reliability and validity as a neuropsychological measure. For example, if a test is designed to be given without a break, giving the patient even a brief break can reduce the accuracy of the confidence with which the test norms can be applied. Changing even the time limits or the language in which a test is given may invalidate the use of the norms. It is also true that some variations in procedure

---

C A U T I O N

Using standard procedures means

- Using exact wording of test questions
- Using specific test materials
- Following specific time limits
- Using specific scoring rules
- Making only standard inquiries
- Always noting deviations from standard procedures

do not affect an examiner's ability to use normative information because the variation falls within the standard error of measurement. Unfortunately, it is usually impossible to know whether a particular variation in procedure is innocuous or will lead to inaccurate results.

Some circumstances necessarily require deviations from standard procedures. Materials may have to be adapted for patients with various handicaps or sensorimotor problems. For example, visually impaired individuals may need an examiner to read items aloud that they otherwise would have read themselves. Alternatively, hearing-impaired individuals may need to read materials that would normally be said aloud. When departures from standard procedures are necessary, this information must be indicated in the test report so that the reader is aware that modifications to testing procedures were made and knows that the normative information may have to be interpreted with caution. Clinicians must use their judgment to discern which data are interpretable from tests that have been adapted to meet a patient's special needs.

Some methods of neuropsychological assessment (e.g., Luria Neuropsychological Investigation; Boston Process Approach) call for the clinician to vary test procedures in a quasi-experimental manner to obtain additional information about a patient's abilities by testing limits. Although in the hands of some clinicians, these variations may lead to equally or even more accurate clinical judgments, no data testing the effects of these experimental violations of test sensitivity and specificity are currently available. Although this text does not take an official position on which test system to use, the clinician should be aware of the costs as well as the potential benefits of using nonstandard variations of procedures on standard tests. We can recommend the following: Clinicians should violate standardized procedures only if they can estimate accurately the effects of such violation on the reliability and validity of the tests or if standard procedures are inappropriate because of special circumstances. If testing the limits is desired for the additional information it can provide, it should occur only after a test has been administered according to standard procedures so as not to influence performance on the remaining items on the test.

In terms of standard procedures, we recommend that even skilled examiners reacquaint themselves occasionally with test procedures by rereading the manuals. As one works with a test, one may change its administration or scoring subtly over time. Periodic review of test procedures helps ensure that examiners use exact wording and do not reinvent the rules for scoring. Experienced

DON'T FORGET

Testing the limits should occur only after a test has been administered according to standard procedures.

examiners should also review the test manuals for revised tests to be certain that well-known procedures have not been changed.

TEST ADMINISTRATION

An examiner has multiple tasks to carry out during an evaluation. He or she must carefully and correctly administer test items in an organized, smooth, and steady fashion while recording exactly a patient's response, observing the patient's behavior, and scoring the patient's responses—all the while attempting to maintain the patient's cooperation. To ensure that the evaluation goes smoothly, an examiner should be thoroughly familiar with the tests being administered and prepared to proceed in a well-planned,

> **DON'T FORGET**
> ....
> **Have the following on hand:**
> • Test manuals and test stimuli
> • Pens and sharpened pencils
> • Extra paper
> • Stopwatch
> • Clipboard

organized fashion. This requires having test materials and the proper supplies ready and on hand so that unnecessary delays are avoided. In addition to the test manuals and stimuli, the examiner's materials should also include sharpened pencils with and without erasers, a pen for the examiner, extra paper, a stopwatch, and a clipboard. Test stimuli, however, should be kept out of sight until they are required and should be taken away as soon as possible after use to minimize the clutter on the tabletop. A small bookshelf on the examiner's side of the table to the examiner's left or right is an appropriate place to store items that should be kept out of the examinee's view. If an examiner is familiar with standard procedures and scoring rules, then moving smoothly from task to task is easier. Rapid Reference 4.4 highlights the steps necessary for test administration.

> **CAUTION**
> ....
> State instructions and questions exactly. Resist the temptation to help the patient by explaining the words in questions, adding additional words, or by repeating directions unless specifically permitted in the test manual.

Test administration requires that test instructions be followed exactly. As part of the standard procedure, general and specific instructions must be phrased exactly as stated in the test manual. Resist the temptation to help the patient by explaining the words in questions unless the manual allows explanations. Resist the temptation to help the patient by adding additional words to the directions or repeating directions unless the manual permits repetition. Inquiries can be made only as instructed in the manual.

≡ Rapid Reference 4.4

Steps in Test Administration

- Establish rapport
- Maintain cooperation
- Provide encouragement
- Probe ambiguous responses
- Have test materials accessible
- Use stopwatch inconspicuously
- Observe behavior
- Administer test items in organized, smooth, and steady fashion
- Record responses verbatim
- Score responses as responses occur

Timing should be done carefully but as inconspicuously as possible. The clinician must be careful not to distract the patient with the stopwatch. It is usually not permissible to tell a patient how much time is allotted for a particular test item. It is better when asked about time limits to remind the patient to tell you when the task is complete or to give an answer as soon as possible.

It is also usually not permissible to provide feedback to a patient about the correctness of a response. Feedback and encouragement should be nonspecific to the patient's response. In other words, the examiner should distribute feedback across the test session and not just when a patient is doing poorly and having difficulty. An examiner who responds only to incorrect answers is inadvertently cuing the patient as to the fact that an answer is wrong and might discourage the patient in the process. In addition, giving answers to questions is also unacceptable, even after an item has been completed. In some instances, it is necessary to elucidate ambiguous responses from a patient by asking the patient to repeat the response or to be more specific. Probing responses must be done only if explicitly allowed in the test manual and only in the ways specified by the manual. The examiner must never ask leading questions when clarifying a patient's response. Answers should be clarified with neutral probes such as, "What do you mean?" or "Tell me more about it."

In some instances, it is necessary to encourage a reluctant patient to try a test item. Given that you want the patient's optimal performance, you should not accept initial "I don't know" responses unless you believe the patient is truly incapable of responding. When patients say, "I don't know," they could be indicating a fear of making a mistake. In those instances, ask the patient to try to answer any way he or she can and remind the patient that you are interested in his or her best effort. Sometimes encouragement takes the form of allowing a patient to work briefly past time limits on tasks he or she is close to completing successfully over time. Abruptly taking away a test item just because time has expired may dull a patient's ambition to do well on subsequent items. In such instances, however, always score the item strictly according to the time limits.

TEST SCORING

The examiner must be able to score as the test progresses because on some tests, the number of correct and incorrect answers determines when to discontinue a test or subtest. It is also important because some answers are not scorable as is and require inquiry. An examiner thoroughly familiar with scoring criteria is able to score a patient's responses as they are given and thus can ask for clarifications when necessary. When examiners encounter responses that are not easily scored, they should inquire for clarification of the response with neutral probes. If upon later rechecking of the scoring it becomes clear that an inquiry was not necessary, the additional response can be ignored in the scoring.

> **DON'T FORGET**
>
> - Be thoroughly familiar with scoring criteria.
> - Score as you go.
> - Score according to the test manuals.
> - Double-check scoring when done.

When scoring, the clinician should not allow the patient to see the scores because this may affect subsequent responses or distract the patient from the task at hand. Usually a clipboard held at an angle or discreet use of one's hands can serve to shield the scores from the patient's view.

Scoring must always be done according to the test manuals, which often set guidelines concerning prototype answers. The examiner who is thoroughly familiar with the scoring guidelines is best able to discern the score value of a response quickly and accurately and better able to follow standard administration procedures. The manuals never list all possible correct or incorrect responses, however, so understanding the intent of a test or a particular item helps in the scoring of questionable responses.

Even experienced examiners make scoring errors. Reviewing test manuals periodically helps to ensure that an examiner has not inadvertently adopted incorrect scoring standards. Scoring should always be checked and rechecked after examination. This applies to all calculations, including the patient's age, the number of correct and incorrect items, additions, and score transfers from one part of the record to another. It also applies to double-checking the correct conversion of raw scores to scaled or standard scores. The examiner should consult books concerning specific tests to learn about common scoring errors that should be avoided. In *Essentials of WISC-IV Assessment,* for example, Flanagan and Kaufman (2009) point out the common errors in obtaining raw and scaled scores, including neglecting to include points from below the basal, transferring total raw scores incorrectly from inside the record form to the summary page, miscalculating a sum when adding scores to obtain the raw score or sum of scaled scores, writing illegibly, using the wrong age reference table, and misreading across the rows of the score conversion tables. Computer scoring programs are available from Pearson and other test publishers for many tests such as the WAIS-IV, WMS-IV, Wechsler Intelligence Scale for Children—Fourth Edition (WISC-IV), Children's Memory Scale, and NEPSY-II; these programs can serve to double-check the figures calculated by the examiner.

SPECIAL NEEDS

Input and Output Channels

Most neuropsychological tests are designed with the assumption that basic motor and sensory functions are intact. The examiner must take into account limitations in visual and auditory acuity and physical disabilities affecting the bones, muscles, or peripheral nervous system when administering and interpreting most neuropsychological tests. Any factors affecting the input of information to a patient or any limitation in a patient's output channels must be noted in a test report and used as part of the interpretative process. Limitations in a patient's input or output channels may undermine an examiner's ability to assess particular areas of function. For example, in patients with nonfluent aphasias, it may be impossible to assess their ability to understand complex issues of reasoning, simply because there may be no reasonable means by which they can demonstrate their knowledge.

One of the challenges to the field of neuropsychology is the question of how to answer clinical questions posed for patients with significant disabilities in vision, hearing, or the use of the upper limbs. In some cases, it may be possible to choose measures that do not require the use of the disabled sensory or motor system. For example, the clinician can use tasks that are primarily auditory for a patient with severe limits in vision or a visual task for a patient with severe limits in hearing. It may also be possible to use tests requiring verbal responses for patients who do not have use of their limbs or manual responses for patients who are severely dysarthric or otherwise unable to speak for reasons unrelated to the central nervous system. In some cases, this approach presents significant limitations on the interpretation of test results and may not allow the neuropsychologist to assess the specific neuropsychological functions that may have been altered or diminished. For example, verbal memory may be of interest in a hearing-impaired patient or naming may be of interest in a patient with severe dysarthria, although it may not be possible to assess these skills in these patients accurately.

Many neuropsychologists find themselves tempted to modify existing measures to be more usable in the presence of a disability. For example, it may be possible to substitute a naming-to-definition task instead of a visual confrontation naming task such as the Boston Naming Test (Kaplan, Goodglass, & Weintraub, 2001) to patients who are severely visually impaired and still be able to determine whether they are anomic. Although sometimes inevitable, these modifications must be made only with great caution and only when there are no published alternatives available. When reporting results from such tasks, the examiner should document the origin of the procedure and the reasons for the modifications (e.g., sensory or motor limitations); also, the clinician should describe the procedure in enough detail to allow another clinician to replicate the observations. Even if no standardization or norms exist for the procedure, occasionally the task may be the only means available for documenting change in performance and may allow data useful for clinical purposes. Whenever modifications are considered, the examiner must determine whether other, more suitable measures already exist for a particular special need instead of (or in addition to) administering commonly used tests with adaptations that might confound test result interpretation.

Testing Patients With Visual Impairments

It may be reasonable to administer to blind patients the verbal portions of standardized tests, such as the Wechsler Intelligence and Memory Scales. Assessing nonverbal or visual skills is obviously more difficult. Tests such as the Tactual Performance Test (TPT), which requires spatial manipulation and nonverbal problem solving as well as blindfold use in sighted individuals, may be one alternative. It should be kept in mind, however, that success on tests like the TPT and even some verbal tests might be dependent on prior visual experiences.

Testing Patients With Hearing Impairments

Testing a deaf patient is difficult because many tasks are dependent on verbal abilities, and verbal tasks pose a particular obstacle for severely hearing-impaired individuals. If the patient and the examiner know American Sign Language (ASL), then verbal tasks can be administered in this fashion. In some instances, written language can be substituted for oral language. Otherwise, verbal tests may have to be omitted entirely. Giving task directions even for nonverbal tasks may be difficult for hearing-impaired individuals. Directions may have to be given in ASL, in writing, and through gesture. Some tasks, such as the Test of Nonverbal Intelligence—Third Edition (TONI-3; Brown, Sherbenou, & Johnson, 1997), the Comprehensive Test of Nonverbal Intelligence (CTONI—2; Hammill, Pearson, & Wiederholt, 2009), the Naglieri Nonverbal Ability Test—Individual Assessment (for children and young adults; Naglieri, 2000), or the Wechsler Nonverbal Scale of Ability (WNV; Wechsler & Naglieri, 2006) may be the most suitable measures of nonverbal reasoning and nonverbal intelligence for the deaf patient because of the language-free format. Response choices are indicated by pointing, and instructions are presented through pantomime. Sattler (1992) offers pantomime instructions for administering the performance subtests from the WISC—Revised to hearing-impaired children. These instructions can likely be adapted for use with the WISC-IV and WAIS-IV performance subtests. Memory tasks may have to be restricted to nonverbal measures; again, however, the examiner must be sure to provide the patient with sufficient directions through the written word, pantomime, and gesture.

Testing Patients With Aphasia

Establishing that a patient with an acquired language disorder has an adequate output channel is the first challenge when testing such a patient. A patient who has no way of indicating responses cannot be tested. Assessment of the pattern and degree of aphasic symptoms can be accomplished with measures such as the Boston Diagnostic Aphasia Examination—Third Edition (Goodglass, Kaplan, & Barresi, 2001) and the Boston Naming Test-2 (Kaplan et al., 2001). Depending on the severity of the patient's language deficits, assessment (as with hearing-impaired individuals) may have to continue with nonverbal tests and other tests that do not depend on language ability (as described earlier for testing patients with hearing impairments).

Testing Patients With Motor Impairments

Patients with motor disabilities may be at a particular disadvantage on speeded tasks and nonverbal tasks requiring coordinated motor movement. In these instances, it may be wise to administer only verbal subtests or motor-free tasks to obtain an assessment of overall cognitive ability. In addition, modifications can be made to accommodate motor disabilities, although standard normative data may not be available to judge performance relative to other individuals with motor disabilities. Also, remember that motor deficits might give false impressions of cognitive ability. Modifications, for example, can involve reading aloud or indicating test choices in turn for a patient and noting patient agreement when even pointing ability is compromised. Another modification might involve testing without time constraints. Rapid Reference 4.5 provides a summary of possible modifications for testing patients who have limitations in input or output channels.

≣ Rapid Reference 4.5

Possible Test Battery Modifications for Individuals With Limitations in Input–Output Channels

Testing Patients with Visual Impairments

- Administer verbal portions of standardized tests.
- Administer nonverbal tests that require spatial manipulation and problem solving but not sight (e.g., the Tactual Performance Test).

Testing Patients With Hearing Impairments

- Use American Sign Language if possible for verbal tasks.
- Substitute written language for oral language.
- Give directions through pantomime, signing, or gesture.
- Use tests such as Test of Nonverbal Intelligence—Third Edition, Comprehensive Test of Nonverbal Intelligence, Second Edition, the Naglieri Nonverbal Ability Test, and the Wechsler Nonverbal Scale of Ability.

Testing Patients With Aphasia

- Establish that an adequate output channel exists.
- Document aphasic features with tests such as the Boston Diagnostic Aphasia Examination—Third Edition.
- Use nonverbal tests.
- Give directions through pantomime and gesture.

Testing Patients With Motor Impairments

- Assess overall cognitive ability with verbal and motor-free tasks.
- Avoid speeded motor tasks.
- Test motor abilities without time constraints.

TEST SELECTION

When selecting the tests to administer in a neuropsychological assessment, the clinician should pay attention to the referral question, the appropriateness of a test for a given individual, the normative data available for a test, and the comprehensiveness of a test battery. On the basis of the reason for referral, the examiner entertains hypotheses about possible deficits and chooses tests that can elicit and measure deficiencies in expected areas. For example, knowing that a patient has had a middle cerebral artery stroke suggests the possibility of acquired language deficits; therefore, the test battery needs to

DON'T FORGET

Select a comprehensive array of tests measuring

- Arousal and attention
- Executive functions
- Intelligence/achievement
- Learning and memory
- Language ability
- Visuospatial skills
- Sensory and motor skills
- Emotion, behavior, and personality
- Effort and compliance

include measures sensitive to aphasic deficits such as the Boston Diagnostic Aphasia Examination—Third Edition (BDAE; Goodglass et al., 2001). In a case in which damage secondary to hypoxia is suspected, then the focus may be directed more toward an in-depth analysis of memory functions. An important issue is whether the test has validity and reliability for the particular application in which it is being considered. The examiner should use tests that are sensitive to dysfunction in the function being examined and be aware of whether particular tests as a sample of function are predictive of behavior in real-life settings.

Tests are also selected on the basis of whether they are appropriate for the particular patient. Considerations of a patient's age and education play a role in test selection, and in some instances language and cultural history may determine test choice. For each test selected for a test battery, good normative data appropriate against which to compare a patient's performance must be available. Even a mature 15-year-old is too young to take the WAIS—Fourth Edition (Wechsler, 2008a) because the normative data do not exist for a 15-year-old. In another instance, if a patient did not acquire knowledge of the English language until late in life, a test such as the Boston Naming Test—2 (Kaplan et al., 2001) may not provide interpretable data. For patients for whom English is a second language, performance may reflect their lack of experience with or exposure to the name of a particular object rather than loss of the ability to name it. Here it is important to use measures fitting for the patient's preferred language, unless, of course, the patient's knowledge base in another language is the issue under examination. Tests are also selected by their ability to add to the comprehensiveness of a test battery. Many areas need to be assessed in the typical neuropsychological evaluation. The examiner may need to develop data to assess premorbid abilities, and it is almost always necessary to measure intelligence to establish a baseline against which other tests will be compared to confirm discrepancies between skills. A comprehensive test battery contains multiple measures of both higher and lower cognitive domains to identify the point of processing at which functions break down and to demonstrate the consistency of that finding. In addition, the clinician must assemble a test battery that permits assessment of the same cognitive domain with multiple measures to explore the reliability of a deficit. A test battery usually needs to include various measures of attention to explore the entire attentional matrix of a patient. A test battery also usually needs to include measures of executive functions such as reasoning, planning, organization, set establishment and maintenance, and measures of verbal and visual learning and memory. In addition, a test battery generally includes tests to assess language skills and perhaps academic skills, as well as visual, tactile, and motor abilities. In many cases, testing must also address issues of motivation, effort, and emotional function and mood. The number of tests that can be administered is determined in part by time available for testing and by patient stamina. It is also incumbent upon the examiner to avoid tests that are obsolete. Rapid Reference 4.6 summarizes the factors involved in test selection.

The particular test battery used is obviously the choice of the neuropsychologist and often reflects the examiner's personal preferences. In some cases, the neuropsychologist chooses to use a predeveloped or fixed battery of tests such as the Halstead–Reitan Neuropsychological Test Battery (HRB), perhaps supplemented by a test of intelligence and another of memory. In other cases, the neuropsychologist assembles a flexible battery of tests designed to answer particular questions about cognitive strengths and weaknesses. Survey data indicate that flexible batteries are used significantly more often now by clinical neuropsychologists than are fixed batteries (Sweet, Nelson, & Moberg, 2006). The tests available for use are varied and too numerous to list here, although we do focus on the various areas of function and discuss some measures for each. For a compilation of neuropsychological tests and commentary and information concerning test administration and norms, the reader is referred to *A Compendium of Neuropsychological Tests* (3rd ed.; Strauss, Sherman, & Spreen, 2006) or to *Neuropsychological Assessment* (4th ed.; Lezak, Howieson, & Loring, 2004). Clinicians should check periodically for updates and revisions of the tests they use. Rapid Reference 4.7 lists the various resources available for assessment measures.

≡ *Rapid Reference 4.6*

Test Selection

Referral question
- Hypothesis generation
- Established validity for task at hand

Appropriateness
- Age
- Education
- Level of difficulty
- Availability of good normative data
- Up-to-date measures

Comprehensiveness
- Assess wide range of functions
- Assess lower and higher domains
- Use multiple measures for the same domain
- Fixed versus flexible battery

≡ *Rapid Reference 4.7*

Assessment Resources

- American Guidance Service (AGS)   www.pearsonassessments.com
  (Pearson Assessments)
- Multi-Health Systems (MHS)   www.mhs.com
- National Rehabilitation Services,   www.nss-nrs.com
  Northern Speech Services (NSS)
- NCS Assessments   pearsonassessments.com
  (Pearson Assessments)
- NFER-NELSON   www.gl-assessment.co.uk
  (GL Assessment)
- PRO-ED   www.proedinc.com
- The Psychological Corporation   www.pearsonassessments.com
  (Pearson Assessments)

(continued)

- Psychological Assessment Resources (PAR)   www.parinc.com
- The Neuropsychology Center   www.neuropsych.com
- Riverside Publishing   www.riversidepublishing.com
- Western Psychological Services (WPS)   www.wpspublish.com
- Wide Range, Inc. (WR)   www3.parinc.com
  (Psychological Assessment Resources)

TEST BATTERIES

Halstead–Reitan Neuropsychological Test Battery

Since 1955 the HRB (Reitan & Wolfson, 1993) has allowed computation of the Halstead Impairment Index from seven scores derived from five tests, including the Category Test, the Finger Oscillation Test, the Seashore Rhythm Test, the Speech Sounds Perception Test, and the total time, memory, and localization scores from the Tactual Performance Test. Also routinely included in the HRB, but not part of the Impairment Index, are the Trail Making Test, the Aphasia Screening Test, the Sensory Perceptual Examination, and Grip Strength. The Impairment Index ranges from .0 to 1.0 and indicates the proportion of test scores that are in the range indicative of brain impairment. The Halstead Impairment Index is calculated by dividing the number of scores in the impaired range by the total number of the seven tests given that are part of the Halstead Impairment Index. Patients obtaining scores of .5 or above are classified as "having brain impairment." The Halstead Impairment Index is used to identify functioning consistent with brain damage, but it does not indicate the type or level of dysfunction.

Several other summary indexes that assist with this limitation are available for use with HRB and its supplemental tests. The Average Impairment Rating is used to document the existence of brain dysfunction and to quantify the amount of impairment. The Average Impairment Rating averages the scaled scores (i.e., 0–4, where 0 is above average, 1 is average, 2 is one standard deviation below the mean, 3 is two standard deviations below the mean, and 4 is three standard deviations below the mean) from the 12 tests that comprise this index. The 12 tests include the seven measures from the original Halstead Impairment Index along with Trail Making B, WAIS Digit Symbol, Aphasia Screening Test, Spatial Relations Test, and the Perceptual Disorders Test. One other index is the General Neuropsychological Deficit Scale, which is based on 42 test variables from the subtests of the HRB and is used to indicate the presence of brain dysfunction by evaluating level and pattern of performance, lateralized motor and sensory findings, and particular deficits and pathognomonic signs. Calculation of the Neuropsychological Deficit Scale for adults is detailed in Reitan and Wolfson (1993). Normative data based on gender, age, race (Caucasian and African American), and education for adults for the HRB are also available from Heaton, Miller, Taylor, and Grant, (2004). Rapid Reference 4.8 provides a description of the HRB, relevant references, and sources.

≡ Rapid Reference 4.8

Halstead–Reitan Neuropsychological Test Battery

Tests for Halstead Impairment Index

Category Test

Finger Oscillation Test

Seashore Rhythm Test

Speech Sounds Perception Test

Tactual Performance Test

Ages

Young child (5–8 years)

Intermediate Child (9–14 years)

Adult

Sources

The Neuropsychology Center

9400 N. Central Expressway

Dallas, TX 75231

1–214–373–3607

www.neuropsych.com

Psychological Assessment Resources

1–800–331–8378

www.parinc.com

Additional Tests

Trail Making Test

Aphasia Screening Test

Sensory Perceptual Examination

Grip Strength

Summary Scores

Halstead Impairment Index

Neuropsychological Deficit Scale

Average Impairment Rating

Relevant Texts

Heaton, R. K., Miller, S. W., Taylor, M. J., & Grant, I. (2004). *Revised comprehensive norms for an expanded Halstead–Reitan Battery: Demographically adjusted neuropsychological norms for African American and Caucasian adults.* Lutz, FL: Psychological Assessment Resources.

Reitan, R. M., & Wolfson, D. (1993). *The Halstead–Reitan Neuropsychological Test Battery: Theory and clinical interpretation.* Tucson, AZ: Neuropsychology Press.

Category Test. This is a complex nonverbal task that assesses concept formation and abstract reasoning. It tests flexible problem-solving abilities and the capacity to learn from experience. The original version uses slides, but a booklet version and a short version are available as well from Psychological Assessment Resources and Western Psychological Services, respectively.

Finger Oscillation Test. This task, also called the Finger Tapping Test, measures fine motor speed of the index finger on each hand. It can be helpful in assessing laterality of brain damage. The finger tapping board can be obtained through the Neuropsychology Center (www.neuropsych.com) and from Psychological Assessment Resources.

Seashore Rhythm Test. This test requires the patient to discriminate between similar and different musical rhythms. This test was derived from the Seashore Tests of Musical Ability (Seashore, Lewis, & Saetveit, 1960) and is dependent on nonspecific functions such as attention.

Speech Sounds Perception Test. This test requires the patient to determine which of four written nonsense words matches a nonsense word said aloud. It is an auditory perception test that is sensitive to attentional problems.

Tactual Performance Test (TPT). This task uses the Seguin–Goddard Formboard to measure the tactual perception and form recognition along with psychomotor problem solving and tactile memory for spatial location and shapes. A portable version of the TPT is available from Psychological Assessment Resources.

Trail Making Test (TMT). The Trail Making Test is a speeded test that measures sustained visual attention, visual scanning, sequencing, and cognitive flexibility. It has two parts, Trail Making A, which requires number sequencing, and Trail Making B, which requires alternation and sequencing between letters and numbers.

Aphasia Screening Test. This is a brief measure of language and nonlanguage skills, such as naming, reading, spelling, writing, identifying body parts, performing arithmetic calculations, drawing shapes, and discriminating left from right.

Sensory Perceptual Examination. This test assesses the patient's ability to perceive tactile, auditory, and visual stimuli on both sides of the body.

Grip Strength. This measure uses a hand dynamometer (available from Psychological Assessment Resources) to assess the strength of each hand.

Kaplan Baycrest Neurocognitive Assessment

The Kaplan Baycrest Neurocognitive Assessment (KBNA) (Leach, Kaplan, Rewilak, Richards, & Proulx, 2000) is designed to evaluate cognitive function in adults aged 20 to 90 for purposes of an overview, diagnosis, treatment planning, and monitoring. The KBNA assesses attention and concentration, immediate and delayed memory recall and recognition, verbal fluency, spatial processing, and reasoning and conceptual shifting. Both index scores (standard scores) and process scores (percentile categories) are available. Administration time is approximately 60 minutes.

Luria–Nebraska Neuropsychological Test Battery

The Luria–Nebraska Neuropsychological Test Battery (LNNB) (Golden, Purisch, & Hammeke, 1985), like the HRB, is a comprehensive test battery designed to measure neuropsychological functioning. The LNNB provides a global measure of cerebral dysfunction along with lateralization and localization of focal brain impairments. Form I of the battery contains 269 items (Form II has 279 items) from which 11 clinical scales can be derived: motor functions, rhythm, tactile functions, visual functions, receptive speech, expressive speech, writing, reading, arithmetic, memory, and intellectual processes. Form II has an additional clinical scale: intermediate memory. From the clinical scales, five summary scales can be derived: pathognomonic, left hemisphere, right hemisphere, profile elevation, and impairment. In addition, since the battery was first published, eight localization scales have been developed pertaining to the two hemispheres and the frontal, sensorimotor, parietal-occipital, and temporal areas of the brain. The LNNB takes 1.5 to 2.5 hours to administer and can be given in a single session or several brief sessions. It has the advantage of being completely portable and can be given at bedside. The LNNB was designed for patients 15 years and older but can also be used for 13 and 14 year olds. A child's version of the LNNB (LNNB-C) has been developed for children aged 8 to 12 years. Scoring and interpretation are complex but can be aided by a computer program. The LNNB and the LNNB-C as well as the computer scoring are available through Western Psychological Services. Characteristics of the battery, neuropsychological findings, and critical considerations about the LNNB are available in Lezak et al. (2004). Rapid Reference 4.9 provides a description of the LNNB, relevant references, and source.

NEPSY-II

The second edition of the NEPSY test battery (Korkman, Kirk, & Kemp, 2007), when supplemented by an intelligence test, provides a comprehensive assessment

≡ *Rapid Reference 4.9*
....

Luria–Nebraska Neuropsychological Test Battery

Tests

Form I (269 items)

Form II (279 items)

Summary Scores

Pathognomonic

Left Hemisphere

Profile Elevation

Right Hemisphere

Impairment

Ages

Child (8–12 years)

Adult (15 years and older)

Relevant Texts

Golden, C. J., Purisch, A. D., & Hammeke, T. A. (1985). *Manual for the Luria–Nebraska Neuropsychological Battery: Forms I and II*. Los Angeles: Western Psychological Services.

Lezak, M. D., Howieson, D. B., & Loring, D. W., with Hannay, H. J., & Fischer, J. S. (2004). *Neuropsychological Assessment* (4th ed.). New York: Oxford University Press.

Source

Western Psychological Services

Phone: 1–800–648–8857

www.wpspublish.com

---

of neuropsychological status in children aged 3 to 16. The NEPSY-II assesses functioning in six theoretically derived content domains: attention and executive functioning, language, sensorimotor, visuospatial processing, memory and learning, and social perception. For each subtest within each domain a primary score (either a scaled score or a percentile rank) can be derived. In addition, various process scores, expressed as scaled scores, percentile ranks, or cumulative percentages, are available to describe specifically some abilities and error rates. Contrast scores are also available as scaled scores to allow statistical comparisons of higher to lower level cognitive functions. A general assessment with this battery takes 45 minutes for preschoolers and 60 minutes for school-age children. A full assessment takes 1.5 hours for younger children and 2 to 3 hours for older children.

Within the attention and executive functioning domain, measures are available to assess selective and sustained attention and distractibility; inhibition, initiation, cognitive flexibility, and planning; working memory; and divided attention. The language subtests examine phonological processing, verbal fluency, comprehension, naming, repetition, and oromotor control and articulation. Within the sensorimotor domain, measures are available to assess fine motor speed, visuomotor precision, tactile sensory ability, motor sequencing, and imitation of motor positions and sequences. The visual and visuospatial processing subtests allow examination of design copying, block construction, and the ability to judge position and directionality, as well as mental rotation ability, visuospatial analysis, visual scanning and discrimination, and spatial localization. Within the memory and learning domain, the test measures evaluate immediate memory for sentences; immediate and delayed memory for names, faces, lists, and designs; memory for narrative stories, and word list interference. The social perception domain includes measures of memory for faces, the ability to recognize and identify emotional states displayed on a person's face, and the ability to understand that others may have thoughts and perceptions different from one's own. The NEPSY-II is available from Pearson. Rapid Reference 4.10 provides a description of the NEPSY-II, relevant references, and source of the test.

☰ Rapid Reference 4.10

NEPSY-II

Tests

Auditory Attention & Response Set	Animal Sorting	Clocks
Design Fluency	Inhibition	Statue
Body Part Naming and Identification	Phonological Processing	Speeded Naming
Comprehension of Instructions	Oromotor Sequences	Word Generation
Repetition of Nonsense Words	Visuomotor Precision	Fingertip Tapping
Imitating Hand Positions	Manual Motor Sequences	Arrows
Route Finding	Picture Puzzles	Design Copying
Block Construction	Geometric Puzzles	Sentence Repetition
List Memory/Delayed	Memory for Designs/ Delayed	
Memory for Faces/Delayed	Memory for Names/ Delayed	

(continued)

Narrative Memory

Affect Recognition

Summary (Domain) Scores

Attention and Executive Functioning

Language

Memory and Learning

Word List Interference

Theory of Mind

Visuospatial Processing

Sensorimotor

Social Perception

Ages

Children and adolescents
(3–16 years)

Relevant Texts

Korkman, M., Kirk, U., & Kemp, S. (2007). *NEPSY-II*. San Antonio,
TX: Harcourt Assessment.

Source

Pearson Assessments

Phone: 1–800–632–9011

www.pearsonassessments.com

Neuropsychological Assessment Battery

The Neuropsychological Assessment Battery (NAB) (Stern & White, 2003) was designed to assess a comprehensive array of cognitive functions in adults. It consists of a screening module (12 tests) and five main modules: Attention, Language, Spatial, Memory, and Executive Functions. The modules can be combined into a fixed or flexible battery or any of the 33 individual tests can be administered alone. There are two parallel, equivalent forms. The entire battery can be administered in about 4 hours. The test is designed for adults aged 18 to 97 years.

Repeatable Battery for the Assessment of Neuropsychological Status

The Repeatable Battery for the Assessment of Neuropsychological Status (RBANS) was developed by Christopher Randolph (1998) as a quick measure of cognitive function in adults aged 20 to 90 with neurological disorders, such as degenerative diseases, vascular accidents, and traumatic brain injury. The RBANS comprises 12 subtests: List Learning, Story Memory, Figure Copy, Line Orientation, Picture Naming, Semantic Fluency, Digit Span, Coding, List Recall, List Recognition,

Story Memory Recall, and Figure Recall. The subtests factor into five domains: Immediate Memory, Visuospatial/Constructional, Language, Attention, and Delayed Memory. There are parallel forms, allowing readministration to track progression and recovery. Administration time is about 30 minutes.

PREMORBID ASSESSMENT

Patients are often referred for assessment after an injury or a decline in ability, but in most instances, no preinjury test scores are available that allow a specific determination of the level of decline or change. Premorbid function therefore has to be estimated on the basis of known demographic variables, including educational and vocational achievement, and performance on tests resistant to decline from injury and predictive of cognitive ability. Vocabulary, fund of general information, and other skills such as word reading are highly correlated with intelligence and are often the best test means for estimating premorbid mental ability. We describe here several measures that can be used to estimate premorbid cognitive ability. Rapid Reference 4.11 lists the tests, the appropriate age ranges, and the publishers.

National Adult Reading Test—2

The National Adult Reading Test—2 (NART-2) was designed to estimate premorbid intellectual ability in adults aged 16 to 70. The NART-2 requires the patient to

≡ *Rapid Reference 4.11*

Tests for Premorbid Assessment

Test	Ages	Source
American National Adult Reading Test/ North American Adult Reading Test	16–70+	Strauss, E., Sherman, E. M. S., & Spreen, O. (2006). *A compendium of neuropsychological tests: Administration, norms, and commentary* (3rd ed.). New York: Oxford University Press.
Shipley-2	14 and older	WPS
Speed and Capacity of Language Processing Test	16–65	Pearson
Wechsler Test of Adult Reading	16–89	Pearson
Wide Range Achievement Test—4—Word Reading	5–94	PAR

read aloud 50 irregularly spelled words. The NART-2 was developed in England and first published in 1982 by Nelson and then by NFER-Nelson (now known as GL Assessment), but is now out of print. The NART has been adapted for the United States and Canada by Blair and Spreen (1989) as the North American Adult Reading Test (NAART) and in the United States by Grober and Sliwinski (1991) as the American National Adult Reading Test (AMNART). The NAART and AMNART can be created using the information provided in Strauss et al. (2006).

Shipley-2

The Shipley-2 (Shipley, 2008) is composed of two subtests: a multiple-choice vocabulary test and a measure of abstraction using logical sequencing. Because vocabulary is fairly resistant to decline from brain damage, the vocabulary test can be used as a measure of premorbid ability and the discrepancy between vocabulary and abstract thinking as a measure of cognitive impairment. Norms are available for individuals aged 7 to 89.

The Speed and Capacity of Language Processing Test

The Speed and Capacity of Language Processing Test (SCOLP) (Baddeley, Emslie, & Nimmo-Smith, 1992) is used to detect language-processing deficits and to measure rate of language processing. It is designed to discriminate long-standing slow processing from that due to brain damage. The SCOLP comprises two tests: the Speed of Comprehension Test and the Spot-the-Word Vocabulary Test. Discrepancies between comprehension speed and vocabulary are then used to rate the probable degree of acquired cognitive impairment. Normative data are available for aged 16 through 65.

Wechsler Test of Adult Reading

The Wechsler Test of Adult Reading (WTAR) was released by the Psychological Corporation (now Pearson) in 2001 (Wechsler, 2001b) and is designed to estimate the premorbid level of intellectual functioning of individuals aged 16 to 89 either by irregular word reading alone or in combination with years of education. The patient is required to read aloud from a list of 50 words with irregular pronunciations. The test is conormed with the WAIS-III and the WMS-III.

Wide Range Achievement Test—4—Word Reading

The Wide Range Achievement Test— 4 —Word Reading (WRAT-4) (Wilkinson & Robertson, 2006) is a screening measure of word reading ability and was designed as a measure of achievement for individuals aged 5 through 94. It requires the patient to read aloud a series of words that become more and more difficult and are less and less common. In patients without verbal deficits, the Word Reading subtest can provide information about premorbid cognitive ability.

INTELLIGENCE

Administering a general measure of intelligence or cognitive ability is an important part of the neuropsychological test battery for several reasons. The results of the IQ test set the baseline against which other test results are measured. Patients generally are expected to perform within a normal range of skills variability around measured IQ on the broad array of cognitive measures included in a neuropsychological battery. Deviations from this range can signal cognitive impairments, especially when a pattern of impairment emerges. In addition, general intelligence tests are multidimensional instruments that allow the examiner to observe how a patient performs across a wide variety of tasks. A patient's performance on the different subtests provides guidelines for the administration of further tests during the evaluation and can elucidate the pattern of impairments.

Intelligence Screening

In some circumstances, it may be necessary because of time constraints, practicality, or the fact that a patient has been tested recently on a full intelligence test to use brief measures to estimate a patient's IQ. Some of the available measures allow measurement of both verbal and nonverbal intelligence, whereas others focus on one skill or the other. Rapid Reference 4.12 lists the tests, the appropriate age ranges, and the publishers.

≡ *Rapid Reference 4.12*

Tests for Intelligence Screening

Test	Ages	Source
Comprehensive Test of Nonverbal Intelligence, Second Edition	6–90	PRO-ED
Kaufman Brief Intelligence Test, Second Edition	4–90	Pearson
Test of Nonverbal Intelligence—Third Edition	6–89	PRO-ED
Raven's Progressive Matrices	5–17+	Pearson
Wechsler Abbreviated Scale of Intelligence	6–89	Pearson
Wide Range Intelligence Test	4–85	PAR

Comprehensive Test of Nonverbal Intelligence, Second Edition

The Comprehensive Test of Nonverbal Intelligence, Second Edition (CTONI-2) (Hammill et al., 2009) is a nonverbal reasoning test consisting of six subtests: Pictorial Analogies, Pictorial Categories, Pictorial Sequences, Geometric Analogies, Geometric Categories, and Geometric Sequences. The subtests were designed to measure analogical reasoning, categorical classification, and sequential reasoning. From these subtests the CTONI-2 provides three composite scores: Nonverbal Intelligence Quotient, Pictorial Nonverbal Intelligence Quotient, and Geometric Nonverbal Intelligence Quotient. Responses to the test are given by pointing. The test is appropriate for individuals aged 6 through 89.

Kaufman Brief Intelligence Test, Second Edition

The Kaufman Brief Intelligence Test, Second Edition (KBIT-2) (Kaufman & Kaufman, 2004b) contains two scales, Verbal (crystallized ability) and Nonverbal (fluid reasoning). The Verbal Scale comprises two subtests, Verbal Knowledge and Riddles, and measures word knowledge, range of general information, verbal concept formation, and reasoning ability, requiring both expressive and receptive language skills. The Nonverbal Scale contains only the Matrices subtest and measures the ability to solve new problems requiring the perception of pictorial relationships and completion of visual analogies. The items are presented via easel, and the test can be administered to individuals ranging in age from 4 through 90.

Test of Nonverbal Intelligence—3

The Test of Nonverbal Intelligence—3 (TONI-3) (Brown et al., 1997) is a brief measure of nonverbal intelligence based on a matrix reasoning task that measures abstract reasoning and nonverbal problem solving. It is a language-free task and is thus useful with individuals who have difficulty with the English language. The test ages are 6 through 89.

The Raven's Progressive Matrices

The Raven's Progressive Matrices are a series of three sets of matrices designed to assess nonverbal ability. The easiest level is the Coloured Progressive Matrices (Raven, 1947/1995), which is appropriate for young children (ages 5–11), mentally impaired adolescents, and the elderly. The average level is the Standard Progressive Matrices (Raven, 1938/1996), which is appropriate for the general population (aged 6–16 and 17+). The most difficult is the Advanced Progressive Matrices (Raven, 1965/1994; Raven, Raven, & Court, 1998), which is intended for the top 20% of the population (aged 12–16 and 17+).

Wechsler Abbreviated Scale of Intelligence

The Wechsler Abbreviated Scale of Intelligence (WASI) (Wechsler, 1999) was designed as a reliable brief measure of general cognitive functioning. The four-subtest version consists of Vocabulary, Similarities, Block Design, and Matrix Reasoning, which result in a Verbal IQ, Performance IQ, and Full Scale IQ. The two-subtest version consists of Vocabulary and Matrix Reasoning, which result in a Full Scale IQ. The test can be administered to patients aged 6 through 89 and has been nationally standardized with 2,245 cases.

Wide Range Intelligence Test

The Wide Range Intelligence Test (WRIT) (Glutting, Adams, & Sheslow, 1999) assesses both verbal and nonverbal abilities with four subtests: Vocabulary, Verbal Analogies, Diamonds, and Matrices. The subtests combine into a Verbal IQ and a Visual IQ, and an overall General IQ. The test can be administered to patients aged 4 through 85 and has been nationally standardized with 2,285 individuals.

Intelligence Tests

Rapid Reference 4.13 lists the tests of intelligence, the appropriate age ranges, and the publishers.

Kaufman Adolescent and Adult Intelligence Test

The Kaufman Adolescent and Adult Intelligence Test (KAIT) (Kaufman & Kaufman, 1993) is a multisubtest intelligence test designed for individuals

≡ Rapid Reference 4.13

Tests of Intelligence

Test	Ages	Source
Kaufman Adolescent and Adult Intelligence Test	11–85+	Pearson
Kaufman Assessment Battery for Children, Second Edition	3–18	Pearson
Reynolds Intellectual Assessment Scales	3–94	PAR
Stanford-Binet Intelligence Scales, Fifth Edition	2–85+	Riverside Publishing
Wechsler Adult Intelligence Scale—Fourth Edition	16–90	Pearson
Wechsler Intelligence Scale for Children—Fourth Edition	6–16.11	Pearson
Wechsler Intelligence Scale for Children-IV Integrated	6–16.11	Pearson
Wechsler Preschool and Primary Scale of Intelligence—Third Edition	2.5–7.3	Pearson

aged 11 through 85+. From the Core Battery, which consists of six subtests, three scores are obtained: Fluid IQ, Crystallized IQ, and Composite IQ. The Crystallized Scale contains three subtests that measure the ability to solve problems using knowledge: Auditory Comprehension, Double Meanings, and Definitions. The Fluid Scale contains three subtests that measure novel problem solving: Rebus Learning, Mystery Codes, and Logical Steps. The Core Battery can be expanded to four more subtests, which permit comparison of immediate versus delayed memory.

Kaufman Assessment Battery for Children, Second Edition

The Kaufman Assessment Battery for Children, Section Edition (KABC-II) (Kaufman & Kaufman, 2004a) is an individually administered measure of cognitive abilities and processing skills based on a dual theoretical model: Cattell–Horn Carroll (CHC) model and Luria neuropsychological model. It was designed to be culturally fair and using the Luria model, it provides a nonverbal option. There are four scales: Simultaneous Processing/Visual Processing, Sequential Processing/Short-Term Memory, Planning Ability/Fluid Reasoning, Learning Ability/Long-Term Storage, and a fifth optional scale: Knowledge/Crystallized Ability. Each model gives two global scores expressed as age-based standard scores: Mental Processing Index or Fluid-Crystallized Index and the Nonverbal Index. The core battery for the Luria model requires 25 to 55 minutes for administration; the core battery for the CHC model requires 35 to 70 minutes. The KABC-II is designed for children aged 3 to 18 years old.

Reynolds Intellectual Assessment Scales

The Reynolds Intellectual Assessment Scales (RIAS) test (Reynolds & Kamphaus, 2003) is an individually administered intelligence test designed for individuals ages 3 to 94 years. The two core indexes are the Verbal Intelligence Index and the Nonverbal Intelligence Index. A Composite Intelligence Index is formed by combining the Verbal Intelligence Index and the Nonverbal Intelligence Index. Each index comprises two subtests. The verbal core measures verbal problem solving and verbal reasoning and the nonverbal core measures reasoning and spatial ability. An additional optional measure of memory is available that evaluates verbal short-term memory skills and recall and pictorial recall, providing a Composite Memory Index. The core battery can be administered in 20 to 25 minutes, and the complete RIAS can be administered in approximately 35 minutes.

Stanford–Binet Intelligence Scales—Fifth Edition

The Stanford–Binet Intelligence Scale—Fifth Edition (SB5) (Roid, 2003) consists of 10 tasks measuring five cognitive areas organized according to the

Cattell–Horn–Carroll factor-analytic framework: Fluid Reasoning, Knowledge, Quantitative Reasoning, Visual–Spatial Processing, and Working Memory. Within each factor, there is a verbal and a nonverbal domain. Fluid Reasoning includes tests of object series/matrices, and early reasoning, verbal absurdities, and verbal analogies. Knowledge includes tests of procedural knowledge and picture absurdities and vocabulary, and Quantitative Reasoning includes tests of quantitative knowledge, math reasoning skills, and word problems. Visual–Spatial Processing includes tests of pattern analysis and paper folding and cutting, along with understanding directions and word problems involving spatial information. The fifth factor of Working Memory includes tests of object memory, visual span, sentence memory, and "last word" memory. Summary scores consist of scaled scores for the subtests and the subtest scores combine to form a factor index, two domain scales (Nonverbal IQ and Verbal IQ). All 10 subtests combine to form the Full Scale IQ. An abbreviated IQ is also available based on performances on Object Series/Matrices and Vocabulary. The Fifth Edition of the Stanford–Binet was standardized on 4,800 individuals aged 2 to 85+. Administration time varies but is estimated to be about 5 minutes per subtest.

The Wechsler Scales

The intelligence scales used most often in the United States are those from David Wechsler. The current adult measure (for ages 16–90) is the WAIS-IV, which was published in 2008 (Wechsler, 2008a). For children aged 6 through 16 years, 11 months, the current test, published in 2003 (Wechsler, 2003), is the WISC-IV. For children aged 2 years, 6 months, through 7 years, 3 months, the current test, published in 2002 (Wechsler, 2002), is the Wechsler Preschool and Primary Scale of Intelligence—Third Edition (WPPSI-III).

The WAIS-IV and WISC-IV provide Full Scale IQ, index, and age-scaled subtest scores. On the WAIS-IV, the Verbal Comprehension Index (VCI) comprises age-scaled scores on subtests of Information, Vocabulary, and Similarities; on the WISC-IV, the VCI comprises age-scaled scores on subtests of Vocabulary, Similarities, and Comprehension. On the WAIS-IV, the Working Memory Index (WMI) comprises age-scaled scores on subtests of Arithmetic and Digit Span, and on the WISC-IV, the WMI comprises age-scaled scores on subtests of Digit Span and Letter–Number Sequencing. The Perceptual Reasoning Index (PRI) comprises age-scaled scores on subtests of Block Design, Matrix Reasoning and Visual Puzzles (WAIS-IV), or Picture Concepts (WISC-IV). The Processing Speed Index (PSI) comprises age-scaled scores on subtests of Coding and Symbol Search. Administration time of the core subtests from the WAIS-IV and the WISC-IV is shorter than their predecessors.

The Wechsler Intelligence Scale for Children, Fourth Edition Integrated

The Wechsler Intelligence Scale for Children, Fourth Edition Integrated (WISC-IV Integrated) (Wechsler et al., 2004) merges the WISC-IV with the revision of the Wechsler Intelligence Scale for Children—Third Edition as a Process Instrument (WISC-III PI; Kaplan, Fein, Kramer, Delis, & Morris, 1999). It was designed to provide a comprehensive approach combining traditional and process-oriented approach to assessing children's intelligence and cognitive processes. The WISC-IV Integrated comprises the WISC-IV and its four core index scores and 16 optional subtests that allow the clinician an opportunity to test the limits and explore the process by which a child solves a problem. In the verbal domain the WISC-IV Integrated offers multiple-choice-based optional process subtests for Similarities, Vocabulary, Comprehension, and Information and Picture Vocabulary Multiple Choice. Other optional process subtests in the verbal domain include Visual Digit Span, Spatial Span, Letter Span, Letter–Number Sequencing Process Approach, Arithmetic Process Approach, and Written Arithmetic. In the visual perceptual domain, the optional process subtests are Block Design Multiple Choice, Block Design Process Approach, Elithorn Mazes, Coding Recall, and Coding Copy. To aid in identification of the bases of a child's cognitive strengths and weaknesses, the WISC-IV Integrated offers more than 25 additional process scores. Normative data specific to the WISC-IV Integrated was obtained from a stratified sample of more than 700 children ranging in age from 6 to 16 years, 11 months, and from children from various special groups, such as children with learning disorders, pervasive developmental disorder, and traumatic brain injury.

ATTENTION

Assessment of attention means evaluating the multiple facets that make up the attentional matrix. This matrix can be conceptualized as involving span of apprehension; the ability to focus, divide, and sustain attention; mental manipulation; and resistance to distraction or interference. Few attentional tasks, however, can be considered to measure only one of these facets, although each may fit more neatly into one category than another. Because intact attention is a building block on which other cognitive abilities rely, it is necessary to measure how well an individual can deploy and maintain his or her attention. To delineate the nature of an attentional problem, multiple tests of attention need to be administered. Rapid Reference 4.14 summarizes the tests, the appropriate age ranges, and the publishers.

≡ *Rapid Reference 4.14*

....

Tests of Attention

Test	Ages	Source
Brief Test of Attention	17–84	PAR
Children Color Trails Test	8–16	PAR
Color Trails Test	18 and older	PAR
Computerized Test of Information Processing	15–74	MHS
Comprehensive Trail-Making Test	8–74	PRO-ED
Connors' Continuous Performance Test, Second Edition	6 and older	MHS
Wechsler Digit Span	6–90	Pearson
Digit Vigilance Test	20–85	PAR
Paced Auditory Serial Attention Test	16 and older	Strauss, E., Sherman, E. M. S., & Spreen, O. (2006). *A compendium of neuropsychological tests: Administration, norms and commentary* (3rd ed.). New York: Oxford University Press.
Ruff 2 & 7 Selective Attention Test	16–70	PAR
Symbol Digit Modalities Test	8–91	WPS
Test of Everyday Attention	18–80	Pearson
Test of Everyday Attention for Children	6–16	Pearson
Test of Variables of Attention	4–80+	The TOVA Company
Trail Making Test	8–89	The Neuropsychology Center
Vigil Continuous Performance Test	6–90	Pearson

Brief Test of Attention

The Brief Test of Attention (BTA) (Schretlen, 1997) is offered as a test of divided auditory attention for individuals aged 17 through 84. A series of numbers and letters is presented aloud via audiotape. In the first half of the test, the client is to disregard the letters and count the numbers in each series. In the second half, the client is to disregard the numbers and count the letters in each series. Time for administration is 10 minutes or less.

Color Trails Test

The Color Trails Test (CTT) (D'Elia, Satz, Uchiyama, & White, 1996) is designed to measure speed of processing, along with sequencing, mental flexibility, and visual search ability. It is similar to the Trail Making Test but uses colors instead of letters to minimize the influence of language and cultural bias. It is individually administered to adults 18 years and older and takes 3 to 8 minutes to administer. For children aged 8 to 16, the Children's Color Trails Test (CCTT) (Llorente, Williams, Satz, & D'Elia, 2003) is available. Administration time for the CCTT is approximately 5 to 7 minutes.

Comprehensive Trail-Making Test

The Comprehensive Trail-Making Test (CTMT) (Reynolds, 2002) comprises five visual search and sequencing tasks that require attention and concentration, resistance to distraction, and set-switching ability. Like other trail-making tasks, the patient must connect a series of stimuli in a specified order as quickly as possible. T-scores are available for each of the five trails, and a composite score is obtained by combining the T-scores from the five trails. It is designed for administration to children and adults ages 8 through 74. Testing time varies from 5 to 12 minutes.

Computerized Test of Information Processing

The Computerized Test of Information Processing (CTIP) (Tombaugh & Rees, 2008) uses three computerized reaction time tests that become progressively more difficult to measure speed of information processing. In addition to measuring the speed at which information is processed, it has been designed to aid in the detection of suboptimal effort in traumatic brain injury. The CTIP is appropriate for ages 15 through 74. Administration time is 15 minutes.

Conners' Continuous Performance Test—Second Edition

The Conners' Continuous Performance Test—Second Edition (CPT-II), Version 5 (Conners, 2004) is used to identify visual attention problems manifested in impaired vigilance and impulsive responding in children and adults aged 6 and older. The test is presented on computer and provides information concerning measures such as number of omission and commission errors, perceptual sensitivity, and reaction time. Administration time is 14 minutes.

Digit Span

This test is one of the working memory subtests in the WAIS-IV and WISC-IV. In Digit Span Forward the patient repeats digits in the exact order they were presented. Digit Span Forward is a measure of elementary attention or span of apprehension. In Digit Span Backward, the patient recalls the digits presented in the exact reverse order. Digit Span Backward is a measure of mental manipulation or control and requires working memory. The WAIS-IV also includes Digit Span Sequencing during which the patient repeats the digits in sequential order from lowest to highest. Like Digit Span Backward, it is a measure of mental manipulation or control and requires working memory.

Digit Vigilance Test

The Digit Vigilance Test (DVT) (Lewis, 1995) is a visual cancellation task that is used to measure sustained attention and that requires visual scanning and psychomotor speed. Measures of omission errors and time-to-task completion are available. Normative data are available for the DVT in Heaton, Miller, Taylor, and Grant (2004) for ages 20 through 85. Time for administration is 10 minutes.

Paced Auditory Serial Addition Test

The Paced Auditory Serial Addition Test (PASAT) (Gronwall, 1977; Gronwall & Sampson, 1974) was designed to measure sustained and divided attention and speed of information processing. The task requires serial addition of pairs of consecutive numbers at varying interval rates. There are multiple versions of the PASAT, including a children's version; ordering information is summarized in Strauss et al. (2006).

Ruff 2 & 7 Selective Attention Test

The Ruff 2 & 7 Selective Attention Test (Ruff & Allen, 1996) is used to measure visual search and cancellation in patients aged 16 through 70. Targets (2 & 7) are embedded among either alphabetical letters or other numbers. The test is scored for both speed and accuracy. Administration time is 5 minutes.

Symbol Digit Modalities Test

The Symbol Digit Modalities Test (SDMT) (Smith, 1991) is a speeded symbol substitution task that requires visual scanning and tracking. With a reference key at hand, the patient pairs specific numbers with specific geometric figures over a 90-second interval. Responses can be both written and oral, allowing a comparison between written and oral responses. The task can be used for individuals aged 8 to 91 years. Time for administration is less than 5 minutes.

Test of Everyday Attention

The Test of Everyday Attention (TEA) (Robertson, Ward, Ridgeway, & Nimmo-Smith, 1994) is designed to measure attention in adults aged 18 through 80 years. The test comprises eight subtests that represent everyday tasks and has three parallel forms. It assesses three aspects of attentional functioning: selective attention, sustained attention, and attentional switching. Administration time is 45 to 60 minutes. There is also a version available for children and adolescents aged 6 to 16 years, the Test of Everyday Attention for Children (TEA-Ch; Manly, Robertson, Anderson, & Nimmo-Smith, 1998). The TEA-Ch has nine subtests and two parallel forms. It assesses selective attention, sustained attention, divided attention, and the ability to switch attention from one task to another and to inhibit responses. Administration time is 55 to 60 minutes.

Test of Variables of Attention
The Test of Variables of Attention (T.O.V.A.) (Greenberg, 2007; Leark, Greenberg, Kindschi, Dupuy, & Hughes, 2007) is a computerized test of attention designed to assist in the screening, diagnosis, and treatment monitoring of attention disorders, such as ADHD in children and adults aged 4 to 80+. The test is language and culture free. Administration time is 21.6 minutes. A new version, the T.O.V.A. 8, also has a Symptom Validity Index for use with adults that can reliably identify cases where symptom exaggeration is present (S. Hughes, e-mail communication, January 17, 2009).

Trail Making Test
Although part of the HRB, the Trail Making Test (TMT), a speeded test that measures sustained visual attention, visual scanning, sequencing, and cognitive flexibility, is often administered apart from the HRB. It has two parts, Trail Making A, which requires number sequencing, and Trail Making B, which requires alternation and sequencing between letters and numbers. The Adult Version is for adults aged 15 to 89 years; the Intermediate Version is for children aged 9 to 14 years. Normative data are available for ages 8 through 85 in Strauss et al. (2006). Time for administration is less than 10 minutes. It is available from the Neuropsychology Center at www.neuropsych.com.

Vigil Continuous Performance Test
The Vigil (Vigil, 1996) is used for children and adults aged 6 through 90 to measure sustained attention or vigilance. The test is administered on computer and includes presentations of both verbal and nonverbal targets. Each test requires 8 minutes of administration time.

EXECUTIVE FUNCTIONS

This category refers to the numerous higher order cognitive functions of establishing, maintaining, and changing set; initiation; planning and organization;

≡ Rapid Reference 4.15

Tests of Executive Functions

Test	Ages	Source
Behavioural Assessment of the Dysexecutive Syndrome	16–87	Pearson
Behavioural Assessment of Dysexecutive Syndrome in Children	8–16	Pearson
Booklet Category Test, Second Edition	15 and older	PAR
Children's Category Test	5–16	Pearson
Short Category Test	20 and older	WPS
Controlled Oral Word Association Test	6–95	Strauss, E., Sherman, E. M. S., & Spreen, O. (2006). A compendium of neuropsychological tests: Administration, norms and commentary (3rd ed.). New York: Oxford University Press.
Delis-Kaplan Executive Function System	8–89	Pearson
Ruff Figural Fluency Test	16–70	PAR
Stroop Color and Word Test	7–90	WPS
Test of Verbal Conceptualization and Fluency	8–89	Pearson
Tower of London-Drexel University, 2nd edition	7–80	PAR
Wisconsin Card Sorting Test	6.5–89	PAR

judgment; reasoning and abstraction; and self-regulation. To capture a patient's abilities and disabilities in the area of executive functions, the tests selected should broadly cover these various processes. Rapid Reference 4.15 provides the test names, the appropriate age ranges, and the publishers.

Behavioural Assessment of the Dysexecutive Syndrome

The Behavioural Assessment of the Dysexecutive Syndrome (BADS) (Wilson et al., 1996) is a battery of tests sensitive to deficits in planning ability, organization, problem solving, and attention that impact behavior in everyday situations. The battery comprises six tests (Temporal Judgment, Rule Shift Cards, Action Program, Key Search, Zoo Map, and Modified Six Elements) and a 20-item Dysexecutive Questionnaire that samples changes related to emotion or personality, motivation, behavior, and cognition. The BADS is normed for ages 16 through 87. An adaptation of the BADS, the Behavioural Assessment of Dysexecutive Syndrome in Children (BADS-C; Emslie et al., 2003) is available for ages 8 through 16 years.

Category Test

Part of the HRB, the Category Test is a complex nonverbal task assessing concept formation and abstract reasoning. It involves flexible problem solving and the ability to learn from experience. The original version uses slides, but a Booklet Category Test (BCT, 2nd ed.; DeFilippis & McCampbell, 1997) is available for adolescents and adults aged 15 years and older from Psychological Assessment Resources. Also, a Short Category Test (Wetzel & Boll, 1987) is available from Western Psychological Services for adults aged 20 and older. In addition, a Children's Category Test (CCT; Boll, 1993) is available from Pearson for children aged 5 through 16.

Controlled Oral Word Association Test

This task is used to measure verbal fluency or the ability to maximally produce words belonging to a particular class. In FAS, the patient must generate as many words as possible beginning with the letters *F, A,* and *S* in 1-minute intervals. Normative data for ages 7 through 95 are available in Strauss et al. (2006), and demographically adjusted norms are available for ages 20 through 85 in Heaton et al. (2004). Normative data are also available for the letters *C, L,* and *F* and for the Thurstone Fluency test in Strauss et al. (2006). In a parallel task, Category Fluency, the patient is required to generate as many words as possible belonging to a particular category—for example, animals, fruits and vegetables, or clothing. Category Fluency norms are available in Strauss et al. (2006).

Delis–Kaplan Executive Function System

The Delis–Kaplan Executive Function System (D-KEFS) (Delis, Kaplan, & Kramer, 2001) comprises nine tests designed to comprehensively assess various executive functions, such as problem solving, flexible thinking, verbal and spatial fluency and concept formation, planning and reasoning, verbal inhibition, hypothesis testing, deductive reasoning, and abstract thinking. The D-KEFS tests include the Sorting Test, Trail Making Test, Verbal Fluency Test, Design Fluency Test, Color–Word Interference Test, Tower Test, 20 Question Test, Word Context Test, and Proverb Test. Norms are available for ages 8 through 89.

Ruff Figural Fluency Test

The Ruff Figural Fluency Test (RFFT) (Ruff, 1998) is designed as a measure of nonverbal fluency or the ability to maximally produce figural responses. The task requires the patient to draw as many unique designs as possible within 60-second intervals by connecting dots on a grid. It is appropriate for ages 16 through 70.

Stroop Color and Word Test

The Stroop Color and Word Test (Golden, 1978) is used to measure cognitive flexibility, resistance to interference from outside stimuli, and the ability to suppress a prepotent verbal response. A patient's performance is compared across three tasks: word reading, color naming, and color word naming. In the latter task the patient must name as quickly as possible the color ink (which is discordant with the color word) in which words are printed rather than reading the word. In the adult version, normative data are available for ages 15 to 90 in the 2002 update (Golden & Freshwater, 2002). A children's version (ages 5 to 14) is also available (Golden, Freshwater, & Golden, 2003).

Test of Verbal Conceptualization and Fluency

This Test of Verbal Conceptualization and Fluency (TVCF) (Reynolds & Horton, 2006) was developed to measure multiple aspects of executive functioning, including verbal fluency, shifting and rule induction, visual search capacity, and cognitive flexibility. It involves both verbal and nonverbal assessment and contains four measures: Categorical Fluency, Classification (a verbal analog to the WCST), Letter Naming, and Trails C. It is appropriate for individuals 8 through 89 years.

Tower of London–Drexel University, Second Edition

The Tower of London–Drexel University, Second Edition (TOL-DX, 2nd Ed.) test (Culbertson & Zilmer, 2000) is designed to assess higher order problem-solving and executive-planning abilities. The children's version is for ages 7 to 15; the adult version is for ages 16 to 80.

Wisconsin Card Sorting Test

The Wisconsin Card Sorting Test (WCST) (Grant & Berg, 1993) is used to measure abstract reasoning, concept generation, and perseverative responding. The task requires the patient to sort the cards according to one of three principles of class membership. Available measures include categories achieved, perseverative responses, perseverative errors, nonperseverative errors, failure to maintain set, and efficiency of learning. The professional manual (Heaton, Chelune, Talley, Kay, & Curtiss, 1993) contains norms for individuals aged 6.5 through 89. A 64-card version is also available (Kongs, Thompson, Iverson, & Heaton, 2000).

LEARNING AND MEMORY

Evaluation of memory requires assessment of numerous, seemingly disparate processes in both the verbal and nonverbal modalities. Evaluation of memory means assessing encoding and acquisition of information, retention and retrieval,

≡ Rapid Reference 4.16

Tests of Learning and Memory

Test	Ages	Source
Benton Visual Retention Test, Fifth Edition	8 and older	Pearson
Brief Visuospatial Memory Test-Revised	18–79	PAR
Buschke Selective Reminding Test	5–91	See Strauss, E., Sherman, E. M. S., & Spreen, O. (2006). *A compendium of neuropsychological tests: Administration, norms and commentary* (3rd ed.). New York: Oxford University Press.
California Verbal Learning Test-Second Edition	16–89	Pearson
California Verbal Learning Test-Children's Version	5–16	Pearson
Children's Memory Scale	5–16	Pearson
Doors and People Test	16–97	Pearson
Hopkins Verbal Learning Test-Revised	16–80+	PAR
Rey Auditory Verbal Learning Test	7–89	WPS
Rey Complex Figure Test and Recognition Test	6–89	PAR
Rivermead Behavioural Memory Test for Children	5–10:11	Pearson
Rivermead Behavioural Memory Test-Third Edition	5–96	Pearson
Test of Memory and Learning, Second Edition	2.5–59	PRO-ED
Wechsler Memory Scale-Fourth Edition	16–90	Pearson
Wide Range Assessment of Memory and Learning, Second Edition	5–90	PAR

rate of decay, and susceptibility to interference, as well as recognition memory versus spontaneous recall. Some memory instruments incorporate measures to assess most of these processes, whereas others measure just one aspect. Rapid Reference 4.16 lists the tests, the appropriate age range, and the publisher.

Benton Visual Retention Test, Fifth Edition
The Benton Visual Retention Test, Fifth Edition (BVRT) (Sivan, 1992) uses recall of geometric designs to measure visual memory in children and adults ages 8 and older. Three test forms allow for retesting without the confound of practice effects.

Brief Visuospatial Memory Test—Revised
The Brief Visuospatial Memory Test—Revised (BVMT-R) (Benedict, 1997) is designed as a measure of visual learning and memory, using a multiple trial, list-learning format. Six geometric designs are presented over three learning trials, followed by a 25-minute delayed recall trial. Six equivalent sets of test stimuli permit repeat testing to measure changes over time. Normative data are available for adults aged 18 to 79 years.

Buschke Selective Reminding Test
The Buschke Selective Reminding Test (SRT) (Hannay & Levin, 1985, after Buschke, 1973) uses a multitrial word list learning task to measure verbal memory. Following the first presentation of the list, only the words the patient did not recall are repeated on subsequent trials. See Strauss et al. (2006) for alternate word lists and normative data for children aged 5 through 15 and adults aged 18 through 91.

California Verbal Learning Test—Second Edition
The California Verbal Learning Test—Second Edition (CVLT-II) (Delis, Kramer, Kaplan, & Ober, 2000) is a word list learning task for adults aged 16 through 89 that permits measurement of verbal learning and memory. The CVLT-II uses a shopping-list format consisting of 16 words from four categories presented over five trials. After the first five trials, an interference list is presented, followed by short-delay recall of the first list and then long-delay recall after 20 minutes. A recognition trial is also available at the end of the test. The CVLT-II provides information about acquisition, recall, retention, and retrieval of verbal information. It also provides information about strategies used in learning. The CVLT-C (Delis, Kramer, Kaplan, & Ober, 1994) is available for children aged 5 through 16.

Children's Memory Scale
The Children's Memory Scale (CMS) (Cohen, 1997) is a comprehensive memory instrument that measures the dimensions of attention and working memory,

verbal and visual memory, short-delay and long-delay memory, recall and recognition, and learning characteristics in children ages 5 through 16. The core subtests result in eight summary scores: Verbal Immediate, Verbal Delayed, Visual Immediate, Visual Delayed, General Memory, Delayed Recognition, Attention and Concentration, and Learning. The core subtests in the auditory (verbal) domain consist of story memory and verbal paired-associate learning. Those in the visual (nonverbal) domain consist of spatial memory and face recognition tasks. Those in the attention and concentration domain consist of digit span and mental control tasks. Available optional memory tasks include word list learning and complex picture memory. The CMS is conormed with the WISC-IV and WPPSI-III, allowing comparisons among intellectual ability, learning, and memory.

Doors and People Test

The Doors and People Test (DPT) was developed by Baddeley, Emslie, and Nimmo-Smith (1994) as a measure of visual and verbal memory, recall and recognition, and forgetting, using doors, shapes, names, and people paired with an occupation. Scaled scores and percentile rankings are available for adolescents and adults aged 16 to 97.

Hopkins Verbal Learning Test—Revised

The Hopkins Verbal Learning Test—Revised (HVLT-R) (Brandt & Benedict, 2001) is a word list learning task for adults aged 16 through 80 years and older that permits measurement of verbal learning and memory. The HVLT-R uses a list format consisting of 12 words from three semantic categories presented over three trials. An incidental long-delay recall is administered 20 to 25 minutes later. A yes–no recognition trial is also available at the end of the test. The HVLT-R provides information about acquisition, recall, retention, and recognition of verbal information. Six equivalent sets of word lists permit repeat testing to measure changes over time.

Rey Auditory Verbal Learning Test

Rey (1958) originally developed the Rey Auditory Verbal Learning Test (RAVLT). It is a superspan list learning task that helps measure verbal learning, memory, proactive and retroactive interference, retention, and encoding and retrieval. The RAVLT requires the patient to learn 15 words over five trials; a second list is then introduced and is followed by short-delay recall, long-delay recall, and recognition of the first list. A handbook (Schmidt, 1996) containing information about administration, scoring, and normative information (ages 7 through 89) for the RAVLT is available from Western Psychological Services. Alternate lists and normative data are also available in Strauss et al. (2006).

Rey Complex Figure Test and Recognition Trial

The Rey Complex Figure Test and Recognition Trial (RCFT) (Meyers & Meyers, 1995) uses four trials (copy, immediate recall, delayed recall, and recognition) to measure visuospatial recall and recognition memory, response bias, processing speed, and visuoconstructional ability. The patient copies the original Rey–Osterrieth Complex Figure (Rey, 1941) and 3 minutes later is asked without warning to reproduce it from memory. After a 30-minute delay, the patient is asked to recall the figure again and perform a recognition trial. The original manual contains normative data for individuals aged 18 through 89. Normative data for children and adolescents aged 6 through 17 are available in the *Manual Supplement* (Meyers & Meyers, 1996). Alternate complex figures and normative data are included in Strauss et al. (2006).

The Rivermead Behavioural Memory Test, Third Edition

The Rivermead Behavioural Memory Test, Third Edition (RBMT-3) (Wilson et al., 2008) is designed to assess the memory problems encountered by patients in their everyday life. For example, it measures remembering appointments, names, and a message to deliver, in addition to story recall, face recognition, picture recognition, and orientation. The RBMT-3 includes a new subtest designed to assess the ability to acquire new skills and adds a separate measure of implicit memory. It is intended for adolescents and adults ages 16 to 89. The Rivermead Behavioural Memory Test for Children (RBMT-C) is also available for children ages 5 years to 10 years, 11 months.

Test of Memory and Learning, Second Edition

The Test of Memory and Learning, Second Edition (TOMAL-2) (Reynolds & Voress, 2007) was designed to evaluate learning and memory abilities in children, adolescents, and adults aged 5 years to 59 years, 11 months. Index scores are available for Verbal Memory, Nonverbal Memory, and Composite Memory. Supplemental indexes include Verbal Delayed Recall, Learning, Attention and Concentration, Sequential Memory, Free Recall, and Associative Recall. Available subtests include Story Memory, Verbal Learning, Sentence Memory, Design Memory, Picture Memory, and Finger Windows (spatial span). The TOMAL-2 comprises eight core subtests, six supplemental subtests, and two delayed recall tasks.

Wechsler Memory Scale—Fourth Edition

The Wechsler Memory Scale—Fourth Edition (WMS-IV) (Wechsler, 2009) is a comprehensive assessment of memory that is conormed with the WAIS-IV, allowing measurement of the relationship between intellect and memory in adults aged 16 through 90. For adults aged 16 to 69, the WMS-IV provides five summary scores or Primary Indexes: Auditory Memory Index, Visual Memory Index, Immediate Memory Index, Delayed Memory Index, and Visual Working Memory Index. The summary scores in the auditory (verbal) memory domain are derived from story memory and verbal paired associate tasks. The summary scores in the visual (nonverbal) domain are derived from spatial memory and design memory tasks. In the visual working memory domain, the primary subtests are a spatial addition task and symbol span. Older adults are not administered the spatial addition task or the spatial memory task. An optional measure, the Brief Cognitive Status Exam, is available to measure orientation, mental control, clock drawing, incidental recall, automaticity and inhibitory control, and verbal production.

Wide Range Assessment of Memory and Learning, Second Edition

The Wide Range Assessment of Memory and Learning test, Second Edition (WRAML2) (Sheslow & Adams, 2003) was designed to evaluate learning and memory abilities in children, adolescents, and adults aged 5 to 90 years. The Core Battery yields index scores for Verbal Memory, Visual Memory, and Attention/ Concentration; from these index scores a General Memory Index can be derived. Also available is a Working Memory Index, composed of symbolic and verbal working memory tasks and recognition subtests for designs, pictures, words, and story information. The core subtests include Story Memory, Verbal Learning,, Design Memory, Picture Memory, Finger Windows (spatial span), and Number– Letter (auditory span).

LANGUAGE FUNCTIONS

The clinician can study many aspects of language ability through behavioral observation. Intact auditory comprehension can be evaluated by a patient's ability to follow directions without requiring repetitions or explanations. Intact repetition can be seen by observing a patient repeat a phrase or a sentence. Other language functions require specific tests to delineate particular deficits. Tests may be necessary to evaluate vocabulary skills, aphasic features, and naming difficulties. Rapid Reference 4.17 summarizes the tests, the appropriate age ranges, and the publishers.

Boston Diagnostic Aphasia Examination—Third Edition

The Boston Diagnostic Aphasia Examination—Third Edition (BDAE) (Goodglass et al., 2001) is a comprehensive measure of language and language-related abilities that aids in the diagnosis of aphasia syndromes in adults. The test measures in detail spontaneous speech and fluency, auditory comprehension, naming, oral reading,

≡ *Rapid Reference 4.17*

Tests of Language

Test	Ages	Source
Boston Diagnostic Aphasia Examination, Third Edition.	Adults	Pearson
Boston Naming Test—2	5–93	Pearson
Expressive One-Word Picture Vocabulary Test, 2000 Edition	2–18.11	PAR
Expressive Vocabulary Test, Second Edition	2.5–90+	Pearson
Multilingual Aphasia Examination, 3rd Ed.	6–12; 16–97	PAR
Peabody Picture Vocabulary Test, Fourth Edition	2.5–90+	Pearson
Receptive One-Word Picture Vocabulary Test, 2000 Edition	2–18.11	PAR
Test of Adolescent/Adult Word Finding	12–80	PRO-ED
Token Test (Multilingual Aphasia Examination, 3rd Ed.)	6–12; 16–97	PAR

repetition, writing, and reading comprehension. Percentile scores are available to compare the patient's performance with that of a sample of persons with aphasia.

Boston Naming Test—2

The Boston Naming Test—2 (BNT) (Kaplan et al., 2001) is used to assess confrontation-naming and word-retrieval deficits. The test evaluates a patient's ability to name pictures of 60 line drawings arranged in order of frequency from high to low. Patients with perceptual problems are allowed categorical or semantic cues; patients with apparent retrieval difficulties are allowed phonemic cues to aid in their production of the object's name. Normative data are available in Strauss et al. (2006) for children aged 5 through 13 and adults aged 25 through 93, and demographically adjusted normative data are available in Heaton et al. (2004) for adults ages 20 through 85.

Expressive One-Word Picture Vocabulary Test

The Expressive One-Word Picture Vocabulary Test, 2000 Ed. (EOWPVT) (Brownell, 2000a) measures expressive vocabulary for English speakers by requiring the child to name pictures. Children and young adults aged 2 through 18 years, 11 months must name an object or group of objects to confrontation. The test is conormed with the Receptive One-Word Picture Vocabulary Test, thus allowing direct, meaningful comparisons between expressive and receptive vocabulary skills.

Expressive Vocabulary Test, Second Edition

The Expressive Vocabulary Test, Second Edition (EVT-2) (Williams, 2006) is used as a measure of English expressive vocabulary and word retrieval. This test requires the examinee to provide labels for pictures, answer specific questions about pictures, and provide synonyms for pictures. For the synonym items, the patient is presented with a picture and a word, after which the patient must produce another single word that means the same thing and goes with the picture. The test contains norms for ages 2.5 to 90+ and is conormed with the PPVT-4 providing comparisons of receptive and expressive vocabulary.

Multilingual Aphasia Examination, Third Edition

The Multilingual Aphasia Examination, Third Edition (MAE) (Benton, deS Hamsher, & Sivan, 1994) is designed as a brief but comprehensive assessment of the presence, severity, and qualitative aspects of acquired language disorders. It includes tests of oral expression, auditory comprehension, reading comprehension, and spelling. The MAE can be used with children aged 6 to 12 and adolescents and adults aged 16 to 97. A Spanish adaptation is available.

Peabody Picture Vocabulary Test—4

The Peabody Picture Vocabulary Test—4 (PPVT-4) (Dunn & Dunn, 2006) is a measure of English receptive vocabulary. The PPVT-4 has norms for individuals aged 2.5 to 90+ and is conormed with the EVT-2. Patients are required to match one of four pictures on a test page with a word spoken aloud by the examiner.

Receptive One-Word Picture Vocabulary Test

The Receptive One-Word Picture Vocabulary Test, 2000 Ed. (ROWPVT) (Brownell, 2000b) measures English hearing or receptive vocabulary. Children and young adults aged 2 through 18 years, 11 months, must match an object or concept with its name. The test is conormed with the EOWPVT-2000, thus permitting direct meaningful comparisons of receptive and expressive vocabulary.

Test of Adolescent/Adult Word Finding

The Test of Adolescent/Adult Word Finding (TAWF) (German, 1990) assesses word finding in adolescents and adults aged 12 through 80. The word finding tasks include naming of both nouns and verbs, naming to description, sentence completion naming, and naming to category. Both speed and accuracy can be assessed, and an optional comprehension section is available to discriminate between difficulties due to poor comprehension versus word-finding difficulties.

Token Test

The Token Test (DeRenzi & Vignolo, 1962) is a brief measure of auditory comprehension and can be used to identify receptive language dysfunction. The Token Test is available as part of the Multilingual Aphasia Examination (MAE; Benton, DeS Hamsher, & Sivan, 1994) and can be used with children aged 6 to 12 and adolescents and adults aged 16 to 97 years.

ACHIEVEMENT TESTS

A comprehensive test battery often must include measures of scholastic achievement. Performance on tests of achievement can provide information about the presence and pattern of learning difficulties or disabilities and an individual's academic strengths and weaknesses. Rapid Reference 4.18 lists the tests, the appropriate age ranges, and the publishers.

Gray Oral Reading Test—Fourth Edition

The Gray Oral Reading Test—Fourth Edition (GORT-4) (Wiederholt & Bryant, 2001) is an individually administered measure of oral reading and comprehension. The GORT-4 provides a Fluency Score that combines rate and accuracy and an Oral Reading Comprehension Score based on number of correct responses to comprehension questions. An Oral Reading Quotient is derived from

≡ *Rapid Reference 4.18*

Tests of Achievement

Test	Ages	Source
Gray Oral Reading Test-Fourth Edition	6–18	PRO-ED
Kaufman Functional Academic Skills Test	15–85+	Pearson
Kaufman Test of Educational Achievement, Second Edition	4.6–25	Pearson
The Nelson-Denny Reading Test	9–Adult	Riverside Publishing
Wechsler Fundamentals: Academic Skills	Grades K–12; Ages 18–50	Pearson
Wechsler Individual Achievement Test, Second Edition	4–85.11	Pearson
Wide Range Achievement Test 4	5–94	PAR
Woodcock-Johnson III Normative Update	2–90+	Riverside Publishing

a combination of the Fluency Score and Oral Reading Comprehension Score. The test is designed for children and adolescents aged 6 through 18.

Kaufman Functional Academic Skills Test

The Kaufman Functional Academic Skills Test (K-FAST) (Kaufman & Kaufman, 1994) uses two subtests, Reading and Arithmetic, to measure an individual's ability to apply reading and mathematics to everyday situations. The items in the K-FAST reflect daily living situations that occur outside of the classroom. The test is normed for adolescents and adults aged 15 through 85 years.

Kaufman Test of Educational Achievement, Second Edition

The Kaufman Test of Educational Achievement, Second Edition (KTEA-II) (Kaufman & Kaufman, 2004c) was designed to measure achievement in reading, mathematics, written language, and oral language. The KTEA-II provides an analysis of errors and prescriptive information for development of intervention planning. It can be administered to individuals aged 4 years, 6 months, through 25 years. A brief form assessing reading, math, and written expression is available for individuals aged 4 years, 6 months, through 90 years (KTEA-II Brief Form; Kaufman & Kaufman, 2004d).

The Nelson–Denny Reading Test

The Nelson–Denny Reading Test (Brown, Fishco, & Hanna, 1993) is designed to assess student achievement and progress in vocabulary, comprehension, and reading rate. It was developed as a survey test for high school and college students and adults. It is a two-part test that measures vocabulary development, reading comprehension, and reading rate.

Wechsler Fundamentals: Academic Skills

The Wechsler Fundamentals: Academic Skills (Wechsler, 2008b) is a brief achievement battery that allows a quick evaluation of academic levels in the areas of spelling, numerical operation, reading comprehension, and word reading. It can be administered individually or in small groups. It is linked with the WASI, allowing a comparison of discrepancies in ability versus achievement. The Wechsler Fundamentals: Academic Skills is designed for children in kindergarten through Grade 12 and adults aged 18 through 50. An alternate version is available and permits monitoring of a student's progress. The Wechsler Fundamentals: Academic Skills is intended to take the place of the Wechsler Individual Achievement Test-II Abbreviated (discussed next).

Wechsler Individual Achievement Test—Second Edition

The Wechsler Individual Achievement Test—Second Edition (WIAT-II) (Wechsler, 2001a) is an achievement battery linked with the WISC-IV, WISC-III, WAIS-III,

WPPSI-III, Differential Ability Scales—Second Edition (DAS-II), and WAIS-IV that allows meaningful comparisons between achievement and ability test performance. The WIAT-II includes eight subtests: Basic Reading, Mathematics Reasoning, Spelling, Reading Comprehension, Numerical Operations, Listening Comprehension, Oral Expression, and Written Expression. The WIAT-II is designed for ages 4 through 85 and includes norms for college students. The WIAT-II Abbreviated contains the subtests Word Reading, Numerical Operations, and Spelling. The WIAT-III is scheduled for publication in early fall 2009. It will feature an Early Reading Skills subtest, three Math Fluency subtests, and an Oral Reading Fluency subtest to measure all eight areas of achievement specified by Individuals with Disabilities Education Act legislation. It will also feature updated norms for prekindergarten through Grade 12 and for ages 4 years through 19 years, 11 months.

Wide Range Achievement Test 4

The Wide Range Achievement Test—Fourth Revision (WRAT-4) (Wilkinson & Robertson, 2006) measures achievement in the areas of word reading, spelling, math computation, and sentence comprehension. The test is normed for children and adults aged 5 through 94. Two forms are available, permitting retesting within short periods of time.

Woodcock–Johnson III Normative Update

The Woodcock–Johnson III Normative Update (WJ III NU) (Woodcock, McGrew, & Mather, 2007) comprises two conormed batteries: the Woodcock–Johnson III NU Tests of Achievement (Woodcock, McGrew, & Mather, 2001b) and the Woodcock–Johnson III NU Tests of Cognitive Abilities (Woodcock, McGrew, & Mather, 2001a) that includes tests designed to assess general intellectual ability, specific cognitive abilities, oral language, and academic achievement in reading, mathematics, written language, and general knowledge. The tests are normed for ages 2 to 90+ years. The WJ III NU Tests of Achievement includes Letter–Word Identification, Reading Fluency, Passage Comprehension, Word Attack, Reading Vocabulary, Spelling, Writing Fluency, Writing Samples, Editing, Understanding Directions, Story Recall, Picture Vocabulary, Oral Comprehension, Academic Knowledge and Spelling of Sounds, and Calculation, Math Fluency, Applied Problems, and Quantitative Concepts. The academic achievement clusters result in summary scores in the areas of Broad Reading, Broad Math, Oral Language, and Broad Written Language. The WJ III NU Tests of Achievement also provides a Total Achievement score. The WJ III NU Tests of Cognitive Ability battery is used to measure verbal ability, thinking ability, and cognitive efficiency, yielding seven broad cognitive clusters: Comprehension–Knowledge, Long-Term Retrieval, Visual–Spatial Thinking, Auditory Processing, Fluid Reasoning, Processing Speed, and Short-Term Memory.

VISUAL, VISUOSPATIAL, AND VISUOTACTILE FUNCTIONS

A comprehensive assessment battery contains measures designed to evaluate visual perception and visuospatial abilities, such as visual construction and visual integration. It also includes measures examining visuotactile functions and the presence or absence of visual neglect. Rapid Reference 4.19 provides a list of the test names, the appropriate age ranges, and the publishers.

The Beery VMI (The Beery–Buktenica Developmental Test of Visual–Motor Integration, Fifth Edition)

The Beery VMI (Beery & Beery, 2006) is designed as a measure of visual–motor integration and to detect visual–motor deficits predictive of learning difficulties. The examinee is required to copy 24 geometric designs that progress from less to more complex. Very young children also produce markings and scribblings for credit. Supplemental measures using the same stimuli as the VMI are available to assess visual perception and motor coordination. The short form test (15 drawings) is normed for children aged 2 through 8 years; the long form (24 drawings) is normed for children and adults aged 2 through 100 years.

The Clock Test

The Clock Test (Tuokko, Hadjistravropoulos, Miller, Horton, & Beattle, 1995) assesses visuospatial construction, visual perception, and abstract conceptualization

≡ Rapid Reference 4.19

Tests of Visual, Visuospatial, and Visuotactile Functions

Test	Ages	Source
The Beery-Buktenica Developmental Test of Visual-Motor Integration, 5th Edition	2–100	Pearson
The Clock Test	65 and older	MHS
Hooper Visual Organization Test	5 and older	WPS
Judgment of Line Orientation	7–74	PAR
Motor-Free Visual Perception Test-3	4–95	PAR
Rey Complex Figure Test and Recognition Trial	6–89	PAR
Tactual Performance Test (Portable)	5–85	PAR
Test of Visual Perceptual Skills, 3rd Ed.	4–19	PAR
Wide Range Assessment of Visual Motor Ability	3–17	PAR

by using the three subtests of Clock Drawing, Clock Setting, and Clock Reading. The task is normed for adults 65 years and older.

Hooper Visual Organization Test

The Hooper Visual Organization Test (VOT) (Hooper, 1958) is a brief screening measure that assesses a patient's mental ability to analyze and integrate visual stimuli. The test stimuli consist of cut-up line drawings of 30 common objects. The test can be administered to both children and adults and norms and cutoff values are available for ages 5 to 91 years in Strauss et al. (2006).

Judgment of Line Orientation

The Judgment of Line Orientation (JOL) test measures spatial perception and orientation as well as visuospatial judgment (Benton et al., 1994). The patient is presented with 30 test items, each depicting a different pair of angled lines. The angled lines must be matched to a display card containing multinumber radii forming a semicircle. Normative data are available for individuals ages 7 through 14 and 16 through 74.

Motor-Free Visual Perception Test—Third Edition

The Motor-Free Visual Perception Test—Third Edition (MVPT-3) (Colarusso & Hammill, 2003) was designed to assess visual perception in children and adults aged 4 through 95. The test measures five categories of visual perception: spatial relationships, visual closure, visual discrimination, visual memory, and figure ground. The client indicates an answer by pointing to one of four choices on the test plate, so no motor involvement is necessary.

Rey Complex Figure Test and Recognition Trial

The Rey Complex Figure Test and Recognition Trial (RCFT) (Meyers & Meyers, 1995) uses four trials (copy, immediate recall, delayed recall, and recognition) to measure visuospatial recall and recognition memory, response bias, processing speed, and visuoconstructional ability in children aged 6 through 17 (Meyers & Meyers, 1996) and adults ages 18 through 89. The patient copies the original Rey–Osterrieth Complex Figure (Rey, 1941) and 3 minutes later is asked without warning to reproduce it from memory. After a 30-minute delay, the patient is asked to recall the figure again and perform a recognition trial.

Tactual Performance Test

The Tactual Performance Test (TPT) is from the HRB and uses the Seguin–Goddard Formboard to measure tactual perception and form recognition along with psychomotor problem solving and tactile memory for spatial location and shapes. A portable version of the TPT is available from PAR. The test is appropriate for both children and adults aged 4 to 85.

Test of Visual–Perceptual Skills, Third Edition

The Test of Visual–Perceptual Skills, Third Edition (TVPS-3) (Martin, 2006) is designed to assess visual perceptual skills in children aged 4 to 19 years. The subtests of the TVPS-R include Visual Discrimination, Visual-Spatial Relationships, Visual Sequential Memory, Visual Figure-Ground, Visual Memory, Form-Constancy, and Visual Closure. The test requires only pointing from the child.

Wide Range Assessment of Visual Motor Ability

The Wide Range Assessment of Visual Motor Ability (WRAVMA) (Adams & Sheslow, 1995) measures visual–motor integration by assessing visual–motor ability, visuospatial ability, and fine motor ability. The subtest scores available for each of these three areas are combined into the Visual-Motor Integration Composite. The test is applicable for children aged 3 to 17.

MOTOR

The clinician should include tests of motor performance in an assessment battery. These tests can identify motor impairment and can provide possible information about lateralized cortical impairment. Rapid Reference 4.20 lists the tests, their appropriate age ranges, and their publishers.

Finger Oscillation Test

This task, also called the Finger Tapping Test and included in the HRB, measures fine motor speed of the index finger on each hand in children and adults. It can be helpful in assessing laterality of brain damage but can also be influenced by peripheral motor problems. The finger tapping board is available through the Neuropsychology Center (www.neuropsych.com) and from Psychological Assessment Resources. Normative data are available for ages 5 through 14 and 16 through 89 in Strauss et al. (2006). Demographically corrected norms are available for ages 20 through 85 in Heaton et al. (2004).

≡ Rapid Reference 4.20

Motor Tests

Test	Ages	Source
Finger Oscillation Test (Tapper)	5–89	PAR
Grip Strength (Hand Dynamometer)	6–90	PAR
Grooved Pegboard	6–85	PAR

Grip Strength

This measure uses a hand dynamometer (available from Psychological Assessment Resources) to assess the strength of each hand. Normative data are available for children and adults ages 6 to 90 in Strauss et al. (2006), and demographically adjusted norms are available for ages 20 through 85 in Heaton et al. (2004).

Grooved Pegboard

This test measures manual dexterity and requires complex visual–motor coordination. The pegboard (available from Psychological Assessment Resources) consists of 25 randomly positioned keyholes; the patient must rotate the pegs (keys) to match the holes before the peg can be inserted into the keyhole on the board. Like the Finger Oscillation Test, Grooved Pegboard can be helpful in assessing laterality of brain damage and is used with both children and adults. Strauss et al. (2006) contains norms for children and adolescents aged 6 through 15 and adults 16 through 70. Heaton et al. (2004) contains demographically adjusted data for adults aged 20 through 85.

RESPONSE BIAS AND SYMPTOM VALIDITY

In some populations (e.g., patients involved in forensic cases) the base rate is quite large for patients exaggerating or simulating impairment. Research has shown clearly that even children can fool seasoned examiners into believing that they have deficits when they do not (Faust, Hart, & Guilmette, 1988). It is therefore crucial to include measures of compliance and motivation in a test battery. The results from such measures indicate to the examiner how much confidence he or she can have in the reliability and validity of the test findings. Rapid Reference 4.21 summarizes the tests, their appropriate age ranges, and the publishers.

The b Test

The b Test (Boone, Lu, & Herzberg, 2002a) uses a letter-recognition and discrimination task to assist the examiner in detecting lack of effort on cognitive measures. An Effort-Score, obtained based on speed of performance, omissions, and commissions, can be compared with the Effort-Scores of 6 "normal effort" groups to identify suspect effort. The test is appropriate for individuals aged 17 and older.

Computerized Assessment of Response Bias

The Computerized Assessment of Response Bias (CARB) (Allen, Conder, Green, & Cox, 2000) is a computer-supported assessment used to detect incomplete

≡ Rapid Reference 4.21

Tests of Response Bias and Symptom Validity

Test	Ages	Source
The b Test	17 and older	WPS
Computerized Assessment of Response Bias	Adults	Cognistat
The Dot Counting Test	17 and older	WPS
Medical Symptom Validity Test	Adults	Green's Publishing Co.
Non-Verbal-Medical Symptom Validity Test	Adults	Green's Publishing Co.
Recall-Recognition Test	Adults	Brandt, J. (1992). Detecting amnesia's impostors. In L. R. Squire & N. Butters (Eds.), *Neuropsychology of memory* (2nd ed., pp. 156–165). New York: Guilford Press.
Rey Memory Test/Fifteen-Item Test	11 and older	Strauss, E., Sherman, E. M. S., & Spreen, O. (2006). *A compendium of neuropsychological tests: Administration, norms and commentary* (3rd ed.). New York: Oxford University Press.
Structured Inventory of Malingered Symptomatology	18 and older	PAR
Test of Memory Malingering	5–12; 16–84	MHS
Validity Indicator Profile	18–69	Pearson
Victoria Symptom Validity Test	18 and older	PAR
Word Memory Test	Children and adults	Green's Publishing Co.
Word Recognition Test	Adults	Frederick, R. I. (1997). *Validity Indicator Profile.* Minneapolis, MN: National Computer System.

effort, symptom exaggeration, response bias, malingering, and feigning of cognitive deficits. The CARB is based on a forced-choice digit recognition paradigm (e.g., Binder, 1993; Hiscock & Hiscock, 1989) and is self-administered via computer. The results from the CARB are analyzed relative to normative information from adult patients with severe traumatic brain injury and neurological disorders.

The Dot Counting Test

The Dot Counting Test (DCT) (Boone, Lu, & Herzberg, 2002b) is used to assess suspect effort in individuals aged 17 and older. The patient is presented with 12 cards containing a set of grouped or ungrouped dots and asked to count the dots on each card as quickly as possible. An Effort-Score is obtained based on average time to count the grouped dots, ungrouped dots, and number of errors. As with the b Test, an individual's Effort-Score can be compared with the Effort-Scores from seven "normal effort" groups to evaluate whether his or her effort is suspect.

Medical Symptom Validity Test

The Medical Symptom Validity Test (MSVT) (Green, 2004) is a 5-minute computerized test based on the original Word Memory Test (Green & Astner, 1995) used to test verbal memory and to detect suboptimal effort. The task requires the patient to learn a list of 10 word pairs. Immediate and delayed recognition are assessed along with paired associate cued recall and free recall. The consistency between the immediate and delayed recognition trials is automatically calculated. Patient performance is compared with normative data obtained from patients with severe traumatic brain injury and other neurological disorders, including dementia and to the performance of multiple other groups including children. The test is available in nine languages.

Non-Verbal-Medical Symptom Validity Test

The Non-Verbal-Medical Symptom Validity Test (NV-MSVT) (Green, 2006) is a nonverbal analog to the MSVT. It is a computerized test used to assess nonverbal memory and test-taking effort. The task requires the patient to learn a list of 10 pairs of pictures. As with the MSVT, the NV-MSVT measures immediate and delayed recognition, paired associate cued recall, and free recall. Patient performance is compared with normative data obtained from patients with severe traumatic brain injury and other neurological disorders, including dementia and to the performance of multiple other groups including children.

Recall-Recognition Test

This test (Brandt, 1992) uses a 20-item word list presented for free recall followed by forced-choice recognition to help differentiate true memory impairment from malingered memory impairment in adults. Comparison of patients with amnesia and assumed malingerers on this task indicated that the assumed malingerers performed more poorly on the forced-choice recognition task than the patients with amnesia did.

Rey Memory Test

The Rey Memory Test (RMT) or Fifteen-Item Test (FIT) (Rey, 1958) is an unsophisticated measure of retrieval that can aid in assessing feigned memory impairment. Clients are asked to recall all 15 items presented on a stimulus card for 10 seconds. In the instructions patients are told that there are 15 unique items to be called in just 10 seconds. They are not told that the items can easily be grouped into five easy sets (uppercase letters A, B, C; lowercase letters a, b, c; numbers 1, 2, 3; Roman numerals I, II, III; and three shapes circle, square, and triangle). Various cutoffs ranging from 7 or fewer items (Lee, Loring, & Martin, 1992) to 11 items (Hiscock, Branham, & Hiscock, 1994) have been cited as suspicious for suboptimal effort or noncompliance. Also suspicious are incomplete rows (with the exception of the row of shapes), reversals, confabulations, or misplaced numbers and letters. The test can be used with children aged 11 and older and with adults.

Structured Inventory of Malingered Symptomatology

The Structured Inventory of Malingered Symptomatology (SIMS) (Widows & Smith, 2005) is a screening measure designed to assess malingered psychopathology and cognitive symptoms. The test consists of 75 true–false items that provide five domain scores and an overall total score for probable malingering. The five domains are as follows: Psychosis, Low Intelligence, Neurologic Impairment, Affective Disorders, and Amnestic Disorders. It is a self-report measure appropriate for ages 18 and older.

Test of Memory Malingering

The Test of Memory Malingering (TOMM) (Tombaugh, 1996) is a visual recognition memory test used to differentiate between bona fide memory impairment and feigned memory impairment. The TOMM consists of two learning trials containing forced-choice recognition and an optional delayed forced-choice recognition task. Normative data are available from various groups: cognitively intact individuals and patients with neurological disorders, including patients with mild traumatic brain injury. It is designed for ages 16 through 84 years, but norms are also available for children aged 5 to 12 (Strauss et al., 2006).

Validity Indicator Profile

The Validity Indicator Profile (VIP) (Frederick, 1997) is used to assess malingering and response style during testing. The VIP consists of two tasks, matrix reasoning (nonverbal) and vocabulary (verbal), and was constructed using a forced-choice format. The results from a patient can be classified as valid or invalid. Invalid performances are further classified as careless, irrelevant, or malingered. The VIP can be administered to adults ages 18 through 69.

Victoria Symptom Validity Test

The Victoria Symptom Validity Test (VSVT) (Slick, Hopp, Strauss, & Thompson, 1999) is a computerized assessment vehicle used to measure effort on memory tests and the presence of exaggeration or simulation of cognitive impairments. The VSVT is based on the forced-choice digit recognition paradigm popularized by Binder (1993) and Hiscock and Hiscock (1989). It is appropriate for adults, ages 18 years and older.

Word Memory Test

Green's Word Memory Test (WMT) for Windows (Green, 2003) is used to test verbal memory and test-taking effort and to detect suboptimal effort, response bias, feigning, and symptom exaggeration. The task requires the patient to learn a list of paired associates, half of which have a close semantic relationship and half of which are only subtly linked. Immediate and delayed recognition are assessed along with multiple-choice recognition, a paired associate cued recall task, free recall, and an optional long-delay free recall. Patient performance is compared with normative data obtained from patients with severe traumatic brain injury and other neurological disorders. The WMT can be administered in 10 languages. Normative data are available for children and adults.

Word Recognition Test

The Word Recognition Test (WRT) (Rey, 1941) is used to evaluate malingering and suboptimal effort on verbal memory tasks in adults by comparing performance on a recognition memory task to first-trial performance on a free recall word list learning task such as the CVLT-II or the RAVLT. The patient is asked to learn a 15-item word list presented orally and then provided (either written or orally) with a 30-item list; the patient is then instructed to identify the words from the 15-item list. In general, recognition memory performance should be better than first-trial free recall performance on the CVLT-II or RAVLT. In addition, fewer than six words recognized or a score of less than 5 when false positives are subtracted from true positives is indicative of failure on this task (Greiffenstein, Baker, & Gola, 1996).

EMOTIONS, BEHAVIOR, AND PERSONALITY

Neuropsychological test results are often not specific to central nervous system impairment and can instead reflect nonneurological influences on test performance. It is therefore important to survey a patient's emotional status and mood to determine whether any negative test findings are exacerbated by or the result of depression or anxiety. In addition, although most neuropsychological tests can provide information about a patient's cognitive strengths and weaknesses, relatively few neuropsychological tests inform the examiner about how a patient functions in his or her daily environment. When questions arise about a patient's functional capacities (for example, when diagnosing mental retardation), a test battery needs to include measures of adaptive abilities. Rapid Reference 4.22 lists the tests, the appropriate age ranges, and the publishers.

Adaptive Behavior Assessment System, Second Edition

The Adaptive Behavior Assessment System, Second Edition (ABAS-II) (Harrison & Oakland, 2003) was designed to assess the adaptive skills of individuals aged birth to 89 years for use in diagnosing and classifying disabilities and disorders, specifying strengths and weaknesses, and monitoring change over time. Parents or primary caregivers, teachers or day-care providers, adult informants, and adult clients can complete the ABAS-II. The 10 areas surveyed include Communication, Community Use, Functional Academics, School Living, Health and Safety, Leisure, Self-Care, Self-Direction, Social, and Work. The test yields three composite domains—Conceptual, Social, and Practical—as well as an overall General Adaptive Composite score.

Adult Behavior Checklist and Adult Self-Report

The Adult Behavior Checklist (ABCL) and Adult Self-Report (ASR) (Achenbach & Rescoria, 2003) are a set of forms for assessing adaptive functioning and problems in adults aged 18 to 59 years. The ASR is a self-report instrument and the ABCL is a parallel form completed by someone who knows the adult well, such as a family member. There are eight syndrome scales: Anxious/Depressed, Withdrawn, Somatic Complaints, Thought Problems, Attention Problems, Aggressive Behavior, Rule-Breaking, and Intrusive. There are also six *Diagnostic and Statistical Manual of Mental Disorders* (4th ed.; *DSM-IV*)–related scales: Depressive Problems, Anxiety Problems, Somatic Problems, Avoidant Personality Problems, Attention Deficit/Hyperactivity Problems, and Antisocial Problems. Both the ABCL and ASR also have scales for Substance Use, Critical Items, Internalizing, Externalizing, and Total Problems. A version adapted for older adults ages 60 to 90+ is also available (i.e., Older Adult Self-Report and Older Adult Behavior Checklist; Achenbach, Newhouse, & Rescorla, 2004).

Attention-Deficit/Hyperactivity Disorder Test

The Attention-Deficit/Hyperactivity Disorder Test (ADHDT) (Gilliam, 1995) is designed to assist clinicians in the diagnosis of ADHD. The test is administered

≡ Rapid Reference 4.22

Tests of Emotion, Behavior, and Personality

Test	Ages	Source
Adaptive Behavior Assessment System, Second Edition	Birth–89	Pearson
Adult Behavior Checklist/Adult Self-Report	18–59	PAR
Attention-Deficit/Hyperactivity Disorder Test	3–23	PRO-ED
Beck Anxiety Inventory	17–80	Pearson
Beck Depression Inventory-II	13–80	Pearson
Beck Youth Inventories, Second Edition	7–18	Pearson
Behavior Assessment System for Children, Second Edition	2–25	Pearson
Behavior Rating Inventory of Executive Function	5–18	PAR
Behavior Rating Inventory of Executive Function-Adult Version	18–90	PAR
Behavior Rating Inventory of Executive Function-Preschool Version	2–5.11	PAR
Behavior Rating Inventory of Executive Function-Self-Report Version	11–18	PAR
Child Behavior Checklist	1.5–5; 6–18	PAR
Conners 3rd Edition	6–18	MHS
Minnesota Multiphasic Personality Inventory-Adolescent	14–18	Pearson
Minnesota Multiphasic Personality Inventory-2	18 and older	Pearson
Minnesota Multiphasic Personality Inventory-2-Restructured Format	18 and older	Pearson
Personality Assessment Inventory	18 and older	PAR
Scales of Independent Behavior-Revised	Infancy-80+	Riverside Publishing
Trauma Symptom Checklist for Children	8–16	PAR
Trauma Symptom Inventory	18 and older	PAR
Vineland Adaptive Behavior Scales, Second Edition	Birth-90	Pearson

to parents, teachers, and others to assess in children and young adults aged 3 through 23 the presence of symptoms in the areas of hyperactivity, impulsivity, and inattention.

Beck Anxiety Inventory

The Beck Anxiety Inventory (BAI) (Beck & Steer, 1993) is a face-valid self-report 21-item measure of common symptoms of anxiety and their severity. The BAI is used to discriminate between anxious and nonanxious individuals aged 17 through 80 years.

Beck Depression Inventory—II

The Beck Depression Inventory—Second Edition (BDI-II) (Beck, Steer, & Brown, 1996) is a face-valid self-report 21-item measure of the common symptoms of depression and the severity of symptoms. The BDI-II can be used to assess the presence and severity of depression in individuals aged 13 through 80.

Beck Youth Inventories, Second Edition

The Beck Youth Inventories—Second Edition (BYI-II) are five self-report instruments (Beck, Beck, Jolly, & Steer, 2005) for children and adolescents between the ages of 7 and 18. Each inventory contains 20 statements about thoughts, feelings, and behaviors in the areas of depression, anxiety, anger, disruptive behavior, and self-concept.

Behavior Assessment System for Children, Second Edition

The Behavior Assessment System for Children, Second Edition (BASC-2) (Reynolds & Kamphaus, 2004) is a set of rating scales and self-report forms for evaluating the behaviors and self-perceptions of children and young adults aged 2 through 25 years. Parents and teachers and the child or young adult whose behavior is of concern can complete the BASC-2. Also available are a Structured Developmental History form and a form for recording and analyzing observed classroom behavior. It is designed to help with the differential diagnosis and educational classification of various emotional and behavioral disorders of children and to help with the design of treatment plans. Composite Scales focus on externalizing problems, internalizing problems, school problems, behavioral symptoms, and adaptive skills. The Adaptive Scales on the Parent and Teacher Rating Scales include Activities of Daily Living, Adaptability, Functional Communication, Leadership, Social Skills, and Study Skills. The Clinical Scales on the Parent and Teacher Rating Scales are Aggression, Anxiety, Attention Problems, Atypicality, Conduct Problems, Depression, Hyperactivity, Learning Problems, Somatization, and Withdrawal.

Behavior Rating Inventory of Executive Function

The Behavior Rating Inventory of Executive Function (BRIEF) (Gioia, Isquith, Guy, & Kenworthy, 2000) is a set of rating forms for parents and teachers to evaluate behaviors related to executive functioning in children and adolescents ages 5 to 18 years. It is intended for evaluations of children with a variety of developmental and acquired neurological disorders. The BRIEF questionnaire consists of 86 items. There are two validity scales—Negativity and Inconsistency—and eight clinical scales—Inhibit, Shift, Emotional Control, Initiate, Working Memory, Plan/Organize, Organization of Materials, and Monitor. The clinical scales combine into two composite indexes: (a) Behavioral Regulation and Metacognition and (b) a Global Executive Composite score. Versions of the Behavior Rating Scales of Executive Function are also available for preschoolers aged 2 to 5 years, 11 months (BRIEF-P; Gioia, Andrews, & Isquith, 2003), and adults ages 18 to 90 (BRIEF-A; Roth, Isquith, & Gioia, 2005). There is also a self-report version for adolescents aged 11 to 18 years (BRIEF-SR; Guy, Isquith, & Gioia, 2004).

Child Behavior Checklist

The Child Behavior Checklist (CBCL) (Achenbach & Rescorla, 2000, 2001) is a parent- and teacher-rated scale designed to measure specific behavioral and emotional problems in children and adolescents, along with competencies, academic performance, and adaptive functioning. There is a version for younger children aged 1.5 to 5 and another for children and adolescents ages 6–18. A self-report scale is also available for youths ages 11 to 18. All forms have parallel Internalizing Problems, Externalizing Problems, and Total Problems scales.

Conners 3rd Edition

The Conners 3 (Conners, 2008) includes three scales (parent, teacher, and self-report) used to assess reports of ADHD and associated features and comorbid disorders. The Conners 3 has validity scales to assess positive impression management, negative impression management, and inconsistency. The six Content scales are Inattention, Hyperactivity/Impulsivity, Learning Problems, Executive Functioning, Aggression, and Peer/Family Relations. The DSM-IV-Text Revision Symptom scales are ADHD Inattentive, ADHD Hyperactive–Impulsive, Conduct Disorder, and Oppositional Defiant Disorder. The parent and teacher scales can be used for children and adolescents aged 6 to 18; the self-report scale can be used with children and adolescents aged 8 to 18.

Minnesota Multiphasic Personality Inventory—Adolescent

The Minnesota Multiphasic Personality Inventory—Adolescent (MMPI-A) (Butcher et al., 1992) is a personality inventory designed to measure adolescent psychopathology and help identify personal, social, and behavioral problems in adolescents 14 through 18 years old. The MMPI-A contains several validity scales including Variable Response Consistency, True Response Inconsistency, Infrequency, Lie, Defensiveness, and Cannot Say. It contains the same 10 Clinical Scales as in the MMPI-2 (discussed next): Hypochondriasis, Depression, Hysteria, Psychopathic Deviate, Masculinity-Femininity, Paranoia, Psychasthenia, Schizophrenia, Hypomania, and Social Introversion. In addition, it contains multiple Supplementary Scales, Content Scales, and Subscales to further delineate pathology.

Minnesota Multiphasic Personality Inventory—2

The Minnesota Multiphasic Personality Inventory—2 (MMPI-2) (Butcher, Dahlstrom, Graham, Tellegen, & Kaemmer, 1989) is a self-administered personality inventory used to assist with the assessment and screening of psychopathology, the identification of appropriate treatment strategies, and the assessment of major symptoms of social and personal maladjustment in individuals 18 years and older. The MMPI-2 is one of the most commonly administered psychological tests in the United States. It consists of multiple validity scales, the three most commonly known as L (Lie), F (Frequency), and K (Defensiveness), along with 10 clinical scales: Hypochondriasis, Depression, Hysteria, Psychopathic Deviance, Masculinity–Femininity, Paranoia, Psychasthenia, Schizophrenia, Hypomania, and Social Introversion. In addition, several other Clinical Subscales, Content Scales, and Supplementary Scales are available. A more recent validity scale incorporated into the MMPI-2 in 2007, the Fake Bad Scale (FBS), is useful in identifying potential exaggeration of somatic symptoms. Specialized interpretative reports are available from Pearson Assessments for various settings, including outpatient mental health, inpatient mental health, general medical, chronic pain, correctional, and college counseling. In addition, Pearson Assessments can provide reports tailored to specific forensic situations, such as child-custody disputes, competency or commitment hearings, personal injury lawsuits, pretrial criminal evaluations, and general corrections recommendations.

Minnesota Multiphasic Personality Inventory—2—Restructured Form

The Minnesota Multiphasic Personality Inventory—2—Restructured Form (MMPI-2-RF) (Ben-Porath & Tellegen, 2008) is a revision of the MMPI-2 featuring new and empirically validated scales to assess mental disorders and the physical, psychological, and social factors that can affect medical treatment. It features 8 Validity scales, 9 Restructured Clinical scales, and 41 revised and newly validated scales. The MMPI-2-RF has 338 items and takes less time to complete than the MMPI-2. Patient profiles are available for patients with medical illness, personal injury and disability, mental illness, and substance abuse.

Personality Assessment Inventory

The Personality Assessment Inventory (PAI) (Morey, 1991) is an objective self-administered personality inventory used to assess clinical syndromes and psychopathology. The PAI is designed for adults 18 years and older. It contains four validity scales measuring consistency of report, endorsement of infrequent items, negative impression management, and positive impression management. It contains 11 clinical scales addressing the areas of somatic complaints, anxiety, anxiety-related disorders, depression, mania, paranoia, schizophrenia, borderline features, antisocial features, alcohol problems, and drug problems. It also contains four treatment scales having to do with aggression, suicidal ideation, stress, nonsupport, and treatment rejection. Two interpersonal scales in this inventory assess dominance and warmth.

Scales of Independent Behavior—Revised

The Scales of Independent Behavior—Revised (SIB-R) (Bruininks, Woodcock, Weatherman, & Hill, 1996) is a rating scale used to assess functional independence and adaptive and maladaptive behavior in a variety of settings, including school, home, employment, and the community. It is administered either as a checklist procedure or a structured interview. The test is designed for ages infancy to 80+ years and is available in three forms: the Early Development Form, the Full Scale, and the Short Form. Each form consists of three problem behavior clusters (Internalized Maladaptive, Asocial Maladaptive, and Externalized Maladaptive) comprising eight problem behavior areas that result in a General Maladaptive Index. A Support Score is also available to help determine the level of support, supervision, and resources an individual will require in his or her daily living.

Trauma Symptom Checklist for Children

The Trauma Symptom Checklist for Children (TSCC) (Briere, 1996) is a self-report measure of posttraumatic distress and related emotional distress. It is intended for children ages 8 to 16 years old who have been exposed to trauma and who may be at risk for posttraumatic stress.

Trauma Symptom Inventory

The Trauma Symptom Inventory (TSI) (Briere, 1995) is a self-report measure of posttraumatic distress and other psychological sequelae of traumatic events. It is intended for adults aged 18 years and older. It contains three validity scales assessing the patient's tendency to deny symptoms, to overendorse unusual or bizarre symptoms, and to respond in an inconsistent fashion. It contains 10 clinical scales concerning trauma-related symptoms: Anxious Arousal, Dissociation, Sexual Concerns, Anger and Irritability, Dysfunctional Sexual Behavior, Intrusive Experiences, Defensive Avoidance, Impaired Self-Reference, and Tension Reduction Behavior.

Vineland Adaptive Behavior Scales, Second Edition

The Vineland Adaptive Behavior Scales, Second Edition (Vineland-II) (Sparrow, Cicchetti, & Balla, 2005) can be used to assess a wide range of adaptive behaviors in the domains of Communication, Daily Living Skills, Socialization, and Motor Skills, which combine to form the Adaptive Behavior Composite. An optional Maladaptive Behavior Index is also available. The Vineland-II is appropriate for young children, school-age children, adolescents, and low-functioning adults with intellectual and developmental disabilities, pervasive developmental disorders, ADHD, progressive dementing disorders, and other disorders. The Survey Interview Form, Expanded Interview Form and Survey, and Parent/Caregiver Rating Form are available for ages birth to 90 years old; the Teacher Rating Form is available for ages 3 to 22 years old.

 TEST YOURSELF

1. **The underlying assumption of neuropsychological testing is that the performances of patients represent their best efforts.**
   True or False?

2. **Patients may not give their best effort because**
   (a) they are depressed.
   (b) they are involved in litigation.
   (c) they are medically ill.
   (d) all of the above.

3. **Any room is sufficient for testing.**
   True or False?

4. **It is preferable to complete testing in 1 day.**
   True or False?

5. **It is easy to determine through simple observation that a patient is applying adequate effort to the task at hand.**
   True or False?

6. **Which of the following is not true?**
   (a) Examiners should score as they go.
   (b) Examiners should observe the patient's behavior.
   (c) Examiners should record every statement by a patient.
   (d) Examiners should keep test materials ready.

7. **It is permissible to violate standardized test procedures for the sake of testing the limits.**

   True or False?

8. **Test administration requires**

   (a) helping patients with explanations of directions.

   (b) following test instructions exactly.

   (c) using a wall clock to time tests.

   (d) informing patients that their answers are correct.

9. **The examiner who is thoroughly familiar with the scoring guidelines is best able to discern the score value of a response quickly and accurately.**

   True or False?

10. **Pantomime and gesture may have to be used when testing individuals with impairments in**

    (a) hearing.

    (b) vision.

    (c) motor impairments.

    (d) memory.

Answers: 1. True; 2. d; 3. False; 4. True; 5. False; 6. c; 7. False; 8. b; 9. True; 10. a

Five

ESSENTIALS OF INTERPRETATION

OVERVIEW

We are now ready to discuss some of the conceptual and logical issues and procedures involved in using neuropsychological tests to answer the kinds of referral questions suggested in Chapter 1. Just as psychologists use a variety of approaches for selecting and organizing test measures (i.e., fixed vs. flexible batteries), they also use a variety of approaches to make inferences about the brain's influence on test performance and behavior. A review of some of the basic issues of psychometric theory relevant to neuropsychological assessment is useful before a discussion of some of the approaches to test interpretation.

TEST VALIDITY

One crucial aspect of psychometrics is whether a test is valid for predicting, measuring, and defining pathology. Correspondingly, each of the various types of validity, including criterion or predictive validity, construct validity, and content validity, must be considered.

The most basic task a neuropsychological test must perform is to detect whether a patient's performance is predictive of the presence of an abnormality of the central nervous system or brain dysfunction. The extent to which a test score successfully allows such a prediction is an example of the concept of test validity and is, in this case, an example of *criterion* or *predictive validity*. Beyond simply predicting the likelihood of brain dysfunction, neuropsychological tests might also be used to predict whether an individual will have adjustment difficulties on the job or in school or even to predict how well an individual will perform in these areas in the future. The ability to predict from neuropsychological test results to real-life functioning is often called *ecological validity*.

One also could ask what psychological function or process the test is measuring. Content validity and construct validity refer to the extent to which a test is actually a measure of a function, whether the function is memory, phonological processing, visual perception, or reasoning and problem solving. Construct validity answers the question: What am I measuring with this test? Content validity answers the question: Is this test a good sample of the construct I am interested in measuring?

The answer to questions of validity may in some cases be directly quantifiable, whereas in other cases, the validity of a test is based on a large corpus of data and concepts. Ideally, a test should be able to predict the presence of a disease or developmental abnormality with perfect certainty or should be clearly interpretable as defining a psychological construct. Unfortunately, in practice neuropsychological tests are never perfectly valid. No test predicts the presence (or absence) of brain dysfunction with perfect certainty, and few measures can be considered in and of themselves perfect or so-called gold standard measurements of any psychological construct. The different types of validity addressed here are defined in Rapid Reference 5.1.

Criterion Validity

Criterion validity refers to the ability of a test to predict or correlate with other measures that define the function of the test. In neuropsychology, tests are most commonly used as predictors of the presence of brain dysfunction. As we discussed in Chapter 1, some assessment systems such as the Halstead–Reitan Neuropsychological Test Battery were originally designed with the ability to predict the presence of brain "impairment" as their primary focus (Halstead, 1947). Ward

---

≡ Rapid Reference 5.1

The Different Types of Validity Defined

Criterion or predictive validity: The ability of a test to predict or correlate with other measures that define the function of a test. Example: The ability of a test to predict the presence of brain dysfunction.

Construct validity: The extent to which a test measures a theoretically defined construct or function. Example: The extent to which a test is a measure of verbal memory.

Content validity: The extent to which the items on a test are actual samples of the construct being measured. Example: That a test of verbal memory uses words to test the function.

Halstead began the process of forming his initial battery through much trial and error. He primarily used tasks that were not necessarily designed to be sensitive to brain impairment (e.g., Seguin–Goddard Form Board; Seashore Musical Aptitude Test) but also those that were considered at the time to be linked to brain function (e.g., Critical Flicker Fusion). His original goal was to develop tests that correctly predicted which patients an independent neurologist clinically classified as having brain damage (and, therefore, likely to show brain impairment). In the 1930s when this work began, skull X-rays, neurosurgeons' reports, and in some cases autopsies were available to provide objective evidence of brain damage. In many cases, it was the neurological examination that determined whether the patient had brain damage. These criteria provided a limited and not necessarily accurate view of the actual state of the brain. Skull X-rays could detect only diseases that impacted the bone and were insensitive to the presence of most strokes, brain tumors, degenerative disease, and even the effects of many closed-head injuries. Neurosurgical reports would be available only for those conditions that required the intervention of a neurosurgeon. This might include brain tumors and certain vascular conditions such as aneurysms, but such reports would not be available for many forms of brain damage. A positive neurological examination showing changes in muscle tone, strength, increased briskness of deep tendon reflexes, and reduced sensitivity to touch, pain, or position might indicate the presence of damage to specific structures related to the sensory and motor systems but might not be sensitive to brain damage in other parts of the brain. The presence of classic symptoms of *aphasia* (acquired disorder of language), *agnosia* (loss of apparent knowledge of sensory information not attributable to primary sensory loss), or *apraxia* (loss of the ability to carry out purposeful movement) might signal the presence of brain damage to other areas, but the absence of these symptoms cannot be used to predict the absence of underlying disease. Autopsy reports can give an accurate picture of the state of the brain at death but do not necessarily reflect the state of the brain when neuropsychological tests are actually administered to the patient. A patient often comes to autopsy months or years after taking a test, in the meantime allowing many intervening changes to occur in the nervous system.

Since Halstead's first attempt to create a valid neuropsychological battery, a number of technological developments in methods have been used to assess the integrity of the central nervous system structures important for normal psychological functions. These include the development of electroencephalography (EEG) and the subsequent development of event-related electroencephalography. The latter technique, referred to as the measurement of event-related potentials (ERPs), consisted of the mathematical summation of EEG information measured at precise times after an external stimulus has been presented to the subject or patient. Although still primarily a research tool, this technique has allowed for the measurement of specific neurophysiological events related to performance and may ultimately prove useful in the evaluation of clinical measures. At this point in time ERPs are still not commonly used to evaluate the neurophysiological correlates of psychological symptoms clinically.

Unquestionably, the most important technological development in the measurement of the state of central nervous system tissue is computerized tomography. Originally developed for use with conventional X-ray in the 1970s, computerized tomography involves the registration of X-ray energy beamed through tissue around a 360-degree axis. Small differences in density of tissue can then be computed for every point that those two beams cross, allowing the development of a cross-sectional image that provides information about soft tissues. Although the original computerized axial tomography (CAT) scan provided a relatively coarse view of specific neural structures, it was more accurate in determining the presence of many kinds of brain damage in a live person than any other technique. It was also relatively safe and noninvasive. Less than a decade later, tomography based on electromagnetic resonance (the energy produced when certain organic molecules are subjected to extremely strong pulsing magnetic waves) allowed for the production of tomographic images of unprecedented detail and sensitivity. Magnetic resonance imaging (MRI) also could be used to produce accurate coronal (i.e., from the front) and sagittal (i.e., from the side) views of the brain, allowing for remarkably clear views of even tiny neural structures. In the 1990s the advancement in this technology allowed for blood-flow measurement so sensitive, it may be used to track extremely subtle localized changes in metabolic rate within populations of neurons. This functional MRI (or fMRI) technique has revolutionized research on cortical function and eventually may prove to be an invaluable tool in diagnosis. The fMRI technique relies on the measurement of the changes in the residual levels of blood oxygen after it has passed through an area with active neurons. This blood oxygen level–dependent (or BOLD) signal is only an indirect measure of neuronal activity. Positron emission tomography (PET) and single photon emission tomography (SPECT) are also functional tomographic techniques that are based on the detection of atomic particles that are emitted during the decay of certain radioisotopes. To do this, radioactive "ligands" that will combine with glucose or oxygen are injected into or inhaled by the research participant or patient. These labeled molecules are absorbed into neurons and can be used to measure their level of metabolic activity directly. PET and SPECT have the advantage or directly gauging neuronal activity but do not have the fine-grained spatial or temporal resolution of the current generation fMRI. Because both techniques rely on the administration of radioactive material, they can only be used sparingly for an individual and are also not commonly used as part of the process of clinical diagnosis.

Neuropsychological tests are constantly being revalidated using these increasingly accurate measures as criteria. The irony is, of course, that as these technologies have become more refined and more economical, the clinical utility of neuropsychological tests as predictors of brain abnormality has become moribund. If the only purpose of a psychological test is to predict the presence of evidence of disease on a neuroimage and both measures cost a similar amount to administer, why not just use the neuroimage? The answer to this question is straightforward: The presence of brain abnormality does not necessarily predict a change in function or level of function. Although the size of a lesion may more or less predict the degree of functional compromise, in many cases, localization is more important than size of a lesion in predicting the kind and severity of functional decline. Localization of a lesion itself, however, is only a modest predictor of function. The presence of a lesion does not guarantee that a specific function is lost, and the loss of a specific function is only a fair predictor of the presence of some kinds of lesions. For example, the presence of aphasia, an acquired disorder of language following brain damage, is usually predictive of a lesion in the territory of the left middle cerebral artery of a right-handed adult. In contrast, the ability to copy drawings or writing is not predictive of a localized lesion in one hemisphere. Although the presence of left hemispatial neglect is usually predictive of the presence of a lesion in the right cerebral hemisphere, that lesion may be in virtually any structure in that side of the brain (McGlinchey et al., 1996). Many classic neuropsychological tests, such as the Tactual Performance Test and the Halstead Category Test from the Halstead–Reitan Neuropsychological Battery, although extremely sensitive to the presence of brain dysfunction, are not valid predictors of the localization of the lesion. Neuropsychological tests must not only predict the presence of brain dysfunction but also indicate and (if possible) describe the psychological function (or functions) that have been compromised.

Ecological validity as described by Sbordone and Saul (2000, p. 178) as "the functional and predictive relationship between an individual's performance on a set of neuropsychological tests and his/her behavior in a variety of real-world settings" can be seen as a subset of predictive validity. Sbordone and Guilmette (1999) caution, however, that no single neuropsychological test can be used at this time to predict accurately or reliably the everyday functioning or ability to work of an individual with brain dysfunction.

Content and Construct Validity

The emphasis on prediction and predictive validity comes from the empiricist tradition that spawned modern clinical neuropsychology in the United States. Although Halstead formulated a concept of *biological intelligence* to describe the fact that the brain is responsible for a range of psychological functions, his holistic leanings caused him to deemphasize descriptions and theoretical analysis of the specific psychological entities that were being measured. For most of its history, the validation of the Halstead–Reitan Neuropsychological Battery, as well as many other neuropsychological tests created before the 1970s, subordinated construct validity to predictive validity. As discussed in Chapter 1, a greater emphasis on understanding the specific mental operations measured by tests followed the reemphasis of cognition as a focus in experimental psychology and the repopularization of localizationist conceptions of brain function in the neurosciences.

The questions of what function a test is measuring and whether the items or tasks are realistic samples of that function are known as *construct validity* and *content validity,* respectively. The current *Standards for Educational and Psychological Testing* (American Educational Research Association, American Psychological Association, & National Council on Measurement in Education, 1999) defines a construct as "a theoretical variable inferred from multiple types of evidence, which might include the interrelations of the test scores with other variables, internal test structure, observations of response processes, as well as the content of the test" (p. 174). It goes on to say that "In current standards, all test scores are viewed as measures of some construct, so the phrase is redundant with validity."

How does a test developer go about establishing the construct validity of a test? In some cases, construct validity is operationalized as a kind of criterion validity in which a correlation between a new test and an established test is demonstrated. This is common in intelligence tests, in which the test scores from a new test are correlated with the Wechsler Adult Intelligence Scales (as of 2008 the WAIS-IV). The Wechsler Intelligence Scales have been extensively investigated in thousands of studies since they were first published in 1939. The scales perform what most clinicians agree is the function of an intelligence test: They predict academic achievement and performance on jobs in which intellectual abilities are considered important. The WAIS also has been used extensively in studies of neurological and psychiatric diseases and as a result has become the standard for tests of intelligence. A substantial correlation of a new test with a current version of the Wechsler Intelligence Scales is usually presented as evidence that the new test also measures intelligence. But is this test really a measure of intelligence? In the literature of human abilities, much controversy surrounds the questions of what constitutes human intelligence and whether the Wechsler Intelligence Scales truly measure what current research considers intelligence to be. An important part of the construct validity of an intelligence test is its relationship to some empirically supported theory of the function it purports to measure. The Wechsler Intelligence Scales may be excellent predictors of school performance and may even have important roles as neuropsychological tests, but what they measure does not necessarily fit into current theoretical notions of intelligence. The Wechsler Intelligence Scales may, in fact, be the most commonly used tests in contemporary neuropsychological batteries, yet even experienced clinicians do not interpret their validity as a construct in a consistent manner. This point can be illustrated by an examination of the Block Design subtest.

In the validity section of the manual for the WAIS-IV, Block Design is shown to load on what is termed a *perceptual reasoning factor* along with the subtests Matrix Reasoning and Visual Puzzles. These data confirm that the scores on these tasks covary across individuals but only scratch the surface of the questions of what the tasks are measuring and how they relate to independently established theories of function. The multitude of functions that Block Design appears to measure have been compiled in a list by Kaufman and Lichtenberg (1999, p. 102–103) and are available in Rapid Reference 5.2.

≡ *Rapid Reference 5.2*

Functions Measured with the Block Design Subtest of the Wechsler Scales

- Visual perception of abstract stimuli
- Auditory perception of complex verbal stimuli
- Discrimination between essential and nonessential details
- Perceptual organization
- Broad visual intelligence
- Fluid intelligence
- Spatial
- Simultaneous processing
- Trial-and-error learning
- Reproduction of models
- Spatial visualization
- Speed of mental processing
- Synthesis of part–whole relationships
- Analysis of whole into component parts
- Visual–motor coordination

Clinicians are often tempted to draw conclusions about the presence of a specific or localized cognitive deficit based on selective impairments detected by such subtests as Block Design. Apart from the issue of whether such a selective impairment may be used to localize a lesion, the clinician must confront how to describe the impaired function represented by a low score. As the list in Rapid Reference 5.2 suggests, Block Design is a test of many functions and is itself the subject of research trying to uncover the psychological components that the test measures. This lack of clear construct validity does not permit consensus among clinicians who must provide some interpretation of test scores on the basis of such complex and often not fully understood measures.

The Wechsler Intelligence Scales and many other tests that have proven valuable as neuropsychological measures were not designed with that purpose in mind and were in most cases not derived from data or theories about how the brain works. In an ideal world, neuropsychological tests would be designed to reflect constructs that have been well elaborated and directly related to brain function, minimizing the need to discover what the test is actually measuring after it already becomes established and popular. Because the construct validity of many neuropsychological measures is not fully established, ideas about the meaning of these measures are constantly evolving. Clinicians must take great care to read the current literature about the tests they are using. The description of a test contained in a manual that is several years old may not reflect current views on the nature of the measure or the neuropsychological function the test purports to measure. The annotated bibliography at the end of this book lists a number of journals and sources that clinicians can use to keep abreast of test measurement developments.

TEST SENSITIVITY AND SPECIFICITY

Sensitivity and specificity are important concepts in the understanding how test validity affects clinical decision making. Consider a psychological test that yields a score that can be used to classify individuals as having or not having "brain dysfunction" and another measure that is considered to be a "gold standard" criterion for the actual presence of that dysfunction (e.g., a direct examination of the brain by a neuropathologist). One can think of four possible outcomes using this test: the correct classification of a patient as having brain dysfunction or a true positive (TP); an incorrect classification of a healthy patient as having brain dysfunction or a false positive (FP); a correct classification of a patient as not having brain dysfunction or a true negative (TN); and an incorrect classification of a patient with brain dysfunction as not having brain dysfunction or a false negative

(FN). In clinical diagnosis, these four outcomes can be used to define the accuracy of a test using several standardized categories: the *sensitivity* of the test is how well the test correctly identifies actual brain dysfunction and is expressed as the proportion of TPs of the total number of TPs and FNs (TP/FN+TP), whereas the *specificity* of the test is how well the test correctly classifies healthy individuals as being healthy and is expressed as the proportion of TNs of the total number of FPs and TNs (TN/TN+FP). Note that the accuracy of a test is also affected by how likely the criterion condition is going to occur in the tested population. This issue is discussed later in the section on base rates.

Some tests are good predictors of the presence of brain dysfunction (i.e., they are sensitive to brain dysfunction) but sometimes are not good predictors of the absence of brain dysfunction—they incorrectly identify healthy individuals or individuals who perform poorly on tests for reasons other than brain dysfunction as having brain dysfunction (i.e., they have poor specificity). The fact that normal individuals sometimes perform poorly on specific neuropsychological tests was recognized early by Halstead. He was one of the first investigators to document formally the poor specificity of individual neuropsychological tests, arguing that it was prudent to create an impairment index based on an individual's performances on multiple measures administered in a battery. To minimize the false-positive rates of the tests in the original versions of the Halstead–Reitan Battery, it was necessary for an individual to obtain a score in the impaired range on 6 of 10 measures.

The problem of false positive errors may be greater in populations at risk for performing poorly on psychological tests for reasons not directly related to brain dysfunction or structural brain damage. For example, patients with psychiatric disorders and those with histories of congenital mental retardation often perform poorly on neuropsychological tests. It is sometimes argued that these cohorts of patients also suffer from some sort of brain dysfunction. However, if the question is whether a pattern of performance is related to an acquired or newly developed neurological pathology, individuals from these groups may have a greater likelihood of obtaining a score in the impaired range than do individuals with no history of less than normal intelligence or psychiatric disorders. An extremely wide range of normal intelligence and academic ability exists in adults and children

DON'T FORGET

Because many individual neuropsychological tests are not specific to brain dysfunction, the risk of false-positive errors is large. False-positive errors arise because neuropsychological tests are sensitive to the effects of many nonneurological factors.

referred for neuropsychological testing. General intellectual abilities and educational level influence performance on many, if not most, neuropsychological tests. Individuals with low normal intelligence or low levels of education have a greater probability of performing poorly on neuropsychological tests than do individuals who have greater than average intelligence and higher levels of education. Many modern neuropsychological tests present normative data for individuals across a range of educational levels to increase both the sensitivity and the specificity of the measures. There exist numerous nonneurological causes of poor performance on neuropsychological tests that must be considered before concluding poor performance is an indication of brain dysfunction. Rapid Reference 5.3 summarizes some of the possible sources for false-positive errors in neuropsychological testing due to the nonspecificity of test results.

 Rapid Reference 5.3

Possible Sources for False Positive Errors in Predicting Brain Dysfunction

- Psychiatric diseases or disorders
- Severe anxiety
- Mental retardation
- Low normal intelligence
- Low levels of education
- Nonnative language speaker
- Cultural background
- Poor socioeconomic conditions
- Sleep deprivation or fatigue
- Physical illness
- Medication effects
- Sensory or motor impairment
- Acute or chronic pain
- Vocational and avocational background
- Lack of cooperation or effort
- Malingering
- Negative patient–examiner interaction
- Test sophistication and practice effects

An individual's cultural background may also be a source of false positive errors on neuropsychological tests. The most obvious cultural factor in neuropsychological test performance is, of course, language. Tests not administered in an individual's native language are more likely to yield false positive errors than those administered in the language in which the individual is fluent. It is possible that even individuals who are fluently bilingual may be disadvantaged on some tasks if their exposure to the language in which the test is administered has been less than that of the native speakers with similar educational backgrounds to whom they will be compared.

The neuropsychological and psychological testing literature is filled with debates on the more controversial claim that subcultural or ethnic differences among individuals who are native monolingual speakers of the language of the test may lead to false positive errors. This debate has centered on the fact that individuals from some minority ethnic backgrounds consistently score more poorly on psychological tests than the majority White population of European background or certain groups of Asian Americans. The issues of both the sensitivity and specificity of psychological tests have received the most public attention in the classification of individuals as mentally retarded and in cases in which test scores are used for job advancement or college admissions. One argument holds that the higher rate of false positives (e.g., reduced specificity) of many psychological tests has led to a greater representation of some ethnic minority groups in special education classes, whereas the lower rate of correct identification (e.g., sensitivity) has led to a lower rate of admissions to college and job promotions.

Perhaps because of the expense and time required to obtain test norms, many neuropsychological test publishers release tests with normative data and validity studies conducted on a cross-section of American adults; these data address differences in performance that may occur with age and education. Separate data for groups with psychiatric illnesses, bilingual groups, and different cultural groups are rarely presented in even the most extensive test manuals. This practice is consistent with the standards for test validity in the *Standards for Educational and Psychological Testing* (American Educational Research Association, American Psychological Association, & National Council on Measurement in Education, 1999; see Standards 1.2–1.4) published by the American Educational Research Association. Standard 1.4 also includes the explicit warning: "If a test is used in a way that has not been validated, it is incumbent on the user to justify the new use, collecting new evidence if necessary."

Because the sensitivity and specificity of neuropsychological tests have not been used until recently to gauge the validity of individual measures, the tendency of individual tests to produce false positive errors tends not be emphasized in test manuals and may be overlooked even by well-trained clinicians. Currently, this situation is extremely problematic for neuropsychologists who frequently assess individuals from the full range of normal intellectual and educational backgrounds, as well as increasing numbers of individuals from diverse cultural backgrounds and linguistic competencies. This practical exigency may be accompanied by a reduction in the validity of many of the available neuropsychological tests and can result in a high rate of incorrect clinical decision making. In some cases, the interpretation of these tests' results forms the basis for decisions in litigation and changes in social policy. The neuropsychologist entering the field needs to be acutely aware of the potential limits of the current technology of measurement because it is not always practical for test publishers to make explicit the limits and cautions that must be considered before a test can be used.

The validity of a test may not only be limited by the tendency of some groups to perform poorly on psychological tests. Test validity may be limited because the measures themselves are not reliable and are sensitive to factors having nothing to do with the quantities being measured.

TEST RELIABILITY

The validity of a test can be limited by multiple factors. Sometimes a test score can be affected by influences aside from the entity it was designed to predict or measure. The extent to which a test is a stable and pure measure of some—in this case, psychological—quantity is its test *reliability*. In classical reliability theory (Crocker & Algina, 1986), it is assumed that every score consists of a *true score* (T) and the influences of various sources of error (e). It is assumed that T is a stable quantity from measurement to measurement. Error (e) is considered to be the sum of random influences that might cause an actual measurement to be greater or lesser at any particular time. Reliability is sometimes expressed as a ratio of a hypothetical true score (T) to the true score (T) plus error (e):

$$reliability = \frac{T}{T+e}$$

It is simple to see that as the level of error increases, the level of the test's reliability decreases. If a test is not reliable, it will (under most circumstances) be limited in its ability to make predictions. If each score contains a high percentage of error, the test scores are less likely to be true reflections of the dimensions they are measuring. Consider a ruler made out of a metal that expands and contracts with small variations in temperature. As a result of its instability, the ruler would yield a different measurement almost every time it was used. Because of the inconsistency of the measures the ruler yields, its validity as a measure of length would be limited by the amount of variation it showed as a function of the irrelevant dimension of temperature. Sometimes the ruler might predict that an item is three quarter inches long, sometimes 1 inch long, and sometimes more. The actual physical dimension or the true score of the item being measured is the same, but the ruler produces different results because of error and therefore yields different predictions of what the actual length is.

Most neuropsychological tests, no matter what they are designed to measure or predict, may be influenced by factors contributing to errors of measurement. Sources of error are numerous and can include factors such as the presence or absence of rapport between the patient and the examiner, patient fatigue, the clarity of instructions, and the clarity of scoring criteria.

Reliability can also be viewed as the extent to which test results are internally consistent and the extent to which a given test result may be generalizable to the findings on other occasions when the measure might be administered. These conceptual variations suggest a variety of ways that reliability may be quantitatively estimated. Instead, however, they should be regarded as different ways that error of measurement may be conceptualized. The correlation among individual test items and the correlation between an individual item and the total score are the most typical measures of internal consistency of a test. These measures are important for tests that consist of multiple items and can gauge the extent to which these items are measuring the same factor. Because multiple measurements of the same quantity ideally should increase true scores and decrease error, psychological tests often consist of many trials or questions. If these individual trials are not well selected, they each may be measuring slightly different factors, hence decreasing rather than increasing reliability. The definition of reliability and the different ways to measure it are listed in Rapid Reference 5.4.

≡ Rapid Reference 5.4

Definition and Types of Reliability

Reliability is the extent to which a test is a stable and pure measure of some quantity. Reliability means consistency.

- *Internal consistency:* The correlation among individual test items or the correlation of individual items and total score.
- *Test–retest reliability:* The correlation of scores obtained from two test times.
- *Interrater reliability:* The correlation between test scores obtained by different examiners.

Interrater and test–retest reliability are the most common ways to assess the generalizability of measures. In these two cases, a high correlation of the scores obtained from two test times suggests that the test scores are stable or generalizable over some time period. Test–retest reliability is in many ways the most intuitive kind of reliability measurement. It would seem that one could not trust a measurement of the same true score that varies from time to time. Imagine the havoc that would occur in the construction industry if tape measures yielded different measurements each day.

In practice, however, tests that appear stable for healthy individuals frequently may not provide stable scores across time for patients with brain dysfunction or for some populations without brain dysfunction such as the elderly, young children, or individuals with psychiatric disorders. In these cases, the underlying true scores may themselves vary, leading to poor or modest estimates of test–retest reliability. Furthermore, internal consistency measures may be limited because some patients' performances can vary within a session. In some cases, increased susceptibility to fatigue and distractibility paradoxically reduce the relative reliability of longer tests and in turn distort estimates of internal consistency.

Interrater reliability (the correlation between test scores obtained by different examiners) is critical for test items that require the judgment of an examiner for scoring. Examples of such tests include the Wechsler Memory Scale—Fourth Edition and many of the subtests of the Wechsler Adult Intelligence Scale—Fourth Edition. Note that a test that has good interrater reliability may not be internally consistent and may not necessarily have good test–retest reliability.

In the medical literature, a different approach to interrater reliability is sometimes used; this approach is known as the reproducibility of diagnosis. Rather than referring to ranges of test scores, as does the concept of interrater reliability, reproducibility refers to the agreement among diagnoses given by different raters for the same patient. Instead of calculating a Pearson's r, or correlation coefficient, as is used to depict interrater reliability across a range of test scores, a kappa or k coefficient is used to depict agreement among raters, giving a positive or negative diagnosis ranging from 0% to 100%. The idea of reproducibility of diagnosis is not often used to evaluate how neuropsychological tests are used to make diagnostic decisions but has some advantages over the mere report of a typical interrater reliability coefficient (Kraemer, 1992). The coefficient of reproducibility provides a metric of the actual reproducibility of a clinical decision, which in many cases is the most important function to be evaluated by the test. Even if the test yields the same score for two raters, it may not yield the same diagnostic decision. Reproducibility of diagnosis depends in large part on an agreement of what constitutes a true diagnosis or the actual presence of the condition that is being diagnosed. This is more an issue of validity or, more specifically, establishing a standard criterion against which the test will be evaluated. Perhaps the idea of reproducibility of diagnosis may not have yet entered the field of neuropsychology because many open issues having to do with diagnostic or predictive criteria themselves still exist. We return to some of the issues surrounding test validation in a moment.

The *Standards for Educational and Psychological Testing* (American Educational Research Association, American Psychological Association, & National Council on Measurement in Education, 1999) suggests that test publishers provide information about the reliability of a test measure and should include the kind of reliability being reported (test–retest, internal consistency, etc.). The clinician needs to evaluate these data carefully and judge whether the kind of reliability reported is relevant to how the test will be used. Reported reliability estimates based on normal control subjects should be extrapolated to any other population with extreme caution. A test that has been shown to be reliable for normal individuals may have limited reliability in other populations, including patient populations.

BASE RATES

Test validity is not calculated in a vacuum. The accuracy of predictions about the presence or absence of a condition varies depending on the occurrence of the condition in the population tested. Although the issue of how base rates will affect the efficiency or accuracy of decisions based on tests is now well known among writers on medical diagnosis (e.g., Kraemer 1992), no analysis of this issue is still more eloquent than that in the classic 1955 article in the journal *Psychological Bulletin* by Paul Meehl and Albert Rosen titled "Antecedent Probability and the Efficiency of Psychometric Signs, Patterns, or Cutting Scores." Consider the following example adapted with slight modernizing adjustments directly from Meehl and Rosen (1955) to illustrate the problem of base rates for the neuropsychologist:

A neuropsychologist is asked to decide whether the patients who have been referred for admission to a rehabilitation hospital have actual deficits related to a head injury or are malingering (i.e., simulating or exaggerating deficits for secondary gain). The screen must be inexpensive and will be used to decide whether patients should be referred for expensive confirmatory radiological testing. In reviewing the literature, the neuropsychologist finds a study that describes a test that will correctly identify 70% of individuals asked to simulate the symptoms of a brain injury (this group will henceforth be called malingerers) who obtain a certain critical score on the test. The test will also correctly identify 70% of individuals with confirmed brain injuries on MRI (henceforth called brain injured).

Assuming that 90% of all the patients referred to the rehabilitation hospital actually have brain injuries that will ultimately be confirmed by radiological evidence, how much confidence should the neuropsychologist have in the candidate test? As Meehl and Rosen point out, on the basis of the base rates and with or without the test, if the neuropsychologist simply adopted the strategy of predicting that every patient referred to the rehabilitation hospital has a brain injury, the prediction would be correct 90% of the time.

As can be seen from Table 5.1, Part A, 7 of 10 malingerers admitted to the rehabilitation hospital receive a malingering score on the test, whereas 63 of 90 patients with brain injuries receive a brain-injured score. If every patient with a malingering score is predicted to be a malingerer, then only 7 of 34 or 21% will be identified correctly. The test is, of course, much better at predicting patients who will be in the brain-injured group because 63 of 66 patients with a brain injury received a brain-injured score.

> **CAUTION**
>
> ....
>
> The accuracy of predictions about the presence or absence of a condition varies depending on the occurrence or base rate of the condition in the population tested.

Table 5.1. Patients Classified as Malingerers or Brain Injured by a Test that Correctly Identifies 70% of Patients with Brain Injury and Patients Who Are Malingering

Prediction by the Neuropsychological Test	Actual Diagnosis		Total Classified by the Test
	Malingerer	Brain injured	
Part A: Rehabilitation hospital admission base rates (90% patients with brain injury, 10% malingerers)			
Malingering score	7	27	34
Brain injury score	3	63	66
Total diagnosed	10	90	100
Part B: Prison hospital base rates (90% malingerers, 10% patients with brain injury)			
Malingering score	63	3	66
Brain injury score	27	7	34
Total diagnosed	90	10	100

Now consider a different situation. The neuropsychologist in our example is now asked to consult for a state prison hospital with the same question. Prison hospital officials are also interested in screening individuals for additional expensive radiological procedures, but their base rates are quite different: 90% of the patients referred to the prison hospital are malingering and end up having no evidence of brain injury, whereas only 10% are found to have actual brain injury. As can be seen from the scores in Table 5.1, Part B, the same test now seems to be a better predictor of malingering because a positive malingering score correctly classifies 63 of 66 or 95% of actual malingerers.

These effects of base rate on the accuracy of clinical prediction are captured in what is now the positive predictive value (PPV) and negative predictive value (NPV) of a test. *Positive predictive value* is defined as the percentage of individuals who are positively diagnosed who actually have the condition and is expressed as the proportion of true positives (TPs) of the total number of positive test results or TPs plus false positives (FPs; i.e., positive predictive value = TP/TP+FP); *negative predictive value* is defined as the percentage of individuals who are not diagnosed with the condition who truly do not have the condition and is expressed as the proportion of true negatives (TNs) of the total number of negative results or TNs plus false negatives (FNs; i.e., negative predictive value = TN/FN+TN). As the reader can readily see, the same test with same sensitivity and specificity can have widely different positive and negative predictive values depending on the actual base rate (or prevalence) of the condition in the population in question. In our admittedly extreme example, the positive predictive value of the malingering test in question ranges from 21% to 95%! Rapid Reference 5.5 summarizes the definitions of the concepts important in evaluating test accuracy.

≡ *Rapid Reference 5.5*

Definitions Pertaining to Test Accuracy

Sensitivity: How well a test correctly identifies actual brain dysfunction and is expressed as the proportion of true positives (TPs) of the total number of TPs and false negatives (FNs) (TP/FN+TP).

Specificity: How well a test correctly classifies healthy individuals as being healthy and is expressed as the proportion of true negatives (TNs) of the total number of false positives (FPs) and TNs (TN/TN+FP).

Positive predictive value: The percentage of individuals who are positively diagnosed who actually have the condition and is expressed as the proportion of

(continued)

TPs of the total number of positive test results (TP/TP+FP). Positive predictive value is influenced by the base rate of the condition in the population tested and is an important measure of the accuracy of a test in the situation it is actually going to be used.

Negative predictive value: The percentage of individuals who are negatively diagnosed who truly do not have the condition and is expressed as the proportion of true negatives of the total number of negative results (TN/FN+TN). Negative predictive value is influenced by the base rate of the condition in the population tested.

A common and frequently overlooked ramification of the effect of base rates on diagnostic accuracy is that tests that have acceptable PPVs and NPVs in consultative practice may not work as well when used as "screening" measures or in situations in which the base rates of positive disorders are rare or not known. Consider the following: The base rate of actual disorders may be quite high for referrals made to neuropsychologists in hospital-based consultative clinical practices because such patients or clients have already been "screened" by the fact that they have symptomatic complaints (that may be rare in the general population of similar adults) and by the fact that one or more professional health care providers (such as a primary care physician or neurologist) have found reason to make the referral in the first place. The same tests might yield unacceptably low levels of PPV and, perhaps more seriously, unacceptable levels of NPV when employed as part of an intake battery for self-referred clients seeking psychotherapy, where the occurrence of actual neuropsychological dysfunction is rarer.

In addition to reflecting the actual probabilities of a diagnosis in a specific setting, the concept of base rates can be used to adjust predictions based on the specific historical facts of an individual patient's life. Patients with a known history of stroke or loss of consciousness are more likely to have a brain injury than individuals with no such history. Unfortunately, in many cases specific data about the base rates of various underlying conditions may not be available. It is therefore critical that the neuropsychologist understand how a test was validated, what the base rates of different conditions were in the validating study, and, if possible, what the prevalence (i.e., actual cases) of the condition is in the population in general and in his or her referral population in particular.

USING TEST NORMS

Normative data are used to answer the first question confronting a neuropsychologist: Is the observed test performance evidence of a healthy or normal individual or evidence of an individual with some form of compromise of brain function? To answer this question, the neuropsychologist must also consider the importance of what norms to choose. Most contemporary neuropsychological tests contain published normative data showing the range of performance on the test for healthy individuals and in most cases for individuals who have been diagnosed with a disease or dysfunction of the central nervous system. In some cases, norms are also provided for individuals with psychiatric disorders or other nonneurological medical illnesses that may affect test performance. As we have discussed, an individual's age and education may affect performance on any psychological test and most neuropsychological tests. For some tests, norms that are stratified by age and education are preferable to norms that simply give scores for patients with brain dysfunction and those with normal brain functioning. Some test publishers go further and publish norms stratified by sex, ethnic group, region, and other common demographic variables used by the U.S. Census. For most purposes, however, age and education are the most critical variables. Ethnic norms may be important in certain settings as well.

The specific advantage of age- and education-based norms is that they allow a more precise determination of what is normal for the individual as opposed to what is normal for the general population. Age- and education-based norms help to control for IQ and level of cognitive ability. A person with above-average cognitive abilities who scores in the average or normal range on tasks normed according to age and education is performing at expected levels. An example can help to illustrate this point. Consider a

DON'T FORGET

It is the responsibility of the neuropsychologist to review test manuals and the scientific literature to make sure that the norms being used are the most up to date and specific to the patient being evaluated.

65-year-old Caucasian man of above average cognitive ability and 16 years of education who requires 68 seconds to complete Trail Making B. Compared with that of other men aged 65 to 69 and with 16 to 17 years of education (Heaton, Miller, Taylor, & Grant, 2004), his performance is average at the 62nd percentile, but compared with other men aged 65 to 69 and with 12 years of education, his performance is high average at the 76th percentile. Likewise, a 65-year-old Caucasian man with 10 years of education who requires 123 seconds to complete Trail Making B and nearly double the time of the previous 65-year-old Caucasian man is actually performing in the average range at the 38th percentile (Heaton et al., 2004) relative to other men his age with similar levels of education. That same performance for the 65-year-old man with 16 to 17 years of education is actually below normal limits for him at the 14th percentile.

The reliability and stability of normative data also are affected by the sample size used. In general, larger samples yield more generalizable and reliable data than smaller samples. In some cases, the test is published with minimal normative data with little stratification but with additional data collected later by investigators. Norms are frequently updated to reflect changes in culture or to extend the data to new populations. It is the responsibility of the neuropsychologist to review the literature relevant to the tests and the settings in which the tests are used to ensure that the norms being used are the most up to date and specific to the patients being evaluated.

What Is Normal?

The question of what is normal performance on a neuropsychological test is really the question: What is normal for the individual being tested? Because the natural variations in genetics and environment (rather than disease) result in a great range of normal variation in ability, the question of what is normal for an individual must be considered carefully. An example of the large variability present in neuropsychological protocols comes from Schretlen, Munro, Anthony, and Pearlson (2003). They demonstrated that substantial intraindividual variability is common in normal adults. In their population, maximum discrepancies between highest and lowest scores on a battery of 15 tests ranged from 1.6 standard deviations to 6.1 standard deviations. More than 60% of these normal adults had maximum discrepancies exceeding 3 standard deviations. The simple presence of variability, therefore, is not sufficient as an indicator of brain dysfunction. As Schretlen et al. (2003) warn these results "underscore the need to base diagnostics inferences on clinically recognizable patterns rather than psychometric variability alone" (p. 864). Often clinicians underestimate the base rates of scatter (i.e., variability between tests) in normal individuals among neuropsychological test results. It is incumbent on neuropsychologists to realize that just because a difference score (i.e., discrepancy between two test scores) is statistically significant at a .05 level in the standardization data does not mean it is clinically or practically significant and, most important, does not necessarily imply the presence of cerebral pathology or brain dysfunction.

The importance of diagnostically meaningful patterns of performance is also underscored by the data collected on normal adults by Heaton, Grant, and Matthews (1991) and Heaton et al. (2004). In the first study, Heaton and his colleagues administered a battery of neuropsychological tests comprising 40 measures to 455 neurologically normal adults. They found that of this group only 10% had no scores in the abnormal range (defined in the study as T-score ≤39 or ≤15th percentile) and, remarkably, 20% had 10 or more scores in the abnormal range. The median number of abnormal scores was 4. In a repeat of this study in 2004, but this time with 25 measures in 1,189 neurological normal adults, they found similar results: Only 13.2% had no scores in the abnormal range, and the median number of abnormal scores was 3. These data make it clear that abnormal scores are not uncommon in normal individuals and that even sensitive neuropsychological tests may have limited "specificity" with a potentially high false positive rate (i.e., classifying individuals without brain dysfunction as being individuals with brain dysfunction). In a recent review, Binder, Iverson and Brooks (2009) conclude: "that *abnormal* performance on some proportion of neuropsychological tests in a battery is psychometrically *normal*. Abnormalities do not necessarily signal the presence of acquired brain dysfunction because low scores and large intraindividual variability often are characteristic of healthy adults" (p. 31). Heaton et al. (2004) correctly indicate that "what distinguishes the normal individuals from persons with acquired brain disorders is not just the number or even the severity of the deficits, but also the nature and pattern of those deficits" (p. 73).

Although it may not provide a complete answer to the question of what is normal for the individual, a comparison to test data drawn from a population that is demographically similar to the patient is usually the first step. In most cases, test norms use a statistical definition of normality based on the assumption that the underlying distribution of scores in a normal population is a normal (or bell-shaped) distribution. The normal distribution is a continuous probability distribution in which the mean, median, and mode are the same and that shows a gradual decrease in the percentage of cases having scores greater or lesser than the mean. In addition to the mean (M), the shape or dispersion of the normal distribution can be described using a statistic called the standard deviation (SD; σ) or:

$$\sigma = \sqrt{\sum_i \frac{x_i - M}{N}}$$

where σ (the symbol for SD) equals the square root of the sum of the differences between the individual scores (x_i) and the mean divided by the number of scores (N). In general, scores within 1 standard deviation from the mean are considered normal. In a true normal distribution, 68.26% of all scores fall within 1 SD of the mean, and an additional 24% (or 92% total) falls within 2 SDs of the mean. The range of scores within a normal distribution can be presented in several standardized forms allowing for comparisons of the relative position of performance on different tests. One form of standardization involves converting raw scores into z-scores or:

$$z = \frac{x - M}{\sigma}$$

Hence, a score is converted into a z-score by computing the difference between the score and the mean of the distribution divided by SD. The score may then be expressed in terms of standard deviation units with $z = 0$ being the mean, and $z = 1$ being 1 standard deviation greater than the mean.

It is common to present raw scores as percentiles of the normal distribution, with the 1st percentile being somewhere between 2 and 3 standard deviations below the mean and the 99th percentile being somewhere between 2 and 3 standard deviations above the mean. In terms of percentiles, the normal range of performance falls between the 16th and 84th percentiles (equivalent to ±1 SD).

There are many other ways of standardizing scores that have been found to be convenient in expressing relative differences across measures. This includes the Wechsler Intelligence Scales (standardized based on a mean of 100 and a standard deviation of 15), the Wechsler subtest scaled scores (based on a mean of 10 and standard deviation of 3), and the T-score (based on a mean of 50 and standard deviation of 10). All these methods produce scores that refer to the shape of the normal distribution and can be used to understand the relative standing of an individual's performance on a test compared with that of other similar individuals.

The normative position of a test score serves as a predictor of whether a score is representative of normal brain functioning or representative of abnormal functioning. Simply because a score falls below the normal range does not immediately translate to brain dysfunction. The accuracy of the score as a predictor of brain dysfunction depends on many factors as just discussed, including the reliability of the test, the likelihood that a deviant score is specific to brain dysfunction, the base rate of brain dysfunction in the population from which the patient comes, and the score the person would have received if that person did not have brain dysfunction. The latter consideration means scores must be cautiously interpreted within the context of the history and background of the patient. This naturally brings us to the topic of the estimation of *premorbid* ability.

PREMORBID CAPACITY

Because normal human abilities are widely distributed, even well-stratified norms may not provide an accurate picture of what mental abilities a patient would have brought to a task before suffering brain dysfunction or disease. In those instances when there is no previous measurement of intellectual ability available to guide a clinician's judgment in this regard, estimating premorbid IQ is the next best means. Although thousands of tests have been published identifying various human abilities, the IQ is by far the best documented and most extensively used measure of premorbid ability. Consider that the normal IQ (i.e., within 1 SD of the mean) ranges from 85 to 115. This range contains individuals with dramatically different expectations of academic and vocational achievement. The relationship between IQ, education, vocational achievement, and other demographic variables such as sex, ethnicity, and geographic origin was recognized by the publication of the WAIS, a test based on a sample that was carefully stratified by these demographic variables. Wilson et al. (1978; Wilson, Rosenbaum, & Brown, 1979) used these data to create equations using demographics to predict IQ. These formulas were updated in 1984 for the WAIS–R by Barona, Reynolds, and Chastain and again in 1996 by Paolo, Ryan, and Troster. Cross-validation studies of these formulas show that demographics are only modestly successful at predicting IQ, with accuracy rates ranging from approximately 60% to 70%.

Such demographic formulas work best for young and middle-aged individuals and less well for children and the elderly. It is not surprising that demographic formulas for children should be less accurate because education is compulsory for most children under 16, allowing for a wide range of abilities to be represented in each grade until the 10th or 11th grades. Demographic variables also do not predict IQ accurately for older adults. This may be due in part to cultural differences in the current cohort of adults older than 65 or 70. As noted earlier, adults who were of school age before World War II often did not complete high school. In fact, because the first compulsory education laws were not put into effect until 1918, many adults born before 1920 stopped their formal education after eighth or ninth grade, in many cases for economic reasons. Adults with a wide range of abilities received an education that today would be unlikely. After World War II, the 1944 GI Bill gave many veterans the opportunity to complete high school and college, increasing the likelihood that adults capable of higher levels of educational achievement could afford to fulfill this potential. These legal landmarks and the underlying cultural changes they reflect are likely to affect the relationship between education and IQ for older adults born in the first 30 years of the 20th century compared with adults born after WWII. It remains to be seen whether education will improve as a predictor of premorbid ability for adults born after WWII.

Comparisons between tests thought to be less sensitive to impairment and tests more sensitive to impairment have a long history as a method for estimating the changes wrought by brain dysfunction for an individual. A comparison among the so-called *hold* and *don't hold* tests of the WAIS was suggested as a way to calculate a *deterioration quotient* by Wechsler. It was argued that such tests as Vocabulary, Information, and others were relatively insensitive to deterioration (specifically the effects of aging), whereas such subtests as the Digit Symbol were relatively more sensitive to the effects of conditions expected to produce a deterioration in IQ (such as brain dysfunction and aging). This method is extremely limited because various forms of brain dysfunction may affect hold tests more than some don't hold tests. For example, patients with aphasia, which form a class of acquired language disorders typically as a result of damage to the left cerebral hemisphere of right-handed adults, are likely to perform more poorly on all language tasks, including Vocabulary, than nonverbal tasks. This is an extreme example, but the general problem is that one has to know what subtests are being affected by the condition in question to calculate a deterioration index, leading to potential circularities when trying to decide what is acquired impairment and what is representative of preserved premorbid functions.

Combining demographic variables with performances on tests appears to have greater utility for estimating premorbid IQ than either demographic variables or test performances alone. With the Oklahoma Premorbid Intelligence Estimate (OPIE) Schoenberg et al. (2002, 2003) have provided formulas for combining subtests from the WAIS-III that are less sensitive to change from brain dysfunction (i.e., Vocabulary, Information, Matrix Reasoning, and Picture Completion) with demographic variables, such as age, education, ethnicity, sex, and region of the country to predict Full Scale IQ. When achievement scores from college board tests (such as Scholastic Aptitude Test [SAT] and American College Test [ACT]) are available, premorbid cognitive functioning can also be estimated using the formula provided by Baade and Schoenberg (2004).

One task that has received much attention in recent years as a potential measure of premorbid IQ is the reading of irregular words. Tests such as the National Adult Reading Test (NART; Nelson & McKenna, 1975) have been extensively investigated as measures of premorbid ability, particularly in older adults with suspected dementia. As a lifelong, overlearned skill, reading appears to be a more stable hold task than such WAIS subtests as Vocabulary (O'Carroll, Baikie, & Whittick, 1987) in the face of such dementing illnesses as Alzheimer's disease, but may still be affected by specific brain lesions that cause reading and language deficits. The Wechsler Test of Adult Reading (WTAR; Wechsler, 2001b) is an excellent example of this approach, containing norms based on the same stratified sample of American adults used to norm the WAIS-III.

Irregular word reading tasks are also dependent on education and may lead to an underestimate of IQ (and therefore an underestimate of impairment) in poorly educated elderly patients and in patients with acquired language disorders. An interesting variation on reading tests of premorbid ability that may minimize this problem are word reading tasks based on identification rather than pronunciation. For example, the Spot-a-Word Test (Baddeley, Emslie, Nimmo-Smith, 1992) presents word pairs consisting of NART words and similar nonwords. Patients are asked to choose which member of each pair is the real word. This task yields an estimate of premorbid intelligence that is resistant to age (Baddeley et al., 1993) but may have limited validity with American patients not familiar with some of the British spelling conventions used on the test. The recently developed Lexical Orthographic Familiarity Test (LOFT; Leritz, McGlinchey, Lundren, Grande, & Milberg, 2008) uses a similar technique but pairs the words from the WTAR with archaic words in English. Patients are asked to choose which word of each pair looks more familiar. This task was found to maintain its correlation with educational levels and the Barona Index even in severely aphasic patients. In contrast, WTAR scores were not found to maintain their correlation with education across the range of aphasia severity. The LOFT has not been fully normed but is promising as an additional method of estimating premorbid potential.

To estimate premorbid potential, the clinician should use a combination of methods that include demographics and performance measures. Methods for estimating premorbid intelligence are outlined in Rapid Reference 5.6.

In many cases, the details of the patient's educational and occupational experience will help with the task of estimating premorbid capacity, although the empirical basis for using such data has not been well studied. However, information such

≡ Rapid Reference 5.6

Methods for Estimating Premorbid Intelligence

- *Hold* vs. *don't hold* tests (e.g., Vocabulary vs. Similarities)
- Demographic formula (e.g., see Barona et al., 1984)
- Demographic formula combined with test performance (e.g., see Schoenberg et al., 2002, 2003)
- Known scores on group achievement measures (e.g., see Baade & Schoenberg, 2004)
- Known educational and occupational attainment (e.g., high school education vs. college; laborer vs. college professor)
- Reading of irregular words (e.g., North American Adult Reading Test, American National Adult Reading Test, or Wechsler Test of Adult Reading)

as school grades, achievement test scores (e.g., SAT, Iowa Tests of Basic Skills), and an analysis of vocational responsibilities (e.g., level and complexity of a job) can be used to make inferences about premorbid ability. Two adults with similar levels of education, such as completion of high school, may have had different grades, curricula, and achievement scores. Sometimes estimates of premorbid ability are especially critical; then it may be particularly necessary to obtain school records and other documentation of premorbid ability and not to rely on a patient's or an informant's self-report alone. Such cases would include those in which the patient has been functioning at a high level of performance with test scores not consistent with this history, cases in which the patient's deficits are subtle, or cases in which no historical reasons can be found for the presence of observed cognitive deficits.

A caution is relevant here. Premorbid estimates of general cognitive ability or IQ may not necessarily generalize to all of the cognitive functions measured by neuropsychological tests. Some measures that may be sensitive to impaired performance in patients with brain dysfunction may not have the same range and distribution as IQ. So, for example, such measures such as the Wisconsin Card Sorting Test and the Rey–Osterrieth Complex Figure may have ceilings (i.e., topmost scores) that are far lower than IQ. This means that although these tests may be able to identify low scorers as impaired, they may not accurately reflect above-average abilities. In addition, it must be kept in mind that IQ may not be a predictor of all the abilities that are measured by tests sensitive to brain dysfunction. In other words, a person with a superior IQ may have only average attentional abilities; this does not mean, however, that he or she has an impairment in attentional abilities. This has also been shown in children who are intellectually gifted. On the Wechsler Intelligence Scale for Children— Fourth Edition (WISC-IV), children who are intellectually gifted often show abnormally large discrepancies between their performances on conceptually based tasks (and hence the Verbal Comprehension Index and the Perceptual Reasoning Index) than their performances on tasks dependent on speeded processing (and hence their Processing Speed Index). For example, the *WISC-IV Integrated Technical and Interpretive Manual* (Wechsler et al., 2004; Table 5.22, page 77) indicates that the mean Vocabulary subtest score for children who are intellectually gifted is 14.6, whereas their mean Coding subtest score is only 11.5. Given how common this pattern is in these children, it would be a mistake to infer the presence of an acquired deficit from scores such as these. The relationship between the various cognitive functions of interest in a neuropsychological examination is not yet well studied, and until this information is available, great caution should be used in drawing inferences about performance across cognitive measures based on IQ.

THE USE OF DESCRIPTORS TO GRADE IMPAIRMENT

In addition to defining a threshold between normal and abnormal, it is often useful to further grade impairment using ordinal terms. These terms are helpful to consumers of neuropsychological reports who may not be familiar with the meaning associated with more quantitative data. The use of ordinal descriptive categories has been a long-standing convention in intelligence testing with the most well-established terminology established for the Wechsler scales. Recently, Guilmette, Hagan, and Giuliano (2008) conducted a survey of board-certified neuropsychologists, asking them to provide the specific terms that they used for various ranges of standardized test scores. A number of terms were used, but the most popular terms were similar to those used in the Wechsler scales, specifically: very superior (≥98th percentile), superior (91st–97th percentile), high average (75th–90th percentile), average (25th–74th percentile), low average (9th–24th percentile), borderline (2nd–8th percentile), impaired (1st–2nd percentile), and severely impaired (<1st percentile).

Russell, Neuringer, and Goldstein (1970) were the first to grade neuropsychological impairment using the descriptors mild, moderate, and severe. Heaton et al.'s (2004) revised demographically adjusted norms use a system that includes the descriptors mild (7th–15th percentile), mild to moderate (2nd–6th percentile), moderate (0.6th–2nd percentile), moderate to severe (0.1st–0.5th percentile), and severe (<0.1th percentile) to grade impairment and above average (≥68th percentile), average (31–67th percentile), and below average (16th–30th percentile) to grade unimpaired performances. Note that these terms do not use 1 standard deviation to define the division between normal and impaired performance. These systems are summarized in Table 5.2.

It is important to be consistent in the description system used in reports, and it is important to report corresponding standard, scaled, or percentile scores with the descriptors because otherwise too much specific information is lost (see Chapter 7 for a more complete discussion of this issue). It is also important to recognize that because of the range of intraindividual variability in the test scores of normal adults, in systems in which labels of "impaired" are applied to scores below the normal range (i.e., according to the area under the normal curve, the 16th–84th percentiles), one cannot directly infer acquired brain dysfunction. An individual can score below the normal range for reasons other than brain dysfunction (see the discussion of test sensitivity and specificity earlier in the chapter).

Table 5.2. Percentile Score Referenced Descriptors Using Systems Based on Wechsler and Heaton et al.

		System	
Percentile Range		Wechsler	Heaton et al.
Above Normal	98+	Very superior	Above average
	91–97	Superior	Above average
	85–90	High average	Above average
Normal	75–84	High average	Above average
	69–74	Average	Above average
	31–68	Average	Average
	25–30	Average	Below average
	16–24	Low average	Below average
Below Normal	9–15	Low average	Mild impairment
	6–8	Borderline	Mild impairment
	2–5	Borderline	Mild to moderate impairment
	1–2	Impaired	Moderate impairment
	0.6–1	Severely impaired	Moderate impairment
	0.1–0.5	Severely impaired	Moderate to severe impairment
	<0.1	Severely impaired	Severe impairment

QUALITATIVE VERSUS QUANTITATIVE DATA

The availability of tests that have been carefully normed is the scientific cornerstone of clinical neuropsychology. Most instruments that have become well accepted provide estimates of the relative standing of an individual to a normal reference population and can thereby predict whether brain function has been compromised. As we have also discussed, some systems combine multiple measures that meet this basic criterion into a battery that is consistently administered to all patients. The use of such batteries may help increase the specificity of neuropsychological predictions and has the advantage of providing a comparable set of measures to be compared from population to population and from individual to individual. It could safely be said that such *fixed battery approaches* are the culmination of the empiricist tradition and the most straightforward method for quantifying the effects of brain dysfunction on behavior. The two best-known examples of quantitative fixed batteries are the Halstead–Reitan Neuropsychological Test Battery (HRB) and the Luria–Nebraska Neuropsychological Battery (LNNB).

Not all neuropsychologists agree, however, that the emphasis on normative data collected within a fixed battery is the optimal method for characterizing the effects of brain dysfunction. As we have noted, many tests, although useful as predictors of the presence of brain dysfunction, were not derived from theories of brain–behavior relationships and are often accompanied by limited or confusing data on construct validity. Several neuropsychology laboratories have advocated assessment techniques that are more like the work of an experimental psychologist applied to an individual. The goal of these approaches is to isolate the specific psychological function or functions that are affected by brain dysfunction. Alexander Luria, who ran a famous neuropsychology laboratory in Moscow for several decades until his death in 1977, wrote several books describing the methods he used to define the effects of brain dysfunction in individual patients. Luria would use some standard materials consisting of pictures, written sentences and words, and objects to create sets of procedures that were designed to isolate various components of more complex functions such as reading, speaking, writing, memory, and many more. Many of his observations were organized according to his theory of brain organization, the basic premise of which was that complex behaviors consisted of sets of more basic functions. He also argued that the brain worked by combining the simpler functions, which were independently localized, into more complex integrated patterns to solve the problems of cognition. Luria's approach may be considered the prototype of what is sometimes called the *qualitative approach* to neuropsychological assessment.

Luria's examinations consisted of sequences of observations organized into various decision trees reflecting the function that was being analyzed. For example, if he observed a patient who had problems writing, he would ask whether the source of the problem was the loss of the recognition of letters as symbols, the loss of the associated sound patterns to the letters, the loss of the rules of sequencing the letters, or the loss of some other component of the writing process. With each task, he attempted to demonstrate whether the patient could perform these various components isolated in this case from writing itself, eventually eliminating as many explanations of the deficit as possible. He might, for example, try to see whether the patient could spell a word out loud or copy nonorthographic figures. He then went on to deduce which lesion might have caused the specific deficit that remained. Luria's methods were difficult to duplicate and learned by only a small number of students who were able to work with him. This situation limited the extent to which his claims and observations were tested by independent neuropsychological laboratories, and the difficulty of his approach prevented his methods from being popularly adopted. However, Luria's approach fit well with the emergence of cognitive psychology in the United States and used a framework that augured the main framework of modern neurosciences. Charles Golden used many of the tasks described by Luria in a fixed battery of tasks he called the LNNB. The LNNB, however, consists of scales representing either functions (such as writing and reading) or potential lesion locations (such as left vs. right hemisphere) and is normed based on the scales or combinations of these scales in much the same way as the HRB. Although the manual contains some suggestions for noting qualitative performance of the patient, the LNNB should be considered a fixed-battery method that is primarily quantitative.

The Boston Process Approach, developed by Edith Kaplan and her colleagues at the Boston VA in the early 1970s, was inspired by a combination of Heinz Werner's theories of cognitive development and the strong influence of cognitive neuropsychology research that was burgeoning at the Boston VA Hospital at that time. The VA Hospital in Boston attracted some of the pioneers of the field such as Harold Goodglass, Norman Geschwind, Nelson Butters, Laird Cermak, Edgar Zurif, and many others. Although these investigators studied such diverse problems as language, memory, and perception, their work had in common the experimental analysis of cognition into basic components that might be localized in neural structures. Dr. Kaplan joined the VA as a research assistant while a graduate student of Werner at Clark University. She was a keen observer of behavior and was immersed in the pioneering research being conducted around her. Werner's central concept was that the achievement or success at solving a problem may be based on a variety of cognitive approaches or processes that change as a child develops. Kaplan applied this distinction of *process and achievement* to uncover the basic cognitive functions that were impaired when patients with brain dysfunction were asked to solve the problems on standard neuropsychological tests.

Over two decades Dr. Kaplan collected a trove of observations and anecdotes about patients' performances on such tasks as the WAIS, the Wechsler Memory Scale (WMS), and other tests that were previously commonly used in neuropsychological batteries. Using her knowledge of cognitive neuropsychology, Dr. Kaplan developed modifications of these tasks, such as adding delayed recall and recognition memory trials to the WMS; these modifications ultimately became standard components of the revised WMS and other memory batteries. Her observations of how patients approach such tasks as the Block Design subtest of the WAIS helped lead to a critical organizing construct for describing differences between the cerebral hemispheres—the distinction between global and local processing of information (e.g., Robertson, 1995). Many of her techniques were incorporated into a special edition of the WAIS called the WAIS as a Neuropsychological Instrument (WAIS-NI; Kaplan, Morris, & Delis, 1991). In addition, she has helped develop a number of important instruments such as the Boston Diagnostic Aphasia Examination, Boston Naming Test, the California Verbal Learning Test (CVLT), and the Delis–Kaplan Executive Function System (D-KEFS), all of which contain elements of her observations. Although not a prolific writer herself, she influenced the practice of many students and practicing neuropsychologists in many countries who consider themselves acolytes of the approach labeled the Boston Process Approach.

Because Dr. Kaplan advocated the use of a core set of tasks including the WAIS, WMS, and so on with the addition of other tasks based on hypotheses developed from the core, the Boston Process Approach should be considered a flexible battery approach. Dr. Kaplan's emphasis on process makes this approach mainly qualitative, although norms may also be used to determine the presence of impairments. In addition, work has been done to quantify the qualitative aspects through new measurement instruments such as the WISC-IV Integrated.

Although Dr. Kaplan's work has certainly had a major influence on the practice of neuropsychology by helping to bring the elements of modern cognitive psychology into the world of psychometric testing, great caution must be used in applying this approach to patients. Although intellectually and intuitively appealing with its emphasis on breaking performance down into elements with potential relevance to rehabilitation and education, the empirical basis of the process approach is not sufficiently well developed to allow for scientifically supportable clinical predictions by all clinicians. Without precise norms and a clearly spelled-out blueprint of how and when these procedures should be used, tremendous variations are likely to occur in the skill and accuracy with which this approach is applied. Unlike Luria, who trained only a few students and was not generally available for training

CAUTION

The empirical basis of the process approach is not sufficiently well developed to allow for scientifically supportable clinical predictions by all clinicians.

workshops outside of Russia, Dr. Kaplan, an inspiring lecturer, has trained many students and still actively presents workshops and seminars effectively exposing a large number of clinicians to her teachings. However, Dr. Kaplan's mastery and the mastery of some students of her techniques do not guarantee that everyone using this approach can be equally successful.

Many of the techniques that comprise the Boston Process Approach have simply not been validated independently of the practitioners who claim expertise in them. Well-normed tests such as the WAIS-IV, WMS-IV, NEPSY-II, CVLT-2, and others that have been influenced by this approach should certainly be considered and deserve a place among the best techniques available to contemporary neuropsychologists. The wholesale adoption of many of the fascinating observational procedures of the Boston Process Approach, however, should not be entertained without specific training in a setting in which the validity of one's clinical expertise can be evaluated.

Appendix A outlines the steps that need to be taken in neuropsychological assessment. This outline considers the assessment process from the point of patient referral through selecting, administering, and scoring tests; interpreting the results of the tests; and finally reporting these results.

 TEST YOURSELF

1. **What principle should guide the clinical neuropsychologist in the choice of assessment tools to predict brain dysfunction?**
   (a) Frequency of use
   (b) Availability
   (c) Empirical validation
   (d) Ease of administration

2. **Which type of validity is involved when one is interested in predicting future behavior from test scores?**
   (a) Concurrent validity
   (b) Predictive validity
   (c) Content validity
   (d) Construct validity

3. **Content validity refers to the extent to which**
   (a) test items adequately cover various aspects of the variable that is being studied.
   (b) test items relate to one another.
   (c) test items predict future behavior.
   (d) test items are clear and understandable.

4. **Which type of validity concerns how well the test score relates to other measures or behaviors in a theoretically expected fashion?**
   (a) Criterion validity
   (b) Predictive validity
   (c) Content validity
   (d) Construct validity

5. **If one subtest of a neuropsychological test measuring memory correlates highly with the total score of the same test, that test has been shown to have**

   (a) internal consistency.

   (b) internal validity.

   (c) test–retest reliability.

   (d) interrater reliability.

6. **One of the problems about base rates in prediction is the fact that**

   (a) most measures lack adequate reliability.

   (b) high-frequency events are hard to predict.

   (c) low-frequency events are hard to predict.

   (d) most measures lack adequate validity.

Answers: 1. c; 2. b; 3. a; 4. d; 5. a; 6. c

Six

SPECIAL ISSUES IN
NEUROPSYCHOLOGICAL ASSESSMENT

OVERVIEW

An almost sure sign of the maturity of neuropsychology as a discipline is the emergence of an increasing number of clinical subspecialties reflecting the variety of settings in which practitioners find themselves based. Although undoubtedly many neuropsychologists would still consider themselves generalists, an increasing number of clinicians have established narrowly focused niches requiring specialized knowledge and skills. Whereas pediatric and geriatric neuropsychology and forensic neuropsychology are emerging as bona fide subspecialties, clinicians who work primarily in psychiatric settings, cross-cultural or bilingual settings, or settings with patients who suffer from significant primary or sensory disabilities must develop expertise in resolving problems that have the potential to severely limit the validity of the available array of testing instruments. In this chapter, we present some of the issues and concerns a clinician needs to address when asked to assess some of these specialty populations.

ASSESSMENT OF CHILDREN

A number of issues are critical in the neuropsychological assessment of children. Rapid Reference 6.1 summarizes the factors that complicate the interpretation of neuropsychological test results in children. First and foremost, the assessment of children is complicated by the fact that children are evolving in their physical and emotional development and in the knowledge structures needed to perform the cognitive functions that must be assessed. Such abilities as attention, language, memory, self-control, and even motor skills rapidly change from birth to adolescence, reflecting the process of neural development occurring in those years. Although certainly normal developmental trends have been documented, the rates of cognitive development may vary widely, particularly in the first 5 or 6 years of life. In some cases, a few months or even weeks can make the difference

≡ Rapid Reference 6.1

Complicating Factors in the Neuropsychological Assessment of Children

- Children are evolving in their physical and emotional development and in their knowledge structures needed to perform the cognitive functions that must be assessed.
- Children differ in their exposure to environments that allow opportunities to acquire new information and skills.
- The database of lesion-based studies for children is far more limited than that available for adults.
- The presence of a deficit in a child is not necessarily associated with the same lesions producing the same deficit in an adult.
- The rate of physiological verification in most clinical settings is low for developmental or academic difficulties in children.
- Parents may not be accurate informants about their child's academic performance.
- On average, children may have greater difficulties than adults sitting through lengthy evaluations because of age-dependent distractibility and fidgety behavior.

in the emergence of a function or ability such as a motor skill or language. While undergoing biological development, children are exposed to environments that present the opportunity to acquire new information and skills. Such exposure may also vary tremendously across individuals. Adult neuropsychological tests are designed to use a standard range of exposure to common facts and information. For example, verbal memory tasks are often designed using words that are controlled for frequency of appearance in written materials and degree of interrelationship or associative strength. The statistics used to compute these variables known to affect memory performance are based on reading materials available to adults and may not represent similar levels of difficulty to a child. Basic skills (e.g., reading, writing, following instructions, and sitting still for an interview) that are usually developed during the elementary school years may not be established in younger children. For these reasons, in most cases it is not sufficient to collect norms for children using the materials developed for an adult test. A test with items that allow for valid neuropsychological predictions and good sensitivity in a teenager or young adult is often inappropriate for use even with older children. A test that is sensitive and specific to the effects of brain dysfunction in older, verbally mature children is usually of no use in the assessment of brain dysfunction in preverbal children or even preschool children.

Test developers can be sensitive to these issues, and numerous tests are designed specifically for use with developing children (e.g., the NEPSY-II). Some developers have attempted to design tests that appear to share content and construct validity with an analogous adult test. The best examples of such tests are again those used to assess IQ, with the Wechsler series the most explicitly designed to provide normative and construct continuity from preschool children to adults.

An even more difficult issue confronting the pediatric neuropsychologist is figuring out how these materials may be used to assess brain functions in children. Although adult neuropsychology—for better or worse—stands on a large accumulated database of lesion-based studies allowing for the development of numerous hypotheses about brain organization in adults, such data are far less available for children. A large literature examines neuropsychological test performance in children with developmental disorders and various forms of acquired brain disorders; however, the diseases and events that most commonly produce the focal lesions that produce effects on behavior and have been studied in adults are far less common in children. Although it is tempting to draw an analogy between similar behavioral disturbances that may be exhibited by both children and adults during the course of a neuropsychological examination, these behavioral disturbances are not necessarily comparable. A particular test result may reflect interactions between changes in normal biological development, incomplete acquisition of knowledge, and the focal effects of a lesion. Neuropsychological data should not be used to make predictions for children in the same way as for adults unless specific data warrant such predictions. The presence of a change in language, memory, or executive functions in a child is not necessarily associated with the same lesions that produce such deficits in adults.

Although neuropsychologists are often asked to evaluate the effects of documented brain damage in children, the most common referral question for clinicians who assess young patients concerns the evaluation of developmental or academic difficulties when no clear-cut event

CAUTION

Similar behavioral disturbances exhibited by an adult and a child may not mean the same thing. A particular test result may reflect interactions between two or more of the following: changes in normal biological development, incomplete acquisition of knowledge, and the focal effects of a lesion.

or disease state can be physiologically verified. In these cases, the choice to use neuropsychological test data to make predictions about the presence of a structural focal deficit should be made with great care and conservatism. The data supporting such assertions are in many cases nonexistent and show a very low rate of physiological verification in most clinical settings. The issues surrounding how such data should be used are complex and beyond the scope of this text. The reader is thus cautioned and advised to consult specialty pediatric neuropsychology texts to learn what scientifically verifiable information can be derived from neuropsychological tests in a pediatric population.

Neuropsychological batteries with children typically include some evaluation of educational achievement, particularly in the domains of reading, spelling, and arithmetic processes. Tests such as the Wide Range Achievement Test—Fourth Revision (WRAT-4; Wilkinson & Robertson, 2006); the Wechsler Individual Achievement Test—Second Edition (WIAT-II; Wechsler, 2001a); the Woodcock–Johnson III Normative Update (WJ III NU; Woodcock, McGrew, & Mather, 2007); and the Kaufman Assessment Battery for Children, Second Edition (Kaufman & Kaufman, 2004a); or the Kaufman Test Educational Achievement, Second Edition (Kaufman & Kaufman, 2004c) might be included. These tests are described in Chapter 4. The clinician should also have detailed information about the child's academic performance. Note that in many cases parents may not be accurate informants about their child's academic performance. The neuropsychologist should obtain recent school records whenever possible, especially any special education records. When the clinician is asked to sort out the effects of a recent neurological illness and longer standing abilities, it may be necessary to evaluate the entire school record to plot the overall course of the child's cognitive development.

A common diagnostic question for which children are increasingly referred for neuropsychological evaluation is the presence of attention-deficit/hyperactivity disorder (ADHD). Although children who obtain this diagnosis sometimes perform poorly on neuropsychological tests, these measures have not been shown to be useful in making the diagnosis itself because of a lack of specificity. The diagnosis of ADHD is currently best made based on behavioral description and history using the *Diagnostic and Statistical Manual of Mental Disorders, Fourth Edition—Text Revision* (*DSM-IV-TR*; American Psychiatric Association, 2000) symptom criteria with the goal of observing consistent patterns of behavior across various environments. In the case of ADHD, the clinician should obtain appropriate data from the child's parents and teachers about behavior patterns at home, at school, and, if possible, in other relevant settings. Several standardized inventories are designed for such purposes, including the Attention Deficit/Hyperactivity Disorder

Test (Gilliam, 1995), the Conners' 3rd Edition (Connors, 2008), and the Behavior Assessment System for Children, Second Edition (Reynolds & Kamphaus, 2004). More information about these measures can be found in Chapter 4. Neuropsychological assessment, although not diagnostic of ADHD, can, of course, provide evidence (or lack, thereof) of the interference of disturbed attention on performance.

Maintaining cooperation and motivation is particularly important in children, who typically cannot sit and attend to testing as long as most adults. Signs of fatigue, wandering attention, and distractibility must be monitored constantly when children are being tested. Extraneous motor activity and some distractibility may be age appropriate and can potentially undermine the reliability of test performance, even in relatively normal children. In the case of some developmental abnormalities and conditions such as ADHD, distractibility may undermine a clinician's ability to obtain reliable test results that can be used for any purpose other than confirming the presence

CAUTION

Neuropsychological tests have not been shown to be useful in making the diagnosis of ADHD. The diagnosis of ADHD at this time is best made on the basis of behavioral description and history using the symptom criteria specified in *DSM-IV-TR*. Support for the interference of attentional problems on cognitive tasks may become available in neuropsychological evaluation, however.

of the deficit in maintaining attention. In these cases, test sessions may have to be shortened considerably, with the provision of breaks and opportunities to move around before testing is resumed.

Rapid Reference 6.2 offers some general considerations necessary for the neuropsychological assessment of children. The Annotated Bibliography at the end

≡ Rapid Reference 6.2

General Considerations in the Neuropsychological Assessment of Children

- Select tests appropriate to the child's age and validated for the desired assessment purpose.
- Gather birth, developmental, medical, psychological, social, and family history from the child's parent or caregiver.
- Corroborate history by requesting and reviewing available records.

(continued)

- Plan the testing session(s) to accommodate the reduced attention span and fidgetiness of some children, and keep distractions to a minimum.
- Work to make the child feel at ease during testing.
- If necessary, especially for very young children, allow a parent to be present at the beginning of an evaluation but avoid administering standardized tests before the child acclimates.
- Encourage the child to be as cooperative as possible.
- Provide encouragement and praise for effort.
- Know the tests to be administered to allow the session to progress smoothly.
- Remember to be cautious when interpreting the deficits seen in children. The deficits seen in children may not occur for the same reasons they do in adults.

of this book includes several texts useful in the neuropsychological assessment of the child.

BILINGUALISM AND CULTURAL ISSUES

The vast majority of neuropsychological tests in use today were originally published in English and normed in the United States. Although some tests originated in other languages such as French (e.g., the Rey Auditory Verbal Learning Test; Rey, 1958) and Italian (the Token Test; De Renzi & Vignolo, 1962), these instruments have been translated into English and renormed using an American population to attain widespread use in the United States or Canada. Performance on these tests depends not only on some mastery of the American dialect of English but also on exposure to experiences and customs that are intrinsic to Western culture. This should not be surprising because the tests are products of the cultural origins and language of their developers. These tests are not necessarily invalid when used outside the cultural and linguistic context in which they are developed. One cannot assume, however, that neuropsychological tests developed in the United States and normed on primarily monolingual English-speaking Americans will retain similar levels of sensitivity and specificity when translated and applied outside this culture. Although an increasing number of neuropsychological tests have been translated and renormed to be used with native speakers in their countries of origin, few data address the critical issue of using English-based tests on individuals who are bilingual and who live a significant portion of their lives speaking languages other than English. These individuals may appear conversationally fluent in both languages, but they may not have comparable levels of exposure as demographically similar monolinguals to information in either language. The data that exist for these populations are contradictory and allow little consistent comparison of similar tests across different bilingual groups. Some data do suggest that some Spanish-speaking bilinguals may be disadvantaged in performance on some tests (Navarrete, 1999), and some bilingual Chinese speakers may be advantaged on others (Hsieh & Tori, 1993). Kaufman (1994) presents data indicating that a large majority of Hispanic children, even those who speak English adequately, showed large differences on the WISC-III between their Verbal Scale IQs (VIQs) and Performance Scale IQs (PIQs) in favor of their PIQs. These studies concerning different kinds of bilingual individuals taking different kinds of tests also vary in subject selection procedures so that the range of age, education, and socioeconomic status of subjects cannot even be compared across studies. Tests that are translated into a second language may work appropriately when used among native monolingual speakers of the language but may not correct the potential inaccuracies that can occur in testing bilingual individuals. Even though the latest Wechsler Intelligence Scales for children and adults no longer contain the VIQ-PIQ structure of previous Wechsler Intelligence Scales, many subtests have significant language demands that could be expected to influence the performances of bilingual individuals.

Even when language is not the primary issue, data suggest that an individual's ethnicity may in itself affect performance on neuropsychological tests. Although it is not clear why members of some groups score more poorly (or at superior levels) than others, a significant number of studies demonstrate ethnic group differences on IQ, language, and achievement tests, even when individuals tested are monolingual English speakers. These differences can potentially affect both the sensitivity and specificity of the neuropsychological tests that have only been normed on the general majority population. Because of the greater likelihood of false positive classifications of impairment for individuals who are members of ethnic groups with tests scores lower than the population for whom the norms are obtained, it is becoming increasingly important to obtain separate norms for some of the larger ethnic groups in the United States. The issue of separate norms is particularly important for African Americans, who constitute a large ethnic minority group in the United States. African Americans frequently perform more poorly on some neuropsychological tests than the majority population. The reason for this is not clear, but this group difference has evoked a range of responses, including a justifiable sensitivity to the political implications of such differences. Social and political arguments have been made both for and against the development and use of separate norms for African Americans; however, most admit that at least under current circumstances, separate norms are critical to ensure the accurate interpretation of neuropsychological test results.

Flanagan and Kaufman (2009) present the Culture–Language Matrix (Flanagan, Ortiz, & Alfonso, 2007) as a tool clinicians can use to evaluate the influence of language and culture on WISC-IV test performances. The Culture–Language Matrix has the advantage of informing the clinician about the degree of linguistic demand and cultural loading for the WISC-IV subtests allowing an analysis of performances on subtests with the lowest cultural loading and linguistic demand (i.e., Matrix Reasoning and Cancellation) versus those with the highest cultural loading and linguistic demand (i.e., Information, Similarities, Vocabulary, Comprehension, and Word Reasoning) so that any systematic effect can be determined and taken into account in the interpretation of the test results. In Appendix D of *Essentials of Cross-Battery Assessment, Second Edition*, Flanagan, Ortiz, and Alfonso (2007) offer test-specific culture–language matrices for multiple standardized norm-referenced tests, including the WAIS-III, WISC-IV, WPPSI-III, WJ III, SB5, KABC-II, KBIT-2, RIAS, CMS, and WMS-III (see Chapter 4 for these tests), to determine the influence of English language proficiency and degree of acculturation on test performances. The Annotated Bibliography at the end of this book describes other textbooks that are also useful to consult when bilingual and cultural issues affect a neuropsychological evaluation.

> **DON'T FORGET**
> ....
> Neuropsychological tests may underestimate language-based and other cognitive abilities in bilingual children and adults.

> **DON'T FORGET**
> ....
> Neuropsychological test results may not generalize across different cultures.

GERONEUROPSYCHOLOGY

Adults over age 65 are the fastest growing population requiring neuropsychological assessment. Even 25 years ago tests were rarely published with norms for adults in their 70s and older. Today, however, many tests are published with norms for adults aged between 70 and 90 years. This change reflects the general demographic shift caused by the large swelling in birth rate that occurred after World War II and the slow but continuous increase in life expectancy since that time. Projections indicate that by the year 2020 the United States will have almost 54 million adults over the age of 65. Furthermore, the population over 75 is projected to be close to 23 million, and the population over 85 is projected to approach 10 million (Centers for Disease Control, 2005). As age increases, so does the presence of diseases that have an impact on cognition. It has been estimated that Alzheimer's disease affects approximately 19.5% of adults aged 75 to 79, with cerebrovascular disease affecting another 8% of adults ages 75 to 84 (Cummings & Coffey, 2000).

As might be expected, neuropsychological assessment of the geriatric patient presents its own issues and challenges; these are summarized in Rapid Reference 6.3. Again, the primary issue is the availability of appropriate norms for tests. The collection of accurate norms for neuropsychological tests in older adults has been hampered by the elusiveness of a clear-cut understanding of what is normal aging and what is not normal aging. Many of the data that are collected comparing different age groups is cross-sectional—that is, data collected from random samples of individuals who have attained different ages within the same time period. Cross-sectional data tend to exaggerate differences between individuals of different ages because their test-taking abilities may reflect variations in the experiences of individuals maturing during different historical eras. In

≡ Rapid Reference 6.3

Complicating Factors in the Neuropsychological Assessment of Older Adults

Appropriate norms may not be available:

- Norms gathered through cross-sectional data may be affected by cohort effects, reflecting differences in the experiences of individuals maturing during different historical eras.
- Because elderly normal populations may have nonneurological medical conditions, neuropsychological tests may have less specificity in older than younger adults.
- Test norms that include data from age-matched individuals with normal brain functioning may include a number of individuals with early signs of dementia or mild cognitive impairment, leading to diminished sensitivity as a function of increased age.
- Tests may be hampered by floor effects.

Elderly patients may be less able to tolerate testing:

- They may fatigue more easily than average younger or middle-aged adults.
- They may suffer from uncomfortable chronic medical conditions.
- They may suffer from undiagnosed but common conditions such as mild depression and sleep deprivation.

addition to such *cohort effects,* data are confounded by the greater likelihood that the older sample is affected by the early stages of diseases that become more prevalent with age. Longitudinal studies, although still affected by the development of diseases as individuals age and sampling bias related to attrition of sample sizes, sometimes eliminate or drastically reduce age differences that are apparent with cross-sectional data. It is likely that geriatric assessment could be improved with items that are created to be more age- and cohort-specific, but the major test publishing houses have not produced such measures.

The problem of what constitutes normal or healthy aging is a serious one for geriatric neuropsychological assessment. The motivation, energy level, and willingness of a geriatric patient to cooperate with the assessment process may be limited by various systemic illnesses, peripheral sensory and motor loss, and the presence of chronic pain. Such conditions as deafness (especially the loss of higher and high-middle-range auditory frequencies), macular degeneration, cataracts, and diabetic retinopathy increase in prevalence with age and have the potential to impair neuropsychological test performance independent of any actual compromise of brain function. For this reason, neuropsychological tests may have far less specificity in older than younger adults. If individuals with these disorders are included in greater numbers in the normal sample used for validation, the criterion score for classifying patients as having brain dysfunction may be too conservative, and the sensitivity of the test will be compromised. Without general health screening in the process of selecting normal subjects, the point at which individuals are classified as impaired may require a higher score than is optimal.

Also, individuals with undiagnosed illnesses that affect the brain can sometimes be included in normal samples. Many geriatric neuropsychological tests are designed and validated to detect the presence of Alzheimer's disease, the most prevalent of the degenerative dementing illnesses. In 1996, Sliwinski, Lipton, Buschke, and Stewart found that many of the individuals who fell one standard deviation below the mean of a group of subjects classified as normal in a memory test validation study went on to receive the diagnosis of dementia 6 to 12 months later. This result suggests that the test norms for older adults may be too conservative. Furthermore, because the prevalence of Alzheimer's disease itself increases with age, test norms that include data from randomly sampled age-matched normally functioning individuals may be expected to include larger numbers of individuals with the early signs of dementia, leading to diminished sensitivity of these tests as a function of the increased age of the individual.

There is a growing body of literature to suggest that some of these individuals belong in a new diagnostic category called "mild cognitive impairment" (MCI). Such individuals have complaints of deficits in memory or other cognitive domains but are nevertheless able to function in their day-to-day lives with relative independence, the latter being the critical feature distinguishing MCI from mild dementia. A recent longitudinal study (Geslani, Tierney, Herrmann, & Szalai, 2005) found that 35% of a sample of 161 patients with a 3-month history of "memory" complaints met criteria for MCI. Of these patients, 41% went on to meet criteria for dementia of the Alzheimer's type after a 1-year follow-up, and 64% went on to meet criteria for dementia after a 2-year follow-up. Because this was a sample of study participants who were selected on the basis of the presence of memory complaints, they were more likely to meet the criteria for MCI than a representative sample of older adults. For the same reason, the reported conversion rates may also be considerably greater in this sample than in the general population within that age range. However, studies such as this suggest that the symptoms of dementia may be preceded by a measureable diminishment in cognitive abilities that may be apparent years before diagnosis.

Finally, an increasing body of data suggests that elevations in such cardiovascular risk factors as blood pressure may impair performance on some neuropsychological tests (Brady, Spiro, McGlinchey-Berroth, Milberg, & Gaziano, 2001; Kuo et al., 2005, 2006; Pugh, Milberg, & Lipsitz, 2001), particularly those associated with executive functions, even when the affected individual has not received a diagnosis of dementia or cognitive impairment. Many other diseases affecting the central nervous system also increase in prevalence as adults age, including strokes, neoplasm, and other neurodegenerative disease, such as Parkinsonism. Such observations highlight why the health status of the individuals comprising the normal samples should be known and specified in the validity studies of neuropsychological tests used with older adults.

Motivation and cooperation must be continuously monitored with older patients because they may fatigue more easily and have a lower frustration tolerance than the average younger or middle-aged adult. Although healthy older adults may be able to tolerate testing as well as younger adults, the prevalence of potentially uncomfortable chronic conditions (such as arthritis and other orthopedic impairments) increases with age, as does the presence of primary sensory impairments in vision and hearing. Furthermore, typically undiagnosed but common conditions such as mild depression, anxiety, and sleep deprivation also increase in prevalence with age. The presence of these conditions may affect the older patient's stamina and ability to maintain attention to the procedures, reducing the reliability of test scores and the reliability and specificity of neuropsychological tests as measures of brain dysfunction, damage, or disease.

As with young children, it may be necessary to employ shorter test sessions with older adults. In fact, whenever possible the clinician should attempt to find the briefest, most efficient, and most relevant tests when testing older adults. Unfortunately, few neuropsychological tests have been designed specifically with the geriatric individual in mind. Even well-normed tests that were originally designed for the range of performance for younger adults may not provide a sufficient range of difficulty to capture the typical level of performance in older adults. Because of the interaction of normal aging effects with disease, many tests show a floor effect with adults whose impairments may only be mild relative to their age cohort. If even mildly impaired adults perform at the bottom of the possible range of a test, the measure will not be able to discriminate between mild and more severely impaired patients and will show a high rate of false positive errors.

The problem of floor effects has plagued such measures as the 16-item California Verbal Learning Test, which has poor specificity in older adults: It classifies a large number of relatively healthy adults as having memory impairments. For this reason, test developers have produced a nine-item *dementia version* that is much more appropriate for this population (Libon et al., 1996). A 9-item short form has also now been incorporated into the CVLT-II (Delis, Kramer, Kaplan, & Ober, 2000). The Hopkins Verbal Learning Test-Revised is also a list learning test that was designed to be more appropriate for this age group (see Chapter 4). Floor effects hamper even tests such as the WMS-IV. A person aged 76 years who recalls only five of the verbal paired associates after a delay will earn a scaled score of 6, placing performance at the 9th percentile and in the low-average range. Should this performance be interpreted as an example of the rapid decay that is the hallmark of Alzheimer's disease, or should it be seen as the expected performance of a 76-year-old with low average premorbid ability? The answer to this question will have to come from other data—perhaps historical data or disease history—because a floor effect prevents the score from being of particular use. To accommodate the growing number of elderly individuals in the population, test revisions and adaptations need to be forthcoming for many of the classic neuropsychological measures that have good sensitivity to neuropsychological deficits in younger adults.

In some cases in which referral and history strongly indicate that the patient is suffering from progressive deterioration of cognitive functions, neuropsychological batteries with elderly patients may include a brief screening battery such as the Dementia Rating Scale—2 (Jurica, Leitten, & Mattis, 2001) or the Neurobehavioral Cognitive Status Examination (Kiernan, Mueller, Langston, & Van Dyke, 1987) and, in some cases, the Folstein Mini-Mental State Exam (MMSE; Folstein, Folstein, & McHugh, 2001). Great caution should be exercised in using such batteries, however, because they have generally poor sensitivity and specificity and often are unable to provide reliable information about the specific cognitive domains affected (Milberg, 1996). These measures may be useful in cases in which the base rate of the presence of dementia is high and in tracking gross changes in a patient's cognitive status over time.

In those cases of assessment in which an initial diagnosis must be made, it is advisable to use a battery consisting of some formal and well-standardized measures of attention, memory, language, executive functions, and perception to target the critical areas for the diagnosis of the most common neuropsychological disorders in the elderly. One of the first such batteries to be shown to have good sensitivity for the diagnosis of Alzheimer's disease was the Consortium to Establish a Registry for Alzheimer's Disease (CERAD) Battery (Welsh et al., 1994). The CERAD consists of a word fluency or word list generation task; Boston Naming Test items; word list memory with immediate, delayed, and recognition trials; and a number of other tests with documented validity in this population. This battery includes the Folstein MMSE to help compare an individual with other patients who have a known diagnosis of Alzheimer's disease (McKhann, 1984). The CERAD is still employed in many research projects on dementia and represents a reasonable prototype for constructing a battery of neuropsychological tests to be used for geriatric patients because it samples the domains of memory, language, and executive functions. However, because it was designed to detect the symptoms of dementia associated with Alzheimer's disease (primarily amnestic in nature), it may not be sensitive to other sources of cognitive impairment in older adults (e.g., cognitive impairment related to vascular disease). Therefore, neuropsychological batteries designed to assess older adults should include a broader range of executive function measures such as the Trail Making Test, Stroop Color and Word Test, and, in some cases, Wisconsin Card Sorting Test. The Repeatable Battery for the Assessment of Neuropsychological Status (Randolph, 1998; see Chapter 4) is also a relatively brief battery of tests that is well normed through 89 years and has an alternate equivalent form that makes it suitable for repeated testing and tracking change over time.

In addition, because mild depression is fairly common in older adults, most batteries should include at least a screen for depression such as the Geriatric Depression Scale (Brink et al., 1982; Yesavage et al., 1983).

≡ Rapid Reference 6.4

General Considerations in the Neuropsychological Assessment of Elderly Adults

- Obtain a full history from the patient and a family member or caregiver.
- Employ a shorter test session.
- Find the briefest, most efficient, and most relevant tests.

(continued)

- If suspicious of a progressive deterioration of cognitive function, include a brief screening battery (e.g., Mattis Dementia Rating Scale, 2nd ed. [DRS-2]; Neurobehavioral Cognitive Status Examination [NCSE]; Mini-Mental State Examination [MMSE]).
- When an initial diagnosis must be made, use formal and well-standardized measures of attention, memory, language, executive functions, and perception to target the critical areas that can contribute to diagnosing the most common neuropsychological disorders in the elderly (e.g., Repeatable Battery of Neuropsychological Status [RBANS]).
- Include a screen for depression.

Rapid Reference 6.4 summarizes the general considerations to be made when performing neuropsychological assessments with elderly adults. In addition, consult the Annotated Bibliography at the end of this book for textbooks relevant to neuropsychological assessment of the elderly patient.

PATIENTS WITH PSYCHIATRIC DISORDERS

Many of the problems concerning the testing of children and older adults also affect the interpretation of the neuropsychological test results for patients with significant psychotic or affective disorders. It is well known that patients with schizophrenia, bipolar disorder, severe obsessive–compulsive disorder, and many other psychiatric conditions show deficits on neuropsychological tests. Although many of these illnesses may have their origins in abnormalities of brain function, they produce symptoms that have an impact on test performance that is not a direct result of the underlying pathology itself.

Psychiatric patients may perform poorly because they are distracted by auditory hallucinations rather than because of a deficit in a specific cognitive function that may typically be measured by the test. Alternatively, as a result of the neurovegetative signs of depression they may work slowly and without full effort during testing, reducing their scores for reasons other than brain dysfunction. As a general rule, patients show greater cognitive deficits as the severity of their thought disorder and affective symptoms increases. Many tests that show excellent specificity when asked to distinguish individuals with brain dysfunction from individuals without brain dysfunction show dismaying levels of false positive errors when asked to distinguish patients with brain dysfunction from patients with psychiatric diagnoses.

The most important adaptation of neuropsychological assessment to this population is the inclusion of interview questions and assessment instruments designed to evaluate the nature and severity of the psychiatric illness. Although it may be advisable to at least screen for the presence of psychiatric symptoms in any evaluation of an adult, detailed data on the presence of hallucinations, delusions, severe depression, mania or hypomania, severe anxiety, phobic symptoms, and the presence of obsessive–compulsive disorder must be available before any

> **CAUTION**
>
> Many tests that show good specificity in distinguishing individuals with brain dysfunction from those without brain dysfunction show high levels of false positive errors when used to distinguish patients with brain dysfunction from patients with psychiatric disorders.

neuropsychological test protocol can be interpreted. In some settings, these data may have been collected by other practitioners and may be available in the patient's medical records.

When working in a psychiatric setting or when there is a strong suspicion that an individual has a psychiatric diagnosis by history or because of the referral question, the neuropsychologist should include test instruments such as the Minnesota Multiphasic Personality Inventory—2 (MMPI-2; Butcher, Dahlstrom, Graham, Tellegen, & Koemmer, 1989), the MMPI-2-Restructured Form (MMPI-2-RF: Ben-Porath & Tellegen, 2008), the Beck Scales such as the Beck Depression Inventory—II (A. T. Beck, Steer, & Brown, 1996) and the Beck Anxiety Inventory (A. T. Beck & Steer, 1993), or other personality or symptom inventories relevant to the question at hand. For the individual who has a long history of abuse or who has been exposed to a traumatic event, the Trauma Symptom Inventory (Briere, 1995) is useful for delineating posttraumatic symptoms. Tests that can be used for the report of emotional symptoms and personality are described in Chapter 4. Neuropsychological tests may still be used to provide a valid profile of abilities for psychiatric patients but should be used cautiously to predict the presence of brain dysfunction in this population. In the future, increasing the specificity of neuropsychological tests may be achieved through the use of multiple longitudinal measurements to determine changes in performance over time. Rapid rates of decline may be used to make inferences about the presence of underlying pathology with greater accuracy than a single data point. This approach is suggested only hypothetically and has not received formal scientific support at this time.

> **DON'T FORGET**
>
> When psychiatric problems may be an issue, include measures of emotional report and personality in the test battery.

As with the other special populations discussed in this chapter, patients with psychiatric problems require careful monitoring for variations in motivation and compliance that can affect test reliability and validity. Like geriatric and pediatric patients, these individuals may require briefer test sessions and frequent reestablishment of attention to the task at hand.

MALINGERING

The vast majority of individuals who are referred for an evaluation by a neuropsychologist can be expected to cooperate with the examination and perform the various tasks comprising a battery of tests to the best of their ability. Although some individuals may fatigue easily, are distractible, or are otherwise limited in their ability to maintain attention to the examination for long periods, they still may be assumed to be expending a reasonable effort to perform well when they are focused on the tasks. This is particularly true in the typical clinical referral, in which patients have little reason to perform poorly. Sometimes, however, individuals who are referred for testing do not try to perform the tests to the best of their abilities or may actually try to perform poorly. Some of these individuals insidiously try to deceive the examiner into concluding that they suffer from deficits or symptoms (or a higher degree of deficits or symptoms) that in reality they do not.

Although included in the *DSM-IV-TR*, *malingering* is not technically a psychiatric disease. Malingering, as defined by the *DSM-IV-TR*, is the intentional or voluntary production or exaggeration of symptoms or deficits or the purposeful suppression of ability for the purposes of secondary gain, such as economic reward in litigation. Malingering is not an all-or-nothing phenomenon; rather, it occurs on various levels. Some individuals have symptoms that they exaggerate, others have had symptoms and maintain them after their resolution, others have had symptoms that predate an event but consciously (and incorrectly) attribute them to a later event, and still others actually simulate or produce deficits. Malingering can involve not only the obvious outright production of false symptoms, which is more rare, but also purposeful suboptimal effort and suppression of ability. Evidence of malingering can be gathered by examining performances on tests specifically designed to measure effort and validity, as well as from unusual neuropsychological test findings and especially from inconsistencies in performance. As is evident from Rapid Reference 6.5, the inconsistencies may be seen between test findings and functional status, between test findings and the degree or type of injury, between different tests measuring similar functions, and between examinations.

Malingering is different from somatoform disorders in that the latter involves the involuntary production of symptoms. In somatoform disorders such as

≡ *Rapid Reference 6.5*

Inconsistencies That Raise the Suspicion of Malingering

- Lack of consistency in the presented deficits
- Lack of consistency between the patient's performances across similar tasks
- Lack of consistency between a patient's verbal report of symptoms and observed behavior
- Lack of consistency between reported symptoms and clinical findings

conversion disorder, psychological factors are assumed to play a role in the production of symptoms (even when those psychological factors cannot be specifically identified) and medical circumstances cannot fully account for a patient's symptoms. Patients adopting a sick or invalid role and emphasizing medical conditions instead of addressing psychological stress may also perform poorly in testing because of decreased effort. Complicating the differential diagnosis, patients with somatoform disorders are also known to do poorly on tests of effort or symptom validity. Understandably, then, sometimes the different causes of low scores on symptom validity tests cannot be differentiated: Just because there is evidence of poor effort, or even medically unexplained symptoms, the question of volitional withholding of effort, or simulated or exaggeration of symptoms may not be easily answered. In clinical situations, the evidence of poor effort or symptom exaggeration should be viewed as part of the broader picture of the patient's psychological health and as problems to be addressed with appropriate counseling or therapy.

The most common situations in which deception or malingering occurs are those in which the individual perceives some actual or secondary gain. Evidence of malingering is most common, for example, among individuals involved in a criminal investigation (especially when pleas of insanity or diminished capacity are involved), civil litigation, or in the course of insurance disability or worker's compensation claims. In other instances, the perceived gain may be of a more psychological or emotional nature, such as increased attention from health care providers or family members; outside the medicolegal arena, in cases such as this, the disorder is called *factitious disorder*. Factitious disorder is like malingering in that the production of symptoms is voluntary but different in that the only obvious secondary gain is the attention that appears to come from being treated as a patient. Because litigation by its very nature is accompanied by secondary

≡ Rapid Reference 6.6

Differential Diagnoses in Motivational Disorders

Malingering—the intentional exaggeration or production of symptoms or willful suboptimal effort or ability for the purpose of secondary gain

Somatoform Disorders—the involuntary production of symptoms in disorders in which psychological factors are assumed to play a role in the production of symptoms and medical circumstances cannot fully account for a patient's symptoms

Factitious Disorder—the intentional production of symptoms motivated by the patient's desire to assume the sick role rather than by a desire for external rewards

gain issues, in forensic cases, the area that typically must be explored is malingering rather than factitious disorder, which more often would present in a medical setting. Rapid Reference 6.6 sets out the *DSM-IV-TR* definitions for malingering versus somatoform disorders versus factitious disorder.

Clinicians who work in medicolegal or forensic settings and other situations in which the base rate of malingering is higher must include tests that are sensitive to motivation, effort, and compliance embedded within a standard battery of neuropsychological tests. Even clinicians who work in more typical neuropsychological settings in which such patients are more unusual nevertheless sometimes find themselves shocked and even hurt that an individual with whom they have entered into an implied contract of trust has tried to deceive them. Clinicians who do see such patients may have the tendency to overlook or underplay evidence of malingering or deception because they find it hard to believe. In addition, clinicians, who are accustomed to being hired by a client and assume the role of patient advocate may feel uncomfortable questioning a patient's motivation and effort. One of the most difficult aspects of dealing with malingering is how to report these findings in a way that is professional and in keeping with the patient's or client's interests. A direct accusation of malingering to a patient is potentially destructive, so the issue must be handled sensitively. The neuropsychologist must find a way to report this information in a manner that allows the client to receive proper treatment. In medicolegal cases, which require a routine examination of the issue of symptom validity, the neuropsychologist must report the information in appropriate ways, keeping in mind that some view the label of *malingerer* as the same as *fake*.

In any case, it is part of the neuropsychologist's responsibility to sort out the potential reasons for a patient's test performance by assessing the contribution of neurological, psychological, and motivational effects on the data. This information ultimately leads to the most appropriate treatment for the issues presented by the client.

To ensure that neuropsychological tests are interpreted accurately, the clinician should be aware of the need to investigate a referral's legal circumstances and to assess effort and symptom validity when warranted. Assessment of effort and compliance is also necessary in forensic evaluations, whether the individual was referred by a plaintiff's attorney or by the defense attorney. In any case, the collection of information about a client's legal history must be handled cautiously and tactfully, without undermining rapport and the clinical working relationship. Sometimes questions about legal factors are suggested naturally by the history of the reported disorder. Problems following an apparent accident or medical procedure are more likely to be affected by issues of effort and symptom validity than by stroke or dementing illnesses, for example.

Some clinicians include questions about ongoing or anticipated litigation or criminal investigations in standard personal history forms, interspersing these questions among less charged inquiries about academic and general medical history. Screening for litigation might begin with a question on the patient information form asking, "Is there litigation pending with regard to this matter?" Many individuals involved in such circumstances will not volunteer information about ongoing litigation or criminal charges unless directly asked and may only provide sufficient detail to answer the specific question at hand. Reports of what appear to be severe functional incapacities following seemingly innocuous circumstances (e.g., minor bumps on the head with no loss of consciousness and no concurrent impairment of mental status), however, or a pattern of increasingly severe symptoms months or years after an event that typically does not result in such progressive declines are circumstances that require careful investigation even when the patient has not been referred explicitly for an evaluation in the context of a legal investigation. When test performance is unexpectedly poor given the patient's office behavior; recent functional, academic, or work history; or the circumstances of the alleged causal event, the clinician should entertain the possibility of less than optimal effort as an explanation and should include in the battery tests that can specifically measure this possibility.

There are many so-called signs that circulate in the clinical lore as being useful in deciding whether a patient is performing with optimal effort or exaggerating pathology. These signs include the presence of overt suspiciousness or inappropriate anger at the clinician, excessive slowness during otherwise normal test performance, frequent complaints about the difficulty of the examination, requests for observers to be in the room during testing, wearing sunglasses indoors, the use of nonmedical canes, and even unexpectedly poor performances. These signs have, for the most part, not been validated scientifically and cannot be used in isolation to document the presence of a malingered performance. The presence of such behaviors, however, does raise the suspicion of malingering and should prompt clinicians to employ some objective methods for determining the level of effort and compliance of the client. These measures also can add to the whole clinical picture when integrated with the history, patient's behavior, and test findings.

Because more and more neuropsychologists in private practice are becoming involved in forensic work and because neuropsychology is now used frequently in the courtroom, the development of measures that are sensitive to motivation has been the focus of considerable research in recent years. The most common strategy for developing these measures has been to find tasks that are performed more poorly by simulators than by patients with actual brain dysfunction or brain lesions. In some cases, these are forced-choice, two-alternative tasks in which results at or below chance can signal purposefully poor effort. Other tests of malingering are designed to appear difficult but are actually so easy that even patients with severe brain injury can succeed. These concepts have been most successfully applied to the detection of malingered memory deficits, one of the most common domains vulnerable to deception or poor effort. A number of measures such as the Portland Digit Recognition Test (Binder, 1993) and the Test of Memory Malingering (Tombaugh, 1996) are based on the observation that even moderately to severely amnesic patients (i.e., patients with functionally incapacitating disorders of new learning) perform at nearly normal levels when given a simple forced-choice, immediate recognition memory task. Individuals who are asked to fake a memory deficit or are at risk for poor effort are more likely to perform such tasks at or near chance or beneath particular criterion levels that distinguish them from patients with bona fide memory impairments.

Multiple tests are available to help identify suspicious performances; these are described in Chapter 4. Several measures should be used in each case to determine whether a consistent pattern of findings occurs across tasks. It is also wise to use symptom validity tests measuring different cognitive domains because patients may choose to fail or give lesser effort only on those tasks that they see as relevant to their primary complaints.

Failures on specific tests of symptom validity are not the only means to judge the reliability and validity of test findings. One of the hallmarks of malingering is inconsistency: This should be assessed by comparing behavior during testing with behavior outside testing, by comparing consistency of level of deficit with expected level of deficit given known injury or disease, and by comparing consistency of performance across different tasks measuring the same functions. Consistency should also be examined by comparing reported symptoms and clinical findings. In addition, consistency should also be assessed by comparing performances on the same tasks during different examinations. When making these comparisons, however, the neuropsychologist should be sure to allow for changes in mood or medical status that could influence test effort in different situations.

An assessment of malingering requires a thorough examination of medical records and other documents. This independent information can be used to corroborate or discredit the patient's self-report. Sometimes reports by family members, friends, and coworkers can be used for corroboration; however, because these individuals may have reasons to be biased in their reports as well, this information should consequently be viewed cautiously.

The clinical interview can also be used in the assessment of malingering. The way a patient answers interview questions may raise suspicions of malingering. Patients may signal dissimulation by giving approximate answers, vague responses, or bizarre responses. They may try to avoid the interview or examination, approach the examiner with hostility, or resist answering questions. Patients' behavior during testing may also raise suspicions of malingering. Patients too eager to demonstrate their deficits, or those who appear to overact and dramatize their presentation, may be signaling dissimulation. Behavior during testing that contradicts reported symptoms, test findings, or both (e.g., a patient who can give a detailed personal history concerning recent events but who has a WMS-IV General Memory Index of 58) can also be a sign of malingering.

The best assessment for malingering is based on multiple sets of patient data. When suspicious of malingering, the neuropsychologist should evaluate historical information and be familiar with expected findings for the particular brain disorder or disease, as well as with the consistency or inconsistency of findings. The neuropsychologist should also evaluate the types of errors made by the patient in evaluation, looking out for errors occurring for the wrong reason or errors discrepant from those seen in patients with documented brain dysfunction. The neuropsychologist should also look for evidence of behaviors performed by the patient inconsistent with neuropsychological test findings, patient complaints, or both (e.g., individuals who complain that they get "lost" in their home but find their way to your office without any difficulty by subway). In addition, the neuropsychologist should evaluate the results of the neuropsychological tests and the specific tests of symptom validity. Particular attention to performances below chance levels is important in the assessment of malingering, because performances below chance levels imply the patient purposely chose at least some incorrect responses during the test. Attention should also be paid to signs on symptom validity tests with high specificity to malingering (see, for example, error types on the b Test or the Dot Counting Test; Boone, Lu, & Herzberg, 2002a, 2002b). In a recent survey of NAN neuropsychologists' beliefs and practices regarding the assessment of effort the most commonly used methods used to detect poor effort or malingering included severity and pattern of cognitive impairment discrepant with the condition; inconsistencies between and among self-report, records, and known behavior; improbable symptoms, improbable changes in test-retest scores; and scores below empirical cutoffs on specific tests of effort, including forced-choice tests (Sharland & Gfeller, 2007). Of the sample, 57% reported they frequently administered measures of effort in neuropsychological evaluations.

Rapid Reference 6.7 summarizes the commonly used signs and symptoms of malingering on tests of cognitive abilities (Tombaugh, 1996). The Annotated

---

≡ Rapid Reference 6.7

Commonly Used Qualitative Signs and Symptoms of Malingering on Tests of Cognitive Abilities

- Any disability that is disproportionate to the severity of the injury or illness
- Recognition scores that are relatively lower than recall scores on tests such as list learning
- Disproportionately impaired attention relative to learning and memory scores (e.g., WMS-III Working Memory Index lower than Immediate Memory Index)
- Failing easy items and passing more difficult ones (e.g., higher scores on backward versus forward digits; on Trails B vs. Trails A; on difficult paired associates versus easy paired associates)
- Unusually high frequency of "I don't know" responses
- Discrepancies between scores on tests measuring similar processes such as verbal or visual learning
- Inconsistencies between memory complaints and behavior observed during the test or outside the testing situation
- Near misses or approximate answers
- Pronounced decrements in delayed recall
- Chance- or near chance-level performance on forced-choice tasks
- Digit span scaled score of ≤4
- Inconsistent pattern between scores on tests and those expected from neurological illness or injury

Source: Test of Memory Malingering, by T. N. Tombaugh, 1996, New York: Multi-Health Systems. Copyright © 1996, Multi-Health Systems Inc. All rights reserved. In the USA, 908 Niagara Falls Blvd., North Tonawanda, NY 14120-2060, 1-800-456-3003. In Canada, 3770 Victoria Park Ave., Toronto, ON M2H 3M6, 1-800-268-6011. Internationally, 1-416-492-2627. Fax, 1-416-492-3343. Reproduced by permission.

Bibliography at the end of this book also includes multiple recently published textbooks that thoroughly explore the issue of malingering and a critical analysis of methods for evaluating malingering.

FORENSIC NEUROPSYCHOLOGICAL EVALUATIONS

Although this book is intended as a resource for the clinical neuropsychologist, the advice and guidance on how to select, administer, score, and interpret neuropsychological tests can also be applied to neuropsychological evaluations that occur in the context of forensic applications. Performing neuropsychological investigations for legal purposes, such as civil or criminal lawsuits, competency hearings, disability evaluations, and workmen's compensation cases—to name a few—has become increasingly common so that many clinical neuropsychologists, even those who do not restrict their work to forensic cases, have had some opportunity to work on cases in which legal issues are involved. There are, however, some special issues that must be addressed for the neuropsychologist who provides expert opinions in legal cases.

One important consideration in forensic neuropsychology is the distinction between "treater" and "expert." A treater is a neuropsychologist hired by the patient or the patient's family to provide neuropsychological services and to serve as a consultant to a patient in a clinical setting and outside a legal setting. A treater's obligation is to the patient: A treater, by necessity, serves as the patient's advocate. An expert, on the other hand, is a neuropsychologist serving as a paid consultant specifically "to inform the attorney(s), as well as the "trier of fact" (e.g., a judge, jury, or hearing officer) of the neuropsychological findings and to present unbiased opinions and answers to specific questions pertinent to the case, based on relevant scientific and clinical evidence (i.e., to be an "advocate of the facts") of the case" (Board of Directors, American Academy of Clinical Neuropsychology [AACN], 2007; p. 215). An expert's obligation is to the facts. The clinician who first serves as a treater and then moves to the role of expert or who tries to combine those roles simultaneously is engaging in multiple relationships, which as defined by Standard 3.05(a) of the American Psychological Association Ethical Principles of Psychologists and Code of Conduct (2002) occurs "when a psychologist is in a professional role with a person and (1) at the same time is in another role with the same person . . . or (3) promises to enter into another relationship in the future with the person." Treaters are not independent of the patient and are subject to being viewed as biased in favor of the patient. The AACN Practice Guidelines (2007) advise: "A neuropsychologist who has treated a patient generally will decline to serve as an expert with regard to that case. If called upon to testify, the treating clinician responds in a manner consistent with the original role limitations and qualifies his/her role when answering questions about the patient" (p. 215). This means limiting testimony to any "facts" a neuropsychologist may have collected in a neuropsychological examination but refraining from offering expert opinions about causality and other issues.

In addition, whereas treaters will typically have a feedback session with a patient to explain the test results and offer advice and recommendations for treatment, the expert will not, even in cases in which they are retained by the plaintiff's attorney. The expert will generally put his or her findings in a report and present the findings to attorneys who retained the expert. The neuropsychologist may also be asked to present findings in a legally sanctioned forum such as a deposition or a courtroom.

A neuropsychologist working in a forensic setting must be thoroughly familiar with the legal responsibilities involved when serving as an expert witness. Forensic neuropsychologists must be prepared to be challenged on their credentials to serve as an expert (e.g., education and clinical training, degrees, research experience, board certification, etc.), and the scope of their testimony (e.g., their ability to measure and define changes in cognitive function or determine whether these changes were caused by brain damage). The expert may also be challenged on the scientific basis and relevance of his or her testimony. The latter is known as the "Daubert Challenge" based on a landmark Supreme Court case that defined the conditions surrounding the admissibility of scientific evidence in court.

Rather than simply offering conclusions and recommendations as a neuropsychologist would do with a patient in a clinical case, the forensic neuropsychologist must typically render opinions to a reasonable degree of neuropsychological or scientific certainty. Therefore, the neuropsychologist offering the opinion must ensure that he or she is up-to-date on the scientific literature pertaining to the issue at hand and to neuropsychological test instruments. Direct review of primary sources is required and, in some cases, consultation with other experts in the area may be necessary. In addition, because of the nonspecificity of neuropsychological tests, the forensic neuropsychologist must thoroughly investigate a forensic case by reviewing medical records and other documents, by interviewing the plaintiff, and, in some instances (and where this is permitted) interviewing collateral sources, and by neuropsychological evaluation, review of prior neuropsychological evaluations, or both. In some cases, another neuropsychological evaluation is not required, and investigations will be limited to review of medical records and other documents, including the deposition transcript of the plaintiff and the raw test data and report of another neuropsychologist.

Forensic neuropsychological evaluations generally require an extensive review of medical records and other documents so that the neuropsychologist has the most complete picture possible available for his or her investigation. Clinicians new to forensic assessments will discover that there are considerably more records for review in a forensic evaluation than are typically seen in a nonforensic evaluation. This discrepancy in the types and number of records available for review in a forensic neuropsychological evaluation is another reason treaters should not become experts: Coming from the role of treater, their opinions are likely to be based on incomplete information. One further note on records: When it is apparent that missing records might be helpful for formulation of an opinion in a case (e.g., educational records), those records should be requested.

In a forensic evaluation, there are also rules to keep in mind when selecting the test battery. Whereas in the clinical setting a neuropsychologist might choose to test the limits on a procedure or use a laboratory-specific, nonstandardized, or novel approach to assessment of a particular skill to provide descriptive information about how an individual went about solving a problem, in the forensic setting, a neuropsychologist must use well-standardized tests with a sound scientific and normative basis that are appropriate for the particular individual and for the alleged disease, disorder, or injury. The forensic neuropsychologist must also be careful to choose norms that permit accurate interpretation of the test results with regard to the individual being examined.

A forensic neuropsychological evaluation must include a range of tests of effort and symptom validity. This is true whether the neuropsychologist has been retained by the plaintiff's attorney or by the defense attorney. Although these tests may not completely answer the question of whether the individual was applying maximum effort throughout the evaluation, the results will help to determine whether confidence can be had in the representativeness of the results of the individual's true level of functioning.

A particularly important issue in forensic evaluations is whether to permit third-party observers. Neuropsychologists are charged with responsibility for administering tests in a standardized fashion and protecting the test environment so that examinees can perform to the best of their ability without the added distraction of observers. The presence of third-party observers in the examination room during testing, including other neuropsychologists, introduces unknown variables into the testing environment and can cause a confounding level of distraction. It has long been recognized that observing an individual's test performance can alter that performance by improving it or worsening it. This interference occurs regardless of the method of observation (e.g., physically present, audio or videotaping, or through a one-way mirror; McCaffrey, Lynch, & Yanz, 2005). The presence of third parties in the examination room during testing violates the procedures for the administration of neuropsychological tests established by the test developers and publishers and compromises the neuropsychologist's ability to adhere to the American Psychological Association (APA) Ethical Principles of Psychologists and Code of Conduct (2002) regarding test administration. Because the scientific integrity of the tests and testing situation may be subject to challenge and impeachment in a forensic case, the request for the presence of third-party observers is "strongly discouraged" (AACN, 2001; Board of Directors, AACN, 2007; National Academy of Neuropsychology [NAN], 2000a) and should be resisted.

Another issue that often arises in forensic cases is whether to release raw test data to nonpsychologists. Neuropsychologists are required by the APA Ethical Principles of Psychologists and Code of Conduct (2002) to maintain test security. Because raw test data often overlap with test materials, requests from nonpsychologists for the raw test data often result in a conflict between adhering to the ethical principles and cooperating with the request. The *Administration and Scoring Manual* for the Wechsler Memory Scale-Fourth Edition (2009) specifies: "It is also the responsibility of the test user to ensure that the test materials, including the Record Forms, remain secure and are released only with written permission to professionals who will safeguard their proper use" (p. 8) One solution—in the absence of a court order—is to offer to send the raw test data to the opposing neuropsychologist. When informed of the reasons behind this solution, reasonable attorneys will usually agree to an exchange of raw test data between the neuropsychologists. In their Official Policy Statement approved October 5, 1999, NAN (2000b) also offers general guidelines for handling requests to release raw test data, recording, or reproducing test data.

One area in which the forensic evaluation is similar to the clinical evaluation concerns disclosures to the plaintiff at the beginning of an evaluation. It is important to make sure the plaintiff is informed about the nature of the assessment (i.e., evaluation only; not the standard doctor–patient relationship) who has retained you, the limits of confidentiality, (including who will and will not receive the report), and what the evaluation will entail. In addition, the examinee is informed that his or her responses will be shared with the referring party and included in any report generated from the evaluation and that it is important to give his or her best effort during testing. Neuropsychologists differ on whether they provide a specific warning that effort tests will be used (Sharland & Gfeller, 2007).

Rapid Reference 6.8 summarizes the general considerations important in forensic neuropsychological evaluations. The Annotated Bibliography at the end of this book contains a host of textbooks relevant to the topic of forensic neuropsychology.

≡ Rapid Reference 6.8

General Considerations in the Forensic Neuropsychological Evaluation

- Recognize the distinction between treater and expert. Refrain from being both a treater and an expert.
- Do not offer examinees advice or recommendations. Present evaluation findings in a report or in consultation with the referral source.
- Prepare for challenges on credentials, scope of testimony, and scientific basis and relevance of testimony.
- Be up-to-date on the scientific literature pertaining to the issues at hand and to the neuropsychological test instruments.
- Conduct a thorough investigation: Review medical records and other documents, interview patient and collateral sources (if necessary and possible), and administer neuropsychological tests (when necessary).
- Be prepared for an extensive review of medical records and other documents. Request missing records (e.g., educational records) that are important in understanding the case.
- Choose well-standardized neuropsychological tests with a sound scientific and normative basis.
- Include a range of tests of effort and symptom validity.
- Resist the inclusion of third party observers in the examination.
- Make a reasonable effort to protect test security.
- Openly disclose at the beginning of the evaluation the referral source, the limits of confidentiality, and the nature of the process.

🐾 TEST YOURSELF 🐾

1. **A test with items that will allow for valid neuropsychological predictions and good sensitivity in a teenager or young adult will often be inappropriate for use even with older children.**
   True or False?

2. **A test result obtained from a child may not mean the same thing as the same result obtained from an adult because**
   (a) children are less educated than adults.
   (b) children's abilities change rapidly from birth to adolescence.

(continued)

204 ESSENTIALS OF NEUROPSYCHOLOGICAL ASSESSMENT

(c) children's brain organization may be different from that of adults.

(d) all of the above.

3. **Tests used for the verbal child may be used with confidence for the pre-verbal child.**

   True or False?

4. **Translation of a test is sufficient to correct potential inaccuracies that can occur in testing bilingual individuals.**

   True or False?

5. **Cross-sectional data tend to underestimate differences between individuals of different ages.**

   True or False?

6. **Testing of elderly adults, young children, and patients with psychiatric problems is similar in that these individuals may not be able to tolerate long testing sessions.**

   True or False?

7. **Malingering, somatoform disorders, and factitious disorders all involve the voluntary production of symptoms.**

   True or False?

8. **Suboptimal effort is synonymous with malingering.**

   True or False?

9. **An expert, by necessity, serves as the patient's advocate.**

   True or False?

10. **A neuropsychologist working in a forensic setting**

    (a) should welcome third party observers in the examination.

    (b) should include SVTs in the evaluation.

    (c) offers advise and recommendations after testing in a feedback session.

    (d) is exempt from disclosing the limits of confidentiality.

Answers: 1. True; 2. d; 3. False; 4. False; 5. False; 6. True; 7. False; 8. False; 9. False; 10. b

Seven

ESSENTIALS OF REPORT WRITING

OVERVIEW

To complete a neuropsychological assessment, the information gathered and the results obtained must be interpreted and compiled in a report that summarizes and communicates this information. Overall, the final step in the assessment process has multiple purposes, including summarizing and communicating information and helping the reader understand the findings and conclusions. It is important for the neuropsychologist to work on the report with as much care as was given to the evaluation. The report serves to inform the referral source and other concerned parties about the patient; it may be used in remediation and treatment plans and may influence readers long after it is written. The neuropsychological report needs to contain particular information organized into separate sections. Each report needs to specify identifying information, the reason for referral, and the source or sources of historical information in the report. Background and historical information should be included, as well as a section detailing relevant behavioral observations. The report also needs to contain a complete list of the tests administered and the results obtained by the patient on each test. In addition, each report needs a summary and conclusions section, followed by recommendations when necessary.

The most important principle the neuropsychological report writer must follow is that the report should be useful to the client. Reports should be written with the intended recipient in mind; they should be readable, objective, and appropriately comprehensive. Referrals may originate from many sources, including other psychologists, physicians, other health professionals, teachers, lawyers, and, in rare instances, patients. Although reports should always be written using the clearest, most succinct information possible, the use of technical terminology and level of detail should reflect who will be reading the report. In most instances, even when the intended recipient is another psychologist, the use of jargon should be avoided. To communicate effectively, reports must be written clearly and in an organized fashion. Reports should contain material relevant to the questions at hand and treat the material objectively. Reports should leave out information that is not pertinent to the referral question and that does not add to understanding the findings. Statements and conclusions in a report should follow clearly from supporting data. Conclusions must follow from interpretation of the test findings in the context of the available historical information and other sources of information such as behavioral observations. The report must address the referral question and include the findings and appropriate recommendations.

The report is not the place to showcase the examiner's depth of knowledge. Reports consisting only of brilliantly justified and exquisitely detailed predictions about lesion localization and offering no usable and specific recommendations may serve either to hasten the rate of deforestation or increase the profit margins of computer disk drive manufacturers, but they are unlikely to be appreciated by those responsible for taking care of patients. The data needed to support conclusions and recommendations should be presented in the report, but the level of detail and comprehensiveness of this information should reflect the setting and the referral questions being asked. An extensive report format that includes details about academic history and information about medical conditions that are not necessarily relevant to brain function might be appropriate in certain pediatric and forensic settings but is often not appreciated in medical settings in which physicians are interested mainly in the consultant's bottom-line conclusions. In some settings, the neuropsychologist may have the luxury of time or may be required to organize and present large amounts of data, as is often the case in forensic evaluations. The reader is referred to Greiffenstein and Cohen (2005) for useful information about the differences between clinical and forensic neuropsychology reports. In other cases, however, the neuropsychologist must judiciously choose to present only the most critical information to allow for rapid and timely feedback.

As we discussed in Chapter 5, the primary function of a neuropsychological assessment no longer is to

CAUTION

General Guidelines for Report Writing

- Avoid jargon and technical terms.
- Refer to the patient by name, not as "the patient."
- Write clearly and concisely.
- Avoid ambiguous terms and words with negative connotations.
- Support your conclusions.
- Use good grammar and sentence structure.
- Be objective.
- Avoid including inappropriate details.

decide whether an individual has brain damage or whether there is evidence of organic brain dysfunction. Although the neuropsychologist may still be expected to sort out the possible causes for changes in intellectual and other psychological functions, in many settings assessment is expected to delineate an individual's cognitive profile and strengths and weaknesses and provide practical recommendations that may assist in short- and long-term patient management and the planning of programs for rehabilitation or educational remediation.

MAXIMS FOR WRITING A NEUROPSYCHOLOGICAL REPORT

Although little scientific research addresses the topic of effective communication of technical neuropsychological information to nonneuropsychologists (e.g., Ownby, 1990, for a rare exception), the so-called art of report writing is a frequent topic in many contemporary texts concerned with neuropsychological assessment. In this section, we present a series of 13 maxims for writing a neuropsychological test report based on some of the themes that occur frequently in these writings. Rapid Reference 7.1 summarizes each of the 13 maxims for quick reference.

≡ Rapid Reference 7.1

Maxims to Keep in Mind for Report Writing

1. Be sure you are reporting properly scored tests and accurate data.
2. Avoid technical words and jargon.
3. Keep the length of the report appropriate to the anticipated reader of the report.
4. Include relevant historical data.
5. Avoid including irrelevant historical data.
6. Describe physical appearance and behavior.
7. Name and describe the test procedures.
8. Include the test scores.
9. Provide the test scores for all tests, not just the impaired test scores.
10. Consider all the evidence when interpreting data, not just test scores.
11. Do not use each test score for lesion localization.
12. Provide useful, specific recommendations.
13. Describe any and all test modifications and their potential impact on interpretation.

1. Be sure you clearly understand the procedures for administering and scoring a neuropsychological test before using it and presenting it in a report. A neuropsychological test report that is based on inaccurately scored or interpreted tests is a potential detriment to the client and may be considered malpractice. All data and test results used in a report should be checked and scored carefully before being included in a report.

2. Avoid technical jargon and follow the rules of clear and readable writing. In almost all cases, a simple common word and declarative sentence structure are more effective in communicating information accurately than the use of obscure or technical words and overly long sentences. Modifiers of the word *memory* such as *primary, anterograde, implicit, semantic,* and *episodic* have rich and specific meanings to someone with some expertise in modern neuropsychology but are likely to be misleading or meaningless to even bright and well-educated nonpsychologists. If you do not think your reader can define the term the same way you do, you should not use it. If you must use a technical term, be sure it is accompanied by a brief nontechnical definition. Using common medical terminology (e.g., coronary infarction or hypertension) is acceptable when communicating to readers who are likely to understand this language and when this information is being reported from other sources such as medical records.

3. Keep the length appropriate to the audience and purpose of the report. Weigh the advantages of comprehensiveness against the reader's need to access and use quickly the most important information in the report. Brevity is generally appreciated. Some circumstances require a complete presentation of case material, a detailed and explicit analysis of data, and a presentation of the logic used for interpretation. In most settings, reports that present conclusions that are clear and easy to follow are more likely to be read. A survey of report-writing practices among neuropsychologists (Donders, 2001b) indicated that the mean length of reports by those surveyed was approximately seven pages; a few clinicians routinely prepared reports that were only one page in length, and a few routinely prepared reports of 30 pages or more. Clinicians who worked in geriatric settings and in medical settings tended to write significantly shorter reports than clinicians working in private practice or in settings that were primarily forensic or pediatric.

4. Include historical data that are relevant to the conclusions and recommendations you will make. In most cases the neuropsychological report should include descriptions of any medical history relevant to the function of the central nervous system. This includes any medications that may affect central nervous system functioning and nonneurological medical procedures that carry a possible risk of affecting brain function (e.g., cardiac surgery). It should also include any history of serious infections (e.g., pneumonia) and any history of diseases and conditions that clearly affect the central nervous system (e.g., closed head injury, stroke, epilepsy, loss of consciousness, degenerative diseases, exposure to environmental toxins, drug and alcohol use, etc.). Information concerned with establishing patterns of premorbid ability, such as educational level and vocational history, is also critical to most neuropsychological reports. Pediatric and forensic reports tend to require greater detail and documentation of this information than other kinds of reports, but all neuropsychology reports should include information about this topic.

5. Avoid presenting historical and behavioral data that are not relevant to either the referral question or to the conclusions you draw. The client's dental history, spouse's hobbies, and recent vacations, although interesting, are unlikely to be used in formulating neuropsychological interpretations. In some circumstances, however, seemingly irrelevant issues may actually be very relevant. For example, vacation history may be important in a case in which a patient has more capacity for leisure than for work; in this situation, the information may contribute to understanding the test findings. In addition, indicate missing historical information that might have been helpful but was not available at the time of the test report. If you feel that additional (but unavailable) information might temper or support your conclusions, this should be indicated.

6. Describe physical appearance and behavior during the interview and formal examination; such information might be relevant to the referral question and the interpretation of the tests. This may include interpersonal behavior (e.g., eye contact and sense of rapport with examiner), demeanor, hygiene and physical appearance, range and appropriateness of affect, characteristics of language production and comprehension, level of attentiveness, and motivation and cooperation.

7. Name and describe the procedures to which you refer in your text. Avoid using theoretical terms and jargon as the only reference to

tests, even if your audience consists of other neuropsychologists. As we discussed in Chapter 5, the construct validity of many neuro-psychological tests is underdetermined or still under investigation. What may be a test of sequencing to Psychologist A may be a test of attention to Psychologist B or a test of working memory to Psychologist C. Always refer to a test by name and by some behavioral description of the procedure (e.g., Digit Span: ability to repeat a sequence of numbers).

8. Provide actual test scores in standard form either in the text of the report or in a summary table. Be sure that you specify which norms you are using to generate the standard scores so that the reader will know the population against which you have compared the test taker. For those tests in which the norms used can vary (e.g., Boston Naming Test), it may be necessary to include the raw score as well. Reporting test scores has come to be a standard practice for neuropsychologists, according to a recent survey of report-writing practices by Donders (2001a, 2001b). Whether you consider yourself to be a traditional Halstead–Reitan expert or an acolyte of the Boston Process Approach, test scores are still the only common referent that may be used by anyone reading a report in the future, regardless of orientation. When test scores (e.g., 50th percentile) rather than labels (e.g., average range) are provided, more precise information is conveyed to the reader. Remember that the average range refers to the 25th to the 74th percentile. Stating that someone performed in the average range is insufficiently precise in many cases, and labels can be subjective. Even though it should not, the description *the high end of the average range* can carry different meanings for different evaluators. Support labels with test scores.

In addition, including test scores allows the next evaluator to measure any change more precisely. *Within normal limits* extends one standard deviation above and below the mean. Consider a situation where a patient scores at the 74th percentile on a test the first time it is taken, but the evaluator reports only that the patient scored within normal limits (a correct statement). Consider now that the patient is tested again a year or two later and now scores at the 21st percentile on the same test, also a score within normal range but quite different from the first. Because the second evaluator has only the description of the patient's prior performance, he or she will not know that a possibly significant downward change may have taken place.

9. Include the scores and some description of all tests in the Test Result section of the report, not just the scores for those tests in which impairment was found. Not all the information presented needs to be repeated in the summary and conclusions.

10. Make sure neuropsychological interpretations make sense. The neuropsychologist must consider *all* the evidence when interpreting the data. When interpreting test results, you should think first about neuropsychologically plausible conclusions from the test data that are derived independently of other sources of data, then weigh these conclusions or predictions against all the evidence before you. Indicate what the neuropsychological, historical, medical, and neuroimaging data each imply and then weigh the consistencies and inconsistencies between these data sources to draw your conclusions. Do not automatically attribute a test finding to an antecedent event or positive neuroimaging finding even if no other known etiology presents itself. The presence of a lesion on magnetic resonance imaging or history of a head injury is not automatically causally related to your test findings. Your evidence should fit together logically, and the test results should be consistent with those expected given the assumed source. If the data cannot be plausibly reconciled with the other information, it is important to say so.

11. Know that test scores cannot guarantee the presence of lesions. There are few single test scores that are good predictors of the presence of a lesion in a specific location. When such predictions can be made, it is because a pattern of deficits or scores is consistent with a specific focal lesion and a plausible reason exists for such a lesion to occur (e.g., nonfluent aphasia following a left middle cerebral artery stroke). If all you are doing in your report is listing a series of test scores as evidence of a series of localizations of lesions, you are not likely to be accurate. In addition, you are unlikely to be providing information that is going to help in the diagnosis of the patient and how to manage the disorder. Individuals who fail a series of neuropsychological tests are unlikely to have a series of verifiable lesions corresponding to those test scores.

12. Know that in most cases, recommendations are the most important and most neglected part of the neuropsychology report. Good recommendations should provide useful guidance to whoever is going to take care of the patient and should be based directly on the data in the report. Most neuropsychological recommendations concentrate

on the cognitive and emotional strengths and weaknesses of the patient, but they may include issues related to social and self-care skills. General principles for helping patients with brain damage such as recommending the *use of structure, verbal mediation,* or a *paper memory* should be illustrated with relevant examples. In addition, these should be specifically tailored to the circumstances of the client (i.e., the classroom, nursing home, job, etc.). Recommendations should be realistic and focus on the actual resources and services that might be available. Do not recommend cognitive rehabilitation when none exists for the particular problems of the patient (e.g., concussion).

13. Be sure to indicate whether any of the tests had to be modified to accommodate a special issue such as bilingualism or even disabilities that interfered with the standard administration of a task. That test modifications may limit the interpretation of the data should be stated clearly in the report.

ORGANIZATION OF THE REPORT

No absolute, single report is right for every evaluation, although certain basic information is contained in each report, and each does follow a certain basic outline, as summarized in Rapid Reference 7.2.

≡ Rapid Reference 7.2

Suggested Report Outline

1. Identifying Information
2. Reason for Referral
3. Records Reviewed or Source of Historical Information
4. Relevant History and Background Information
5. Behavioral Observations
6. Tests Administered
7. Test Results
8. Summary and Impressions
9. Recommendations
10. Examiner and Report Writer Signature(s)

1. *Identifying Information.* At the beginning of each report, the writer should present information that specifically identifies the patient. This usually includes the patient's name, the patient's date of birth, the patient's age, the date(s) of testing, the date of the report, the examiner's name (if different from report writer), and perhaps the referral source.

2. *Reason for Referral.* This section should state clearly why the neuropsychological assessment was conducted and what the specific referral questions are. It may also include a summary of the symptoms and behaviors that prompted the referral. In addition, this section should name the referral source and his or her relationship to the patient. This information establishes some boundaries for the report because it indicates who will read the report and the specific purpose of the evaluation. This information in turn limits the scope of the evaluation and the report. Who referred the patient and why defines the tests and procedures that are administered, the interpretation of the results, and the applications of the results. In this section, the writer may also include the patient's chief complaints and concerns. Putting the patient's subjective report here permits a comparison between the information obtained from the referral source and that from the patient.

   This section should also indicate whether the patient was informed about who requested the evaluation and the purposes of the evaluation. In addition, if the testing is being performed at the request of a third party, such as the court, this section informs the reader whether the patient was instructed about the limits of confidentiality.

3. *Records Reviewed.* In this section, the author should list all the sources from which background and historical information was obtained and the relevant dates of the material. It is important that the reader know from where the information in a report has come. The source of information informs the reader of the comprehensiveness and accuracy of the information and (perhaps) any bias. In some instances, historical information comes solely from the patient; in other cases, information is also available from relatives, caregivers, and the referral source. In forensic reports, an inventory of both records reviewed and the sources of this information is especially crucial because any opinions will be based on the available facts.

4. *History and Background Information.* In this section, you should report the history taken from record review, clinical interview, and the

reports of others. The information reported should be relevant to the questions at hand and should include any information that will be used to support your conclusions. Birth and developmental, educational, vocational, medical, social, and family history should be reported in this section as necessary to establish a good description of the patient. It should also include information from prior neuropsychological evaluations. Typically it is sufficient to highlight the primary findings to allow a comparison between earlier test performances and the current one.

5. *Behavioral Observations.* This part of the report should contain the information learned from observing the patient during interview and testing. Important here are observations of interpersonal behavior, demeanor, hygiene and physical appearance, range and appropriateness of affect, characteristics of language production and comprehension, level of attentiveness, and motivation and cooperation.

6. *Tests Administered.* In some form or another (list or paragraph format), all the tests and procedures administered to the patient should be provided in this section of the report. This informs the reader what particular tests were administered and what versions of those tests (e.g., Wechsler Intelligence Scale (WAIS)-III vs. WAIS-IV) were used.

7. *Test Results.* In this section, the examiner has the opportunity to provide the specific results obtained during testing by reporting the test scores and the patient's level of performance on each test. A handy way to organize the report is by cognitive function, so that a report from a comprehensive neuropsychological examination might contain subheadings of Intellectual Functions, Attention and Executive Functions, Learning and Memory, Language Functions, and so on. This section should be organized so that the reader can easily find specific information about particular areas being measured by finding the appropriate subheading.

8. *Summary and Impressions.* This section of the report should bring together all the test findings in the context of available history and observations, providing an interpretation of the data. The pattern of strengths and weaknesses should be summarized and discussed here. The interpretation of the findings requires including the information supporting the conclusions.

9. *Recommendations.* This final section should include any treatment and case management recommendations that can be provided to guide patient care. Recommendations should be specific and clearly stated.

10. *Examiner's and Report Writer's Signatures.* This identifies for the reader who administered the tests and wrote the report and provides his or her credentials.

SAMPLE REPORT

Neuropsychological Evaluation

Name:	Susan Smith	**Date of Testing:**	12/30/08
DOB:	08/09/73	**Date of Report:**	01/02/09
Age:	35 years	**CONFIDENTIAL**	

Reason for Referral

Dr. Susan Smith is a 35-year-old, right-handed, single physician referred for neuropsychological assessment by her treating psychologist. An evaluation was requested to investigate whether any cognitive deficits correspond to Dr. Smith's subjective complaints of difficulties affecting her daily functioning in her job as a physician.

As her presenting complaint, Dr. Smith reported that despite her accomplishments, she has difficulty remembering the faces of people she has seen or met. She reported that this is not simply a matter of recognizing someone and not being able to remember a name, but rather not recognizing the face at all. She reported that this happens daily in her medical practice and can occur within an hour or two of having met someone. Dr. Smith indicated that she remembers things about the people that she has seen, including parts of faces, but it is as though she is unable to process the face itself. She also indicated that she has no difficulty recalling details about an individual's medical case, despite not recalling the individual's face.

Dr. Smith reported that she is able to recognize people that resemble family members and that she does eventually recognize faces after multiple repetitions. She reported having particular trouble remembering undistinguished faces. Dr. Smith reported that as a result she often avoids situations, such as parties, in which problems with not recognizing faces are likely. She indicated that she

> # DON'T FORGET
>
> ### Information to Include in the Reason for Referral Section of the Report
>
> - The referral source
> - The referral questions
> - The patient's complaints and concerns

tends to have more intensive one-on-one relationships rather than casual relationships. She indicated that she has no real strategies for dealing with the problem and that she is not sure whether she attends well to a person's image beyond identifying characteristics such as moles and other features relevant to medicine.

Historical information in this report came from an interview with Dr. Smith and from her referring psychologist. Dr. Smith appeared to be a reliable historian.

Relevant History and Background Information

Dr. Smith reported that she works in internal medicine in the Basic Care Clinic at a local hospital. She indicated that she works full time in this position but that she also does a considerable amount of computer work, managing a Web site on the Internet. She described herself as a successful investor and indicated that she loves numbers. She reported that before coming to her present hospital position, she had moonlighted there for 2 years and that she had been at another local hospital before that for about 6 months.

DON'T FORGET

Information to Include in the Relevant History and Background Information of the Report

- Age, sex, handedness, ethnic identity
- History of presenting complaint
- Educational history
- Employment or vocational history
- Birth and early development
- Medical history
- Neurological history
- Psychiatric history
- Current and past medication(s)
- Substance abuse history
- Psychosocial history, including stressors
- Family medical, neurological, and psychiatric history
- Other relevant information gathered in interview

Dr. Smith reported that from fourth through twelfth grades, she attended a so-called elitist test school where various experimental learning programs were tried. Dr. Smith reported that she graduated from university in 1994 with a B.A. in physics and that she had attended on a full-tuition scholarship. She then earned her M.D. from the Southwest University Medical School in 1998; she did her residency and attended 1 year in the emergency room at an urban hospital in the Southwest. She described going to university as the first real break from her family. Following that, she moved to a large northeast city because she had a close friend living in the area, and she began to work at a private city hospital doing home-based primary care. Unhappy with that job, however, she then worked at a large suburban medical clinic and then at the local hospital mentioned previously until she began her present position. Dr. Smith reported she has always done well academically, and she believes she has done well because she worked very hard.

Dr. Smith reported that she spends a lot of time working both at the hospital and on the Internet, and she has very few social activities outside of visiting with her closest friends for dinners and movies, about once every other month. She reported that she has taken tai chi classes, she swims every other day, and she used to play the piano regularly. Dr. Smith reported that her family (mother, father, and three sisters) lives in a dangerous neighborhood in another northeastern city. She reported that of her two eldest sisters, one has never married and one is about to be married. She reported that her oldest sister is a letter carrier and that her second oldest sister is a pediatrician. Her youngest sister suffers from mental retardation and has had behavioral difficulties, at least of late. She indicated that her father is a draftsman who has been unemployed since he was in his fifties because his shop closed. She also reported he has been diagnosed with lung cancer, which he has refused to treat after receiving radiation treatment. She reported that her mother graduated from high school and worked as a waitress before having children. She believes her father attended school until about 11th grade. She reported that they were very insular as a family and that her mother pushed her academically.

For purposes of confidentiality, Dr. Smith's psychiatric history is only summarized briefly. Dr. Smith reported that as a youngster, she witnessed considerable abuse within her family, and she has had episodes of suicidal ideation since the mid-1990s as a result. She has never been in a psychiatric hospital and took antidepressants only for a brief period many years ago before discontinuing them. Dr. Smith reported her past medical history as basically unremarkable. She denied any history of head injury or loss of consciousness. She denied any known exposure to toxins and any neurological symptoms or history. Dr. Smith also denied any history of alcohol or drug abuse. She does not smoke cigarettes, and her consumption of caffeine is minimal. She reported being on no medications at the time of testing.

Behavioral Observations

Dr. Smith presented on time for the evaluation. She was neatly and appropriately dressed in casual attire. She was cooperative during testing, and her manner was pleasant. She was clearly nervous, at least initially, as evidenced in some hesitation and embarrassment in discussing her difficulties. As the testing progressed, she appeared to grow more comfortable and confident.

DON'T FORGET

Information to Include in the Behavioral Observation Section of the Report

- Physical appearance and grooming
- Level of alertness and arousal
- Attention span
- Level of cooperation
- Activity level
- Response to failure or success
- Response to encouragement
- Speech and discourse abilities
- Emotionality
- Appropriateness of social skills
- Sensorimotor functioning
- Thought content and processes
- Unusual habits or mannerisms

At some points during testing, it appeared that Dr. Smith did not concentrate as fully as she could; she seemed to note this herself when, for example, during administration of an arithmetic test, she remarked, "Boy I'm not concentrating, am I?" Dr. Smith also reported that she found the tests to be intimidating and tried to instruct herself to relax "a little bit." Also, at some points during testing, Dr. Smith appeared to have difficulties primarily because she imposed complexities on simple tasks and as a result made some tasks more difficult than intended. This was notable, for example, on the Wisconsin Card Sorting Test—64, in which she searched for unusual patterns; the same tendency was probably also present during Animal Naming, in which she initially attempted to recite animal names in alphabetical order. Dr. Smith indicated that she did not want to learn what her actual IQ was because she believes it is either low average or just average. She believes she attained what she has as a result of her hard work rather than her natural abilities.

Speech was fluent and well articulated with no instances of word-finding difficulties occurring in spontaneous speech. Dr. Smith had no difficulties understanding test directions or the examiner's language. Because of Dr. Smith's cooperation and behavior during testing, the test findings are considered to be a reliable and valid measurement of her current level of cognitive functioning.

Test Results

Tests Administered

Dr. Smith was administered the following battery of tests: Wechsler Adult Intellectual Scale—Fourth Edition (WAIS-IV); Trail Making A and B; Stroop Color and Word Test; Wisconsin Card Sorting Test (WCST); Controlled Oral Word Association Test (FAS); Animal Naming; Wechsler Memory Scale—Third Edition (WMS-III); Rey Complex Figure Test and Recognition Test (RCFT); Boston Naming Test; and the Hooper Visual Organization Test (VOT). In addition, Dr. Smith completed the Beck Depression Inventory—II (BDI-II) and the Beck Anxiety Inventory (BAI).

DON'T FORGET

Information to Include in Test Result Section of the Report

- List of tests and procedures used
- Test descriptions
- Test scores
- Test score ratings
- Summary data
- Indication of norms used
- Findings organized by domain or test-by-test basis
- Findings integrated across domains or tests

Intellectual Functions

To assess intellectual functioning, Dr. Smith was administered the WAIS-IV. The WAIS-IV test groups an individual's ability into four global areas: Verbal Comprehension Index (VCI), which measures verbal ability; Perceptual Reasoning

Index (PRI), which involves the manipulation of concrete materials or processing of visual stimuli to solve nonverbal problems; Working Memory Index (WMI), which measures short-term memory; and Processing Speed Index (PSI), which measures cognitive processing efficiency/speed. On the WAIS-IV, Dr. Smith earned a Full Scale IQ (FSIQ) of 115, which is ranked at the 84th percentile and classified as high average and at the upper end of normal limits. At a 95% confidence interval, this would place her true score between 111 and 119 or in the high average to the superior range. There was an unusually large discrepancy, however, between her Verbal Comprehension Index and her Perceptual Reasoning Index of 36 points, indicating that her FSIQ cannot be interpreted as a meaningful representation of her overall global ability. Given the rarity of Dr. Smith's cognitive profile (0.5% in individuals in standardization sample with comparable FSIQ), Dr. Smith's intellectual profile is best understood by examining her VCI and PRI separately. Each of these indexes was interpretable because the scatter within each of the indexes was normal. Overall Dr. Smith's performance on the WAIS-IV indicated her verbal skills are significantly stronger than her visual processing and visuospatial skills.

On the WAIS-IV, Dr. Smith earned the following Index scores:

Scale	Standard Score	Percentile	Range
VCI	136	99	Very Superior
PRI	100	50	Average
WMI	122	93	Superior
PSI	92	30	Average

Examination of the indexes indicated that Dr. Smith has exceptional verbal comprehension skills and superior working memory skills, but only average perceptual reasoning and processing speed skills. Given the lack of recent onset of new symptoms or cognitive problems, this pattern is most consistent with a long-standing pattern of neurodevelopment.

The VCI, a measure of crystallized intelligence, represents Dr. Smith's ability to reason with previously learned information and verbal conceptualization ability. This ability develops largely as a function of both formal and informal educational opportunities and experiences and is highly dependent on exposure to mainstream U.S. culture. Her ability here was assessed by tasks that required her to define words, draw conceptual similarities between words, and answer questions involving knowledge of general information. The variability among Dr. Smith's performances on these tasks was normal (scatter = 3, where 5 or more is abnormal), indicating that her overall ability in this area can be adequately summarized in a single score (i.e., the VCI). Her VCI was 136, which is ranked at the 99th percentile and classified as very superior and well above normal limits. Her performances on the VCI subtests ranged from superior to very superior as is evident from the table that follows:

Subtest	Scaled Score	Percentile	Description
Information	17	98	Very Superior
Vocabulary	17	98	Very Superior
Similarities	14	91	Superior

The PRI, a measure of nonverbal thinking and visuospatial problem solving, represents Dr. Smith's ability to integrate visual stimuli, reason nonverbally, and apply visuospatial and visuomotor skills to solve the kinds of problems that are not school taught. Her ability in this area was assessed by tasks that required her to recreate a series of modeled or picture designs using blocks, identify the missing portion of an incomplete visual matrix from one of five response options, and identify an important missing detail from incomplete pictures. The variability among her performances on these tasks was normal (scatter = 4), indicating that her overall ability in this area can be adequately summarized in a single score (i.e., the PRI). Dr. Smith earned a PRI of 100, which is ranked at the 50th percentile and classified as average and within normal limits. Dr. Smith's scores on the PRI subtests ranged from average to high average as follows:

Subtest	Scaled Score	Percentile	Description
Picture Completion	8	25	Average
Block Design	10	50	Average
Matrix Reasoning	12	75	High Average

Although none of Dr. Smith's performances on the visual subtests even approached the impaired range, none was as highly developed as her verbal comprehension abilities.

The WMI, a measure of short-term memory, represents Dr. Smith's ability to apprehend and hold, or transform, information in immediate awareness and then use it within a few seconds. Her ability in this area was assessed by two tasks: Digit Span, which required her to repeat a sequence of numbers in the same order as presented by the examiner and also in the reverse order and in chronological sequence, and Arithmetic, which required her to solve mental arithmetic problems. Dr. Smith obtained a WMI of 122, which is ranked at the 93rd percentile and is classified as superior and above normal limits. Dr. Smith's performances in this area were consistent (scatter = 2). Span of apprehension was measured in the high average range, and mental arithmetic was measured in the superior range. Her scores in the area of working memory were as follows:

Subtest	Scaled Score	Percentile	Description
Digit Span	13	84	High Average
Arithmetic	15	95	Superior

The PSI, a measure of processing speed, represents Dr. Smith's ability to perform simple clerical-type tasks quickly. Her ability in this area was assessed with two tasks: one required Dr. Smith to quickly copy symbols that were paired with shapes according to a key, and the other required her to identify the presence or absence of a target symbol in a row of symbols. Dr. Smith showed normal variability between her performances on these two tasks (scatter = 3), indicating that her PSI is a good estimate of her processing speed. Dr. Smith obtained a PSI of 92, which is ranked at the 30th percentile and is classified as average and within normal limits. Her processing speed subtest scores were as follows:

Subtest	Scaled Score	Percentile	Description
Symbol Search	10	50	Average
Coding	7	16	Low Average

Attention and Executive Functions

Dr. Smith was alert and oriented during testing. Performance on the Information and Orientation subtest from the WMS-III was well within normal limits; all questions were answered correctly. Mental control of overlearned sequences, however, was only average (50th percentile). Dr. Smith's speed on this test was inconsistent, and in one instance, she lost the sequence when alternating serial 6s and days of the week.

As noted earlier, Working Memory Index on the WAIS-IV was measured in the superior range at the 95th percentile. Digit Span Forward was 8, and performance here was high average (84th percentile). Digit Span Backward was 7, and superior at the 91st percentile. In addition, Digit Span Sequencing was 7 and superior at the 91st percentile. None of these span scores was significantly different from any other. Mental arithmetic ability was measured in the high average range at the 84th percentile. Dr. Smith noted that she was not concentrating well during this portion of the examination.

As noted earlier, Processing Speed Index on the WAIS-IV was 92, which is ranked at the 30th percentile and classified as average and within normal limits.

This was another area of weakness relative to verbal abilities for Dr. Smith. Psychomotor speed on a graphomotor transcription test was low average and at the lower end of normal limits, whereas speeded visual search was average and within normal limits. In contrast, speeded processing on Trail Making A, which requires visual scanning and number sequencing, was at expected levels relative to age, sex, race, and education at the 38th percentile (norms: Heaton, Miller, Taylor, & Grant, 2004). Dr. Smith made no errors on this task and scored within expected limits, requiring just 22 seconds to complete the task. In contrast, on Trail Making B, a complex tracking test requiring alternation and sequencing between letters and numbers, Dr. Smith scored below expected levels at the 10th percentile relative to demographically adjusted norms. She worked relatively slowly on this task in general (74 seconds) and slowed herself further with one error involving loss of set.

On the Stroop, a test measuring self-regulatory and inhibitory skills, Dr. Smith scored in the average range relative to age at the 27th percentile when reading color-words, and in the low average range at the 16th percentile when naming colors. On the Inhibition trial, when naming the color ink in which a color-word was printed, she also scored in the low average range at the 21st percentile. Although within normal limits, Dr. Smith worked relatively slowly on these tasks. On the WCST, a card-sorting test requiring concept formation and set flexibility, Dr. Smith scored at expected levels overall relative to age and education norms. She scored within normal limits (>16th percentile) in terms of categories completed (6), trials to complete the first category (11), and failures to maintain set (0). Total number of errors (21st percentile), perseverative errors (18th percentile), nonperseverative errors (21st percentile), and percent conceptual level responses (19th percentile) were all in the low average range, but within normal limits relative to age and education. Dr. Smith's scores on this measure may have stemmed from the fact that once she sorted the first two most salient categories, she then attempted unusual combinations and patterns before she finally succeeded in recognizing the third category. After this was done, she quickly completed the remainder of the test.

Verbal fluency was also at expected levels relative to demographically adjusted norms for phonemic categories. Dr. Smith named 42 F-A-S items in a 3-minute interval, scoring at the 27th percentile. The words presented tended to be those of an articulate person with a good vocabulary. Performance was also at expected levels for category fluency, although she slowed herself initially by attempting to alphabetize her list; Dr. Smith named 21 animals in a 1-minute interval. This placed her performance at the 21st percentile relative to demographically adjusted norms.

Learning and Memory Functions

On the WMS-III, Dr. Smith earned scores on the various Primary Indexes ranging from the borderline range (3rd percentile) to the high end of the average range (70th percentile), with most performances low average or average relative to age. Her primary index scores are contained in the following table:

Primary Indexes	Index Score	Percentile
Auditory Immediate	105	63
Visual Immediate	71	3
Immediate Memory	87	19
Auditory Delayed	108	70
Visual Delayed	81	10
Auditory Recognition Delayed	95	37
General Memory	93	32

Upon comparison of these scores to each other, a statistically significant difference is apparent between the Auditory Immediate and Visual Immediate Indexes and between the Auditory Delayed Index and the Visual Delayed Index. Both of these differences were also relatively unusual in the normative sample (4.2% and 7.9%, respectively). The direction and degree of findings parallels that seen on the WAIS-IV with auditory immediate and delayed memory significantly better than visual immediate and delayed memory.

Relative to measured ability, Dr. Smith's performances on the WMS-III suggested that she was not learning on the WMS-III tasks as expected, especially significantly so in the area of visual learning and memory. The differences were in the direction that would be expected, given Dr. Smith's subjective complaints of difficulty recognizing faces. The problem seems to be more extensive than that, however, as is evident later in the report.

Acquisition of prose passage information was only average relative to age (50th percentile) with performance comparable after a delay (50th percentile) and with percent retention of the information average (63rd percentile). Acquisition of verbal paired associates was above average (75th percentile) and good recall of this information was seen after a delay (84th percentile) with full retention. Recognition for auditory information after a delay was in the average range (37th percentile). Dr. Smith had an easier time recognizing word pairs from among foils than she had recognizing prose passage information. Although overall learning in the area of prose passages was less than expected given Dr. Smith's excellent verbal abilities, no decay or loss in memory was apparent over time.

Immediate recognition of faces was low average (16th percentile), and delayed recognition of the same faces was relatively better (37th percentile), because no information was lost over time (100% retention). Of particular note was Dr. Smith's performance on a visual memory task requiring her to acquire visual details from complex visual scenes. On this particular test, immediate acquisition of information was in the borderline range (2nd percentile). No decay was seen after a delay (5th percentile), however. Incidental delayed recall of the Rey Complex Figure was within normal limits but less than expected relative to age at the 21st percentile. Dr. Smith recalled only the major outline figure and appeared to have forgotten most of the internal details, earning 18.5 of 36 points. No further information was lost after a filled delay (18.5/36), however, with performance at the 18th percentile. Delayed recognition of the figure was average and within normal limits at the 46th percentile.

Language Functions

As noted earlier, Dr. Smith is an articulate woman with a very good vocabulary. Basic language functions, such as auditory comprehension and verbal expression were intact to observation. Confrontation naming, as measured by the Boston Naming Test, was at expected levels relative to demographic variables at the 24th percentile with 57 of 60 items named correctly and three additional correct responses to phonemic cues. As noted earlier in this report, Dr. Smith's performances on verbal fluency tests were at expected levels relative to measured ability.

Visuospatial Functions

Basic visual perception was intact on object-naming and figure-copying tasks. Ability to mentally assemble cut-up pictures of objects on the VOT was normal at the 62nd percentile with 27.5 of 30 points earned. Ability to integrate and organize visual information was also intact relative to age (>16th percentile), as measured by copy of a complex design (34/36).

Self-Report of Mood

On the BDI, a face-valid and self-report measure of depressive symptomatology, Dr. Smith scored in the *minimal* range (5). She did not endorse a significant number or degree of depressive symptoms. On the BAI, she also scored in the *minimal* range (7). The combination of minimal symptoms of anxiety and minimal symptoms of depression suggests Dr. Smith is not experiencing significant emotional distress at this time.

Summary and Impressions

Dr. Smith is a 35-year-old, right-handed physician referred for neuropsychological testing by her psychologist because she wished to undergo neuropsychological testing to evaluate her subjective report of difficulty remembering faces. Dr. Smith's description of her complaint suggested that the problem was long-standing and detrimental to her work. Dr. Smith's educational and medical history is unremarkable for problems, whereas her psychiatric history suggested some long-standing emotional issues centered on self-esteem and interpersonal difficulties.

DON'T FORGET

Important Considerations for the Summary and Impressions Section of the Report

- Summarize critical history concisely
- Summarize strengths and weaknesses
- Summarize most important test findings
- Consider all sources of information
- Integrate and interpret the findings
- State or resolve inconsistencies
- Make diagnostic formulations
- Support your conclusions and diagnosis

Measurement of intellect at this time indicated very superior verbal skills in contrast to average nonverbal abilities. Although nonverbal abilities were generally average, they were deficient relative to verbal abilities, which were uniformly superior to very superior. This large discrepancy between verbal and visual skills is likely to be long-standing and is probably the source of Dr. Smith's subjective complaint of difficulty remembering faces. Elementary attentional skills were intact and indicated an excellent span of apprehension. In contrast, performance on tests measuring various aspects of executive functions revealed slower-than-expected processing and a tendency to make tests more complicated than they needed to be. Slower than expected processing speed was evident on the PSI tasks from the WAIS-IV, Trail Making B, and the Stroop. Auditory learning and memory tended to be average and mildly beneath what would be expected, given verbal cognitive abilities. Visual learning and memory, however, were clearly discrepant with expected performance at this time relative even to perceptual reasoning abilities. Although Dr. Smith tended to learn auditory information at average to above average levels, her acquisition of visual information presented as faces and as visual scenes was clearly below average. No decay was seen in memory over time, indicating that what Dr. Smith learned, she retained. Basic language functions were intact, as was basic visual perception. Visuointegration and visuoconstruction were also intact. At the time of testing, Dr. Smith did not report an unusual number or degree of depressive or anxiety symptoms.

The results from Dr. Smith's neuropsychological evaluation indicated an individual with a clear, significantly and abnormally large, and probably long-standing advantage for verbal over visual skills that was evident on both cognitive tests and tests of learning and memory. Although Dr. Smith showed no evidence of impairment in basic visuospatial skills, including visual perception, visual integration, and visual organization, she had difficulties relative to her verbal abilities in processing and using visual detail information. She also had difficulties relative to normal in learning visual information such as faces and visual scene information. The relatively slowed processing speed is not an unusual finding for a verbally gifted individual.

The source of Dr. Smith's relative visual difficulties is unclear, but given that the dysfunction is apparently long-standing, it is likely to be congenital in nature. This pattern of discrepancy with verbal abilities so much better than visual abilities can be viewed as a nonverbal learning disability, a disability that can be associated with interpersonal difficulties. Such difficulties often appear to stem from difficulties in understanding the visual cues and visual information that occur during interpersonal interaction.

Recommendations

Given the likely long-standing nature of the dysfunction seen in testing, Dr. Smith would do best to develop compensatory strategies to deal with these difficulties. This examiner is not aware of any specific rehabilitation that is available to deal with these problems, but Dr. Smith would likely benefit from social skills training, perhaps through behavioral treatment, which helps her to understand social interaction and that allows her to be comfortable with social interaction. She might also consider developing strategies for recalling faces and visual scenes. These strategies would include specifically examining people's faces upon meeting them and noting all characteristics that she can then use verbally-based mnemonic devices to retrieve. Although this strategy might never fully compensate for failing to recall the visual image, it would help her to have information available to her with which to recognize an individual later. This will require, however, that Dr. Smith actively encode

> **DON'T FORGET**
> ....
> **Important Considerations for the Recommendations Section**
> - Practicality and viability
> - Clear and understandable presentation
> - Intervention goals
> - Possible treatment and rehabilitation strategies
> - Use of strengths and weaknesses in remediation
> - Recommendations for follow-up evaluations

such information. When meeting with a patient, she might wish to record this information on her initial history and physical exam sheet, and she might wish to review the information on any subsequent meetings. She could also begin putting photographs of her patients in their medical records. Dr. Smith would also be wise to allow others to aid her in dealing with her difficulties with recognizing faces. When encountering persons she does not know, she might wish to ask a friend quietly the facts about the individuals in her visual field, thus using others to help her recognize people. The examiner is also aware of programs using experimental therapies designed to enhance facial recognition (DeGutis at al., 2008). If Dr. Smith is interested, the examiner would be happy to put her in contact with a program enrolling patients such as her in clinical trials.

Given the suspected long-standing nature of this problem, further workup does not appear to be necessary. Should Dr. Smith discover that her abilities appear to be declining, a full neurological evaluation with repeat neuropsychological testing and imaging by magnetic resonance imaging should be considered.

Jane Doe, Ph.D.
Board Certified in Clinical Neuropsychology,
American Board of Professional Psychology

TEST YOURSELF

1. **Test reports should be written like a scholarly paper with formal citations and bibliography.**
   True or False?
2. **All neuropsychological reports should contain complete medical histories.**
   True or False?
3. **The Behavioral Observations section in a report should include all but the following:**
   (a) Observations relevant to the patient's cooperation and motivation
   (b) Observations relevant to the patient's mood and affect
   (c) Observations relevant to the patient's favorite clothing designer
   (d) Observations relevant to the patient's ability to pay attention
4. **As an expert, it is important to include in a report the most current theoretical terms used by experimental psychologists to describe test results.**
   True or False?
5. **In describing test results in a report, it is important to do the following:**
   (a) Never include test scores.

(b) Use jargon and technical terms.

(c) Present only impaired scores.

(d) Provide names of the tests that you are describing.

6. **It is not necessary to support your conclusions with data included in the test report.**

True or False?

7. **Test reports should reflect the questions asked by the referral source.**

True or False?

Answers: 1. False; 2. False; 3. c; 4. False; 5. d; 6. False; 7. True

Appendix A

A General Guide for Neuropsychological Assessment

A. PLANNING THE ASSESSMENT

1. Obtain information about the referral question and the patient's history from the referral source.
2. Request and review available historical information and records concerning the patient's medical, social, psychological, educational, and vocational history.
3. Select neuropsychological tests validated for the assessment purpose. These may form a fixed or flexible battery that is brief or comprehensive or consists of a single targeted test depending on the referral question, the possible diagnosis, and the ability of the patient to cooperate or tolerate testing.

B. THE ASSESSMENT

1. Interview the patient and, when necessary (e.g., child, patient with severe traumatic brain injury, patient with known or presumed Alzheimer's disease), the accompanying parent or caregiver to gather medical, social, psychological, educational, and vocational history.
2. Administer the neuropsychological tests following all directions explicitly. Note any deviations from standard protocol. Adjust or revise the tests to be administered on the basis of information obtained through interview or observation.
3. During interview and test administration, observe and note patient behavior relevant to test interpretation (e.g., effort, anxiety, language difficulties, emotional upset).
4. Score the tests as testing proceeds to ensure proper inquiries for each test question.

C. SCORING THE ASSESSMENT FINDINGS

1. Finish scoring any individual responses not completed during the evaluation.
2. Tabulate raw scores and make conversions to scaled scales, standard scores, and other scores such as percentile scores. Calculate any composite scores or impairment indexes as necessary for test battery.
3. Double-check all scores to ensure proper tabulations and conversions.
4. Compare scores across tests as necessary (e.g., WAIS-IV composite scores and WMS-IV index scores).

D. INTERPRETATION OF THE FINDINGS FROM ASSESSMENT

1. *Stage One:* Setting the stage for interpretation—base rates or prevalence of likely conditions.
   a. What was the referral question? What was the purpose of the assessment (e.g., rehabilitation, diagnosis, overall global assessment of functioning)?
   b. What is the likelihood that the patient has cognitive impairment given the referral source and history? Consider the base rate or prevalence of brain dysfunction given the referral source (e.g., acute hospital ward, worker's compensation, school psychologist) and the patient's history (e.g., cardiovascular accident, closed head injury with no loss of consciousness, severe academic difficulties, native language).
   c. Do the behavioral observations provide information about the possible source of or contribution to any impairment found (e.g., sleepiness, distractibility, suboptimal effort, thought disorder, word finding difficulties, poor comprehension)?
   d. What factors other than brain damage could have affected the patient's performance (e.g., age, education, motivation, effort, anxiety, cultural background, psychiatric difficulties)?
2. *Stage Two:* Determining premorbid level of function.
   a. What premorbid level of functioning do the patient's educational and vocational achievements suggest?
   b. What premorbid level of function does performance on hold tests (e.g., WAIS-III Vocabulary) suggest?

    c. What premorbid level of function does performance on tests re-
       quiring reading of irregular words (e.g., AMNART or WTAR)
       suggest?

    d. What premorbid level of function does the Barona et al. (1984) IQ
       demographic formula estimate?

3. *Stage Three:* Determining whether evidence of brain damage or dysfunction is present.

    a. Was the patient sufficiently attentive, cooperative, and effortful so
       that the test results are likely to be a reliable and a valid reflection
       of their optimal current performance?

    b. If specific tests of motivation and compliance (e.g., TOMM, VIP)
       were administered, did the patient's performance suggest suboptimal
       effort or symptom exaggeration that could diminish the reli-
       ability and validity of the test results?

    c. Were any factors such as culture or primary language different
       from those of the standardized tests used? Could these have af-
       fected test performance and reduced the validity of the tests to
       measure the functions for which they were designed and to pre-
       dict the presence of the conditions in question?

    d. Was there evidence of a psychiatric disorder that could account for
       some (or all) of any findings?

    e. Do the test scores fall in a range for normal individuals similar to
       the patient in terms of age and education?

    f. Are the test scores in the range that would be expected from the
       patient's specific educational and vocational achievements?

    g. How discrepant are the results from the expected findings? In
       other words, what do the results suggest about the degree of
       deficit: mild, moderate, or severe?

    h. Do the results provide consistent evidence of a deficit in one or
       more cognitive domains?

    i. Are the results consistent in both type and degree with those ex-
       pected, given the referral question and suspected etiology?

4. *Stage Four:* Making inferences about brain damage or dysfunction.

    a. Does the pattern of deficits suggest that the deficits are relatively
       isolated with a clear-cut pattern of strengths and weaknesses
       (e.g., memory versus perception or language)?

    b. Do the deficits fall into one of the classic neurobehavioral catego-
       ries (e.g., aphasia, agnosia, apraxia, neglect, alexia, or amnesia)?

   c. Do the deficits suggest a generalized pattern of deficits affecting many cognitive domains, including IQ?

   d. Does the history of the symptoms suggest an etiology with focal (e.g., single incident stroke), multifocal (e.g., closed head injury), or diffuse (e.g., toxic and metabolic disease) impact on the brain?

   e. Does the history suggest a slow (e.g., neoplasm) or sudden (e.g., cardiovascular accident) onset or a long-standing problem (e.g., mental retardation)?

   f. Does the progression of symptoms and deficits follow a particular etiology? In other words, was the deterioration gradual and consistent, suggesting disorders such as Alzheimer's or Parkinson's disease, or was the deterioration irregular and inconsistent, suggesting disorders such as multiple sclerosis?

E. COMMUNICATING THE FINDINGS FROM THE ASSESSMENT

1. Write a report that contains the referral information, relevant history, behavioral observations, tests administered, test results, interpretation, and recommendations.

2. Communicate results to the referral source and, if appropriate, have feedback session with patient.

Appendix B

Essentials of the Neurobehavioral Syndromes

In this appendix, we provide the reader with a list of some of the main clinical phenomena that lie at the center of many neuropsychological referrals. An understanding of these and similar syndromes is critical to the development of skills in neuropsychological assessment. Because this text focuses primarily on the procedures and logic of the clinical assessment of brain–behavior relationships, it presents little of the clinical phenomenology of clinical neuropsychology and neurology and does not contain a presentation of anatomy and neuropathology. An even cursory examination of these areas would be far beyond the scope of this volume. In Chapter 2, we reviewed the important areas that form the basis of the clinician's basic material knowledge, and in the annotated bibliography, we provide a listing of texts and journals that can be used to access this scientific substance of clinical neuropsychology. Appendix B is provided only to help orient the reader to the kinds of specific syndromes that may occur in isolation as a result of specific brain lesions. Some information about typical causative lesions is provided with many of these examples. Readers should familiarize themselves with basic neuroanatomy to understand the terminology used for this purpose. Where relevant, we present the names of the syndromes using the Greek prefix *a* to mean *without* to refer to disorders of specific functions rather than the Latin prefix *dys* meaning *impaired*. Both are used in the literature, but the form used in this book is the form most often used in the United States.

Acalculia. Acalculia refers to a number of disorders affecting a patient's ability to perform calculations. The problem may be secondary to a loss of comprehension of written symbols (i.e., *alexia* for numerals) or to difficulties using the spatial information needed to align correctly the columns in written arithmetic problems. Acalculia may also be caused by an inability to recall or use arithmetic facts or to a primary loss of conceptual arithmetic knowledge. Acalculia may occur with any lesion of the left cerebral hemisphere that produces aphasia but is most likely to be associated with lesions of the posterior temporal or parietal region.

Agnosia. Agnosia refers to a series of disorders that cannot be explained by primary sensory loss and that involve the loss of recognition of previously learned information. Agnosia may occur in any sensory modality (e.g., visual or auditory) and may involve specific kinds of material (e.g., prosopagnosia for faces). Agnosia rarely occurs in isolation of other limitations in cognition but may do so in the presence of highly specific lesions. Agnosia is usually caused by a lesion to the primary sensory area of the affected modality and is more likely to occur with bilateral rather than unilateral lesions.

Agraphia. Agraphia is an acquired disorder of writing. In rare instances, agraphia may occur in relative isolation, but it is usually seen as part of a general disorder of language. Patients may lose the mechanics of writing, the ability to spell, or they may not be able to write because of a loss of understanding of the written symbol (i.e., alexia). An agraphia is most likely to occur with a lesion in the left cerebral hemisphere, particularly in the areas of the frontal, parietal, and temporal lobe surrounding the Sylvian fissure.

Alexia. Alexia is an acquired reading disorder that may occur in isolation but is most commonly seen accompanying symptoms of aphasia. Several subtypes of alexia exist, including pure alexia, in which patients can read single letters but not words, and deep dyslexia, in which patients make numerous syntactic and semantic errors. Pure alexia is most likely the result of a lesion in the occipital–temporal area of the left hemisphere, whereas deep dyslexia is most likely the result of a lesion that includes Broca's area of the left hemisphere (see *aphasia*). The term *dyslexia* is typically used to refer to developmental disorders of reading.

Amnesia. This classic acquired disorder of memory is characterized by an inability to retain new information. Patients with amnesia are still alert and may be capable of recalling information that was learned before the onset of the disorder. *Anterograde amnesia* refers to an inability to learn or recall information that has been presented since the injury, and *retrograde amnesia* refers to an inability to recall information that was known before the injury. Some patients have attention or retrieval difficulties that may affect memory performance significantly. These disorders are considered distinct from true amnesia. Many patients with amnesia may show a remarkable ability to learn practiced motor skills and may show evidence of perceptual learning. A lesion affecting the hippocampus or the adjacent structures of the medial temporal lobes is considered critical for the presentation of the disorder, although lesions in such structures as the anterior thalamus, fornix, mammillary bodies, and amygdala may also be important.

Anosognosia. Anosognosia refers to a disorder of awareness of the sensory, motor, or cognitive deficits that occur as a consequence of neurological disease. Anosognosia frequently accompanies *hemispatial neglect* (see entry), but may occur with other neurological disorders such as dementia and amnesia. Patients with anosognosia are difficult to treat with physical or occupational therapy. Anosognosia is a predictor of poor long-term outcome.

Aphasia. Aphasia is an acquired language disorder that is typically characterized by word-finding difficulties and word errors. Some aphasias are characterized by fluent speech lacking meaningful nouns and verbs with varying degrees of word substitution errors or *paraphasias* (e.g., semantic = cat for dog; phonemic = rog for dog). These patients may use stock phrases (e.g., "I'm fine, thank you"), common or overlearned expressions (e.g., "You know how it is"), and circumlocutions (e.g., "The thing you eat with") without being able to express specific ideas with language. *Fluent aphasias* are often accompanied by poor comprehension of written and auditory language. In its mildest form, fluent aphasia may appear as word-finding difficulties or *anomia*.

Other aphasias are characterized by effortful, sparse speech emphasizing nouns, pronouns, and some common verbs but lacking in sentence structure. These patients may also make paraphasic errors, typically of the phonemic variety and may also make gross violations of the conventions of word order and sentence structure (e.g., "There I" for "I went there"). Patients with *nonfluent aphasias* typically appear to have much better comprehension of auditory and written language than patients with fluent aphasias but may nevertheless misinterpret longer or complex sentences.

Many aphasias affect all language-related response systems, including abilities to repeat, to read, and to write. In some cases, these response systems may be selectively impaired or preserved, depending on the specific localization of the causative lesion. Some of the classic syndromes of aphasia include *Broca's aphasia* (nonfluent; poor repetition, reading, and writing, but relatively preserved comprehension), *Wernicke's aphasia* (fluent; empty speech with varying degrees of paraphasic errors and poor comprehension, repetition, reading, and writing). Some patients with aphasias fit into these categories but show relatively preserved repetition ability. These patients are classically referred to as having *transcortical aphasias* and may be fluent or nonfluent. Some patients with aphasia may repeat more poorly than would be suspected from their spontaneous speech. These patients are classically classified as having *conduction aphasia*. Aphasia is most often a disorder of the left cerebral hemisphere (in most right-handed and a significant number of left-handed adults). Patients with nonfluent aphasia tend to suffer from lesions affecting the frontal and sometimes anterior parietal lobes, whereas patients with fluent aphasia tend to suffer from lesions affecting the temporal and inferior parietal lobes. Small variations in lesion location can make a large difference in clinical presentation of aphasia.

Apraxia. Apraxia is loss of the ability to perform previously known movements both voluntarily or to command. Although this term is sometimes used to describe disorders that may reflect attention or sensory problems (e.g., *dressing apraxia, constructional apraxia,* or *optic apraxia*), it is usually considered to be a disorder related to the highest level of motor programming that is not due to primary muscle weakness or spasticity. Classic forms of apraxia include *ideational apraxia,* in which patients have difficulty executing organized sequences of movements (e.g., washing dishes or cooking) and *ideomotor apraxia,* in which patients cannot perform gestures to command (e.g., "show me how you comb your hair"). Sometimes patients with ideomotor apraxia are able to produce the general limb movement without the detailed hand or finger positioning needed to produce the required gesture correctly (e.g., the patient may use a hand as a comb when asked to show how to comb hair). This phenomenon is known as *body part as object.* Motor apraxic symptoms are more likely to be caused by lesions to the left hemisphere and often accompany aphasic symptoms.

Delirium or Confusional State. This is a disturbance of the ability to maintain basic attention and a consistent stream of thought. It may be accompanied by difficulties with wakefulness or in some cases by hypervigilance. Delirium usually reflects a widespread central nervous system impairment that may be caused by an infection, toxic or metabolic disturbance, or any brain disease causing significant disruption of central nervous system functioning. Delirium may have an acute onset and be time limited or may have a slow onset and chronic course, depending on the causative illness (e.g., central nervous system infection versus dementia, respectively).

Dementia. Dementia refers to a set of disorders characterized by a progressive decline in cognitive functions. Patients with dementia usually suffer from a loss of multiple functions that may include language, perception, and executive functions (see dysexecutive syndrome), but must also have a disorder of memory to receive the diagnosis. The most common illness producing dementia is *Alzheimer's disease.* Other illnesses such as *vascular dementia* and *Pick's disease* may present initially with difficulties with executive functions or language and then later progress to a memory disorder. Illnesses producing dementia are more prevalent in older adults, becoming increasingly common in the seventh decade of life and later.

Dysexecutive Syndrome. Although not a classical syndrome, disorders of what are termed *executive functions* have been increasingly recognized in recent years. Executive functions refer to a variety of abilities ranging from the mental maintenance and manipulation of information (i.e., working memory) and the initiation and termination or inhibition of behavioral responses to such high-level functions as planning and social judgment. A number of clinical manifestations of dysexecutive disorders occur, ranging from patients who appear inert with diminished spontaneous behavior, to patients who appear to act out in socially inappropriate manners with sexual or aggressive behavior, and to patients who appear to be sufficiently disorganized with disrupted work and daily activities. Dysexecutive syndromes are often attributed to lesions of the frontal lobe, but they vary considerably depending on the exact localization within this large cortical structure. Clinicians must be particularly cautious in relating dysexecutive behavior to a specific lesion, however, because these disorders may appear as a result of lesions to other cortical and subcortical structures or may be related to psychiatric illness.

Hemianopsia. This is a primary visual disorder affecting one visual field. Hemianopsia or hemianopia usually results from a visual system lesion that occurs in the optic tract beyond the optic chiasm or in the occipital cortex itself. Hemianopsia is equivalent to blindness affecting a visual field rather than an eye.

Hemispatial Neglect. This is an acquired disorder in which, despite normal sensory function, patients fail to acknowledge or respond to information that is present on one side of space. Neglect is considered a disorder of attention rather than sensation and affects the side of space on the side of the patient's body opposite that of the causative lesion. Neglect is most likely to occur and is most severe with a lesion of the right cerebral hemisphere rather than the left cerebral hemisphere. Neglect may result from lesions to various brain structures, including the frontal and temporal lobes, but it is most severe and enduring with lesions in the area of the parietal lobes. Neglect is often marked by anosognosia for its symptoms (see above).

Prosopagnosia. This is a disorder of the recognition of familiar faces that may occur even when the ability to distinguish similar but novel faces and vision acuity is otherwise normal. It may occur as either an acquired disorder or a congenital or developmental disorder. Currently it is estimated that the latter may affect 2.5% of the adult population (Kennerknecht et al., 2006). Lesions of the fusiform gyrus of the right inferior temporal–occipital cortex are often implicated as a causal lesion for prosopagnosia, although it appears that the most severe cases are accompanied by bilateral lesions. Prosopagnosia has attracted considerable interest from researchers in recent years because it supports the idea that face recognition is accomplished by a specially adapted and localized brain mechanism that could be unique to advanced primates.

References

Achenbach, T. M., Newhouse, P. A., & Rescorla, L. A. (2004). *Manual for the ASEBA older adult forms & profiles*. Burlington, VT: University of Vermont Research Center for Children, Youth, & Families.

Achenbach, T. M., & Rescorla, L. A. (2000). *Manual for the ASEBA preschool-age forms & profiles*. Burlington, VT: University of Vermont Research Center for Children, Youth, & Families.

Achenbach, T. M., & Rescorla, L. A. (2001). *Manual for the ASEBA school-age forms & profiles*. Burlington, VT: University of Vermont Research Center for Children, Youth, & Families.

Achenbach, T. M., & Rescorla, L. A. (2003). *Manual for the ASEBA adult forms & profiles*. Burlington, VT: University of Vermont Research Center for Children, Youth, & Families.

Adams, K. M., & Rourke, B. P. (Eds.). (1992). *The TCN guide to professional practice in clinical neuropsychology*. Amsterdam: Swets & Zeitlinger.

Adams, W., & Sheslow, D. (1995). *Wide Range Assessment of Visual Motor Ability*. Lutz, FL: Psychological Assessment Resources.

Allen, L. M., Conder, R. L., Jr., Green, P., & Cox, D. R. (2000). *Computerized Assessment of Response Bias*. Durham, NC: Cognisyst.

American Academy of Clinical Neuropsychology. (2001). Policy statement on the presence of third party observers in neuropsychological assessments. *The Clinical Neuropsychologist, 15,* 433–439.

American Board of Professional Neuropsychology. (2007). The board of directors' meeting. *The Professional Neuropsychologist, Volume 12, Issue 2.* Retrieved December 23, 2008, from www.neuropsychologyboard.org/newsArticle.aspx?id=3.

American Educational Research Association, American Psychological Association, & National Council on Measurement in Education. (1999). *Standards for educational and psychological testing*. Washington, DC: American Educational Research Association.

American Psychiatric Association. (2000). *Diagnostic and Statistical Manual of Mental Disorders, Fourth Edition, Text Revision*. Washington, DC: American Psychiatric Association.

American Psychological Association. (2002). Ethical principles of psychologists and code of conduct. *American Psychologist, 57,* 1060–1073.

Anderson, J. A. (1995). *An introduction to neural networks*. Cambridge, MA: MIT Press.

Armstrong, K. E., Beebe, D. W., Hilsabeck, R. C., & Kirkwood, M. W. (2008). *Board certification in clinical neuropsychology: A guide to becoming ABPP/ABCN certified without sacrificing your sanity*. New York: Oxford University Press.

Baade, L. E., & Schoenberg, M. R. (2004). A proposed method to estimate premorbid intelligence utilizing group achievement measures from school records. *Archives of Clinical Neuropsychology, 19,* 227–243.

Baddeley, A., Emslie, H., & Nimmo-Smith, I. (1992). *The Speed and Capacity of Language-Processing Test*. Suffolk, England: Thames Valley Test Company.

Baddeley, A., Emslie, H., & Nimmo-Smith, I. (1993) The Spot-A-Word Test: A robust estimate of verbal intelligence based on lexical decision. *British Journal of Clinical Psychology, 32,* 55–65.

Baddeley, A., Emslie, H., & Nimmo-Smith, I. (1994). *Doors and People*. Bury St. Edmonds, England: Thames Valley Test Company.

Barona, A., Reynolds, C. R., & Chastain, R. (1984). A demographically based index of premorbid intelligence for the WAIS-R. *Journal of Consulting and Clinical Psychology, 52,* 885–887.

Beck, A. T., & Steer, R. A. (1993). *Beck Anxiety Inventory.* San Antonio, TX: Psychological Corporation.

Beck, A. T., Steer, R. A., & Brown, G. (1996). *Beck Depression Inventory—II.* San Antonio: Psychological Corporation.

Beck, J. S., Beck, A. T., Jolly, J. B., & Steer, R. A. (2005). *Beck Youth Inventories, Second Edition for Children and Adolescents manual.* San Antonio, TX: Harcourt Assessment.

Beery, K. E., & Beery, N. A. (2006). *The Beery VMI For Children and Adults with supplemental developmental tests of visual perception and motor coordination: Administration, scoring and teaching manual, 5th ed.* Minneapolis, MN: NCS Pearson.

Belar, C. D., & Perry, N. W. (1992). National conference on scientist–practitioner education and training for the professional practice of psychology. *American Psychologist, 44,* 60–65.

Ben-Porath, Y. S., & Tellegen, A. (2008). *MMPI-2-RF: Manual for administration, scoring, and interpretation.* Minneapolis: University of Minnesota Press.

Benedict, R. H. B. (1997). *Brief Visuospatial Memory Test—Revised.* Odessa, FL: Psychological Assessment Resources.

Benton, A., & Adams, K. M. (2000). *Exploring the history of neuropsychology: Selected papers.* New York: Oxford University Press.

Benton, A. L., deS Hamsher, K., & Sivan, A. B. (1994). *Multilingual Aphasia Examination, 3rd ed.* Iowa City, IA: AJA Associates.

Benton, A. L., Sivan, A. B., deS. Hamsher, K., Varney, N. R., & Spreen O. (1994). *Contributions to neuropsychological assessment* (2nd ed.). New York: Oxford University Press.

Binder, L. M. (1993). An abbreviated version of the Portland Digit Recognition Test. *The Clinical Neuropsychologist, 7,* 104–107.

Binder, L. M., Iverson, G. L., & Brooks, B. L. (2009). To err is human: "Abnormal" neuropsychological scores and variability are common in healthy adults. *Archives of Clinical Neuropsychology, 24,* 31–46.

Bihrle, A. M., Bellugi, U., Delis, D., & Marks, S. (1989). Seeing either the forest or the trees: Dissociation in visuospatial processing. *Brain and Cognition, 11,* 37–49.

Blair, J. R., & Spreen, O. (1989). Predicting premorbid IQ: A revision of the National Adult Reading Test. *The Clinical Neuropsychologist, 3,* 129–136.

Board of Directors. (2007). American Academy of Clinical Neuropsychology (AACN) practice guidelines for neuropsychological assessment and consultation. *The Clinical Neuropsychologist, 21,* 209–231.

Boll, T. (1993). *Children's Category Test.* San Antonio, TX: Psychological Corporation.

Boone, K., Lu, P., & Herzberg, D. (2002a). *The b Test.* Los Angeles: Western Psychological Services.

Boone, K., Lu, P., & Herzberg, D. (2002b). *The Dot Counting Test.* Los Angeles: Western Psychological Services.

Brady, C. B., Spiro, A., McGlinchey-Berroth, R., Milberg, W., & Gaziano, M. (2001). Stroke risk predicts verbal fluency decline in healthy older men: Evidence from the Normative Aging Study. *Journal of Gerontology: Psychological Sciences, 56B,* 340–346.

Brandt, J. (1992). Detecting amnesia's impostors. In L. R. Squire & N. Butters (Eds.), *Neuropsychology of memory* (2nd ed., pp. 156–165). New York: Guilford Press.

Brandt, J., & Benedict, R. H. B. (2001). *The Hopkins Verbal Learning Test-Revised.* Odessa, FL: Psychological Assessment Resources.

Briere, J. (1995). *Trauma Symptom Inventory: Professional Manual.* Odessa, FL: Psychological Assessment Resources.

Briere, J. (1996). *Trauma Symptom Checklist for Children: Professional Manual*. Odessa, FL: Psychological Assessment Resources.

Brink, T. L., Yesavage, J. A., Lum, O., Heersema, P. H., Adey, M., & Rose, T. L. (1982). Screening tests for geriatric depression. *Clinical Gerontologist, 1,* 37–43.

Brown, J. I., Fishco, V. V., & Hanna, G. S. (1993). *Nelson-Denny Reading Test*. Itasca, IL: Riverside.

Brown, L., Sherbenou, R. J., & Johnson, S. K. (1997). *Test of Nonverbal Intelligence—III*. Austin, TX: PRO-ED.

Brownell, R. (2000a). *Expressive One-Word Picture Vocabulary Test*. Novato, CA: Academic Therapy.

Brownell, R. (2000b). *Receptive One-Word Picture Vocabulary Test*. Novato, CA: Academic Therapy.

Bruininks, R. H., Woodcock, R. W., Weatherman, R. F., & Hill, B. K. (1996). *SIB-R: Scales of Independent Behavior-Revised*. Itasca, IL: Riverside Publishing Company.

Brunswick, E. (1956). *Perception and the representative design of psychological experiments, 2nd ed.* Berkley, CA: University of California Press.

Burgess, P. W., Alderman, N., Forbes, C., Costello, A., Coates, L. M-A., Dawson, D. R., Anderson, N. D., Gilbert, S. J., Dumontheil, I., & Channon, S. (2006). The case for the development and use of "ecologically valid" measure of executive function in experimental and clinical neuropsychology. *Journal of the International Neuropsychology Society, 12,* 194–209.

Buschke, H. (1973). Selective reminding for analysis of memory and learning. *Journal of Verbal Learning and Verbal Behavior, 12,* 543–550.

Butcher, J. N., Dahlstrom, W. G., Graham, J. R., Tellegen, A. M., & Kaemmer, B. (1989). *MMPI-2: Manual for administration and scoring*. Minneapolis, MN: University of Minnesota Press.

Butcher, J. N., Williams, C. L., Graham, J. R., Archer, R. P., Tellegen, A., Ben-Porath, Y. S., & Kaemmer, B. (1992). *MMPI-A: Manual for administration, scoring, and interpretation*. Minneapolis, MN: University of Minnesota Press.

Centers for Disease Control and Prevention, National Center for Health Statistics. (2005). *Health, United States, 2005: With chartbook on trends in the health of Americans*. Hyattsville, MD: Centers for Disease Control and Prevention.

Christensen, A. –L. (1974). *Luria's neuropsychological investigation*. Munksgaard, Copenhagen, Denmark.

Churchland, P. M. (1989). *A neurocomputational perspective*. Cambridge, MA: MIT Press.

Cohen, M. (1997). *Children's Memory Scale*. San Antonio, TX: Psychological Corporation.

Colarusso, R. R., & Hammill, D. D. (2003). *Motor-Free Visual Perception Test—3*. Novato, CA: Academic Therapy.

Conners, C. K. (2004). *Conners' Continuous Performance Test II, Version 5*. Toronto, Canada: Multi-Health Systems.

Conners, C. K. (2008). *Conners 3rd Edition*. North Tonawanda, NY: Multi-Health Systems.

Constantinou, M., Ashendorf, L., & McCaffrey, R. J. (2002). When the third party observer of a neuropsychological evaluation is an audio—recorder. *The Clinical Neuropsychologist, 16,* 407–412.

Constantinou, M., Ashendorf, L., & McCaffrey, R. J. (2005). Effects of a third party observer during neuropsychological assessment: When the observer is a video—camera. *Journal of Forensic Neuropsychology, 4,* 39–47.

Crocker, L., & Algina, J. (1986). *Introduction to classical and modern test theory*. Fort Worth, TX: Holt, Rinehart and Winston.

Culbertson, W. C., & Zilmer, E. A. (2000). *Tower of London-Drexel University (2nd ed.)*. North Tonawanda, NY: Multi-Health Systems.

Cummings, J. L., & Coffey, C. E. (2000). Geriatric neuropsychiatry. In C. E. Coffey & J. L. Cummings (Eds.), *Textbook of geriatric neuropsychiatry* (2nd ed., pp. 3–15). Washington, DC: APA Press.

Damasio, A. R. (1995). *Descartes' error: Emotion, reason, and the human brain.* New York: Avon Books.

Dana, R. H. (1993). *Multicultural assessment perspectives for professional psychology.* Boston: Allyn and Bacon.

De Renzi, E., & Vignolo, L. (1962). The Token Test: A sensitive test to detect receptive disturbances in aphasics. *Brain, 85,* 665–678.

DeFilippis, N. A., & McCampbell, E. (1997). *Manual for the Booklet Category Test (2nd ed.).* Odessa, FL: Psychological Assessment Resources.

DeGutis, J., Robertson, L., Nakayama, K., McGlinchey, R., & Milberg, W. (2008). Learning faces: Plasticity and the rehabilitation of congenital prosopagnosia [abstract]. *Journal of Vision, 8,* 184a.

D'Elia, L. F., Satz, P., Uchiyama, C. L., & White, T. (1996). *Color Trails Test.* Odessa, FL: Psychological Assessment Resources, Inc.

Delis, D. C., Kaplan, E., & Kramer, J. H. (2001). *Delis–Kaplan Executive Function System.* San Antonio, TX: The Psychological Corporation.

Delis, D. C., Kramer, J. H., Kaplan, E., & Ober, B. A. (1987). *California Verbal Learning Test— Adult Version.* San Antonio, TX: Psychological Corporation.

Delis, D. C., Kramer, J. H., Kaplan, E., & Ober, B. A. (1994). *California Verbal Learning Test— Children's Version.* San Antonio, TX: Psychological Corporation.

Delis, D. C., Kramer, J. H., Kaplan, E., & Ober, B. A. (2000). *California Verbal Learning Test— Second Edition.* San Antonio, TX: Psychological Corporation.

Division 40. (1997). Bylaws of the Division of Clinical Neuropsychology. Retrieved December 24, 2008, from http://www.div40.org/APA Division_40_Bylaws 2005.pdf.

Division 40. (1989). Definition of a clinical neuropsychologist. *The Clinical Neuropsychologist, 3,* 22.

Donders, J. (2001a). A survey of report writing by neuropsychologists: I. General characteristics and content. *The Clinical Neuropsychologist, 15,* 137–149.

Donders, J. (2001b). A survey of report writing by neuropsychologists: II. Test data, report format, and document length. *The Clinical Neuropsychologist, 15,* 150–161.

Dunn, L. M., & Dunn, D. M. (2006). *Peabody Picture Vocabulary Test, fourth edition.* Minneapolis, MN: Pearson Assessments.

Emslie, H., Wilson, F. C., Burden, V., Nimmo-Smith, A., & Wilson, B. A. (2003). *Behavioural Assessment of the Dysexecutive Syndrome in Children.* Bury St. Edmunds, England: Thames Valley Test Company.

Faust, D., Hart, K., & Guilmette, T. J. (1988). Pediatric malingering: The capacity of children to fake believable deficits on neuropsychological testing. *Journal of Consulting and Clinical Psychology, 56,* 578–582.

Finger, S., & Stein, D. G. (1982). *Brain damage and recovery: Research and clinical perspectives.* New York: Academic Press.

Flanagan, D. P., & Kaufman, A. S. (2009). *Essentials of WISC-IV assessment, 2nd ed.* New York: Wiley.

Flanagan, D. P., Ortiz, S. O., & Alfonso, V. C. (2007). *Essentials of cross-battery assessment, 2nd ed.* New York: Wiley.

Flourens, P. (1960). Recherches Expérimentales sur les Propriétés et les Fonction du Système Nerveux dans les Animaux Vertébrés. Paris: Crevot. Translated and reprinted in G. von Bonin (Ed.), *Some papers on the cerebral cortex.* Springfield, IL: Thomas. (Original work published 1824)

Fodor, J. A. (1983). *The modularity of mind: An essay on faculty psychology*. Cambridge, MA: MIT Press.

Folstein, M. F., Folstein, S. E., & McHugh, P. R. (2001). *Mini-Mental State Examination: Clinical guide*. Odessa, FL: Psychological Assessment Resources.

Frederick, R. I. (1997). *Validity Indicator Profile*. Minneapolis, MN: National Computer Systems.

Freedman, M., Leach, L., Kaplan, E., Winocur, G., Shulman, K. I., & Delis, D. C. (1994). *Clock drawing: A neuropsychological analysis*. New York: Oxford University Press.

Gall, F. (1835). *On the functions of the brain and each of its parts: With observations on determining the instincts, propensities, and talents, or the moral and intellectual dispositions of men and animals, by the configuration of the brain and head* (Vol. 3; W. Lewis Jr., Trans.). Boston: Marsh, Capen and Lyon.

German, D. J. (1990). *Test of Adolescent/Adult Word Finding*. Austin, TX: PRO-ED.

Geslani, D. M., Tierney, M. C., Herrmann, N., & Szalai, J. P. (2005). Mild cognitive impairment: An operational definition and its conversion rate to Alzheimer's disease. *Dementia and Geriatric Cognitive Disorders, 5,* 383–389.

Gilliam, J. E. (1995). *Attention-Deficit/Hyperactivity Disorder Test: Examiner's manual*. Austin, TX: PRO-ED.

Gioia, G. A., Espy, K. A., & Isquith, P. K. (2003). *Behavior Rating Inventory of Executive Function—Preschool Version*. Lutz, FL: Psychological Assessment Resources.

Gioia, G. A., Isquith, P. K., Guy, S. C., & Kenworthy, L. (2000). *Behavior Rating Inventory of Executive Function*. Lutz, FL: Psychological Assessment Resources.

Glutting, J., Adams, W., & Sheslow, D. (1999). *Wide Range Intelligence Test Manual*. Lutz, FL: Psychological Assessment Resources.

Golden, C. J. (1978). *Stroop Color and Word Test*. Chicago, IL: Stoelting.

Golden, C. J., & Freshwater, S. M. (2002). *Stroop Color and Word Test: Revised Examiner's Manual*. Wood Dale, IL: Stoelting.

Golden, C. J., Freshwater, S. M., Golden, Z. (2003). *Stroop Color and Word Test Children's Version for Ages 5–14*. Wood Dale, IL: Stoelting.

Golden, C. J., Hammeke, T. A., & Purisch, A. D. (1978). Diagnostic validity of a standardized neuropsychological battery derived from Luria's neuropsychological tests. *Journal of Consulting and Clinical Psychology, 46,* 1258–1265.

Golden, C. J., Purisch, A. D., & Hammeke, T. A. (1985). *Manual for the Luria–Nebraska Neuropsychological Battery: Forms I and II*. Los Angeles: Western Psychological Services.

Goldstein, K. (1939). *The organism*. New York: American Book Company.

Goodglass, H., & Kaplan, E. (1983). *The assessment of aphasia and related disorders* (2nd ed.). Philadelphia: Lea & Febiger.

Goodglass, H., Kaplan, E., & Barresi, B. (2001). *Boston Diagnostic Aphasia Examination* (3rd ed.). Philadelphia: Lippincott Williams & Wilkins.

Grant, D. A., & Berg, E. A. (1993). *Wisconsin Card Sorting Test*. Odessa, FL: Psychological Assessment Resources.

Green, P. (2003). *Green's Word Memory Test for Windows*. Edmonton, Canada: Green's Publishing.

Green, P. (2004). *Green's Medical Symptom Validity Test for Microsoft Windows*. Edmonton, Canada: Green's Publishing, Inc.

Green, P. (2006). *The Nonverbal Medical Symptom Validity Test: MS Windows computer program*. Edmonton, Canada: Green's Publishing.

Green, P., & Astner, K. (1995). *Test Manual for the Oral Word Memory Test*. Durham, NC: Cognisyst. [Out of print but available through Green's Publishing, Inc.].

Greenberg, L. M. (2007), *The Test of Variables of Attention* (Version 7.3) [Computer Software]. Los Alamitos, CA: The TOVA Company.

Greiffenstein, M. F., Baker, W. J., & Gola, T. (1996). Comparison of multiple scoring methods for Rey's malingered amnesia measures. *Archives of Clinical Neuropsychology, 11,* 283–293.

Greiffenstein, M. F., & Cohen, L. (2005). Neuropsychology and the law: Principles of productive attorney-neuropsychologist relations. In G. J. Larrabee (Ed.). *Forensic neuropsychology: A scientific approach* (pp. 29–91). New York: Oxford University Press.

Grober, E., & Sliwinski, M. (1991). Development and validation of a model for estimating premorbid verbal intelligence in the elderly. *Journal of Clinical and Experimental Neuropsychology, 13,* 933–949.

Gronwall, D. M. A. (1977). Paced Auditory Serial-Addition Task: A measure of recovery from concussion. *Perceptual and Motor Skills, 44,* 367–373.

Gronwall, D. M. A., & Sampson, H. (1974). *The psychological effects of concussion.* New Zealand: Auckland University Press.

Guilmette, T. J., Hagan, L. D., & Giuliano, A. J. (2008). Assigning qualitative descriptions to test scores in neuropsychology: Forensic implications. *The Clinical Neuropsychologist, 22,* 122–139.

Guy, S. C., Isquith, P. K., & Gioia, G.A. (2004). *Behavior Rating Inventory of Executive Function—Self-Report.* Lutz, FL: Psychological Assessment Resources.

Halstead, W. C. (1947). *Brain and intelligence.* Chicago: University of Chicago Press.

Hammill, D. D., Pearson, N. A., & Wiederholt, J. L. (2009). *Comprehensive Test of Nonverbal Intelligence, Second Edition.* Austin, TX: PRO-ED.

Hannay, H. J., Bieliauskas, L., Crosson, B. A., Hammeke, T. A., deS. Hamsher, K., & Koffler, S. (Eds.). (1998). Proceedings of the Houston Conference on Specialty Training in Clinical Neuropsychology, September 3–7, 1997. *Archives of Clinical Neuropsychology, 13,* 157–249.

Hannay, H. J., & Levin, H. S. (1985). Selective reminding: An examination of the equivalence of four forms. *Journal of Clinical and Experimental Neuropsychology, 7,* 251–263.

Harrison, P. L., & Oakland, T. (2000). *Adaptive Behavior Assessment System: Manual.* San Antonio, TX: Psychological Corporation.

Heaton, R. K., Chelune, G. J., Talley, J. L., Kay, G. G., & Curtiss, G. (1993). *Wisconsin Card Sorting Test manual: Revised and expanded.* Odessa, FL: Psychological Assessment Resources.

Heaton, R. K., Grant, I., & Matthews, C. G. (1991). *Comprehensive norms for an Expanded Halstead–Reitan Battery: Demographic corrections, research findings, and clinical applications.* Odessa, FL: Psychological Assessment Resources.

Heaton, R. K., Miller, S. W., Taylor, M. J., & Grant, I. (2004). *Revised comprehensive norms for an expanded Halstead-Reitan Battery: Demographically adjusted neuropsychological norms for African American and Caucasian adults.* Lutz, FL: Psychological Assessment Resources, Inc.

Hiscock, C., Branham, J., & Hiscock, M. (1994). Detection of feigned cognitive impairment: The two-alternative forced-choice method compared with selected conventional tests. *Journal of Psychopathology and Behavioral Assessment, 16,* 95–109.

Hiscock, M., & Hiscock, C. K. (1989). Refining the forced-choice method for the detection of malingering. *Journal of Clinical and Experimental Neuropsychology, 11,* 967–974.

Hooper, H. E. (1958). *The Hooper Visual Organization Test.* Beverly Hills, CA: Western Psychological Services.

Hsieh, S. L. J., & Tori, C. D. (1993). Neuropsychological and cognitive effects of Chinese-language instruction. *Perceptual and Motor Skills, 77,* 1071–1081.

Ivnik, R. J., Haaland, K. Y., & Bieliauskas, L. A. (2000). The American Board of Clinical Neuropsychology (ABCN), 2000 update. *The Clinical Neuropsychologist, 14,* 261–268.

Jackson, J. H. (1894). The factors of insanities. *Medical Press and Circular, 2,* 615–619.

Joy, S., Fein, D., Kaplan, E., & Morris, F. (2001). Quantifying qualitative features of Block Design performance among healthy older adults. *Archives of Clinical Neuropsychology, 16,* 157–170.

Jurica, P. J., Leitten, C. L., & Mattis, S. (2001). *Dementia Rating Scale—2: Professional manual.* Odessa, FL: Psychological Assessment Resources.

Kaplan, E. F., Goodglass, H., & Weintraub, S. (2001). *The Boston Naming Test (2nd ed.).* Philadelphia: Lippincott, Williams & Wilkins.

Kaplan, E., Fein, D., Kramer, J., Delis, D., & Morris, R. (1999). *Wechsler Intelligence Scale for Children—Third Edition as a Process Instrument manual.* San Antonio, TX: Psychological Corporation.

Kaplan, E., Fein, D., Morris, R., & Delis, D. C. (1991). *WAIS-R NI for use with WAIS-R manual.* San Antonio, TX: Psychological Corporation.

Kaufman, A. S. (1994). *Intelligent testing with the WISC—III.* New York: Wiley.

Kaufman, A. S., & Kaufman, N. L. (1993). *Kaufman Adolescent and Adult Intelligence Test.* Circle Pines, MN: American Guidance Service.

Kaufman, A. S., & Kaufman, N. L. (1994). *Kaufman Functional Academic Skills Test.* Circle Pines, MN: American Guidance Service.

Kaufman, A. S., & Kaufman, N. L. (2004a). *Kaufman Assessment Battery for Children, Second Edition.* Circle Pines, MN: AGS.

Kaufman, A. S., & Kaufman, N. L. (2004b). *Kaufman Brief Intelligence Test, Second Edition.* Circle Pines, MN: AGS.

Kaufman, A. S., & Kaufman, N. L. (2004c). *Kaufman Test of Educational Achievement, Second Edition.* Circle Pines, MN: American Guidance Service.

Kaufman, A. S., & Kaufman, N. L. (2004d). *Kaufman Test of Educational Achievement, Second Edition, Brief Form.* Circle Pines, MN: American Guidance Service.

Kaufman, A. S., & Lichtenberger, E. O. (2000). *Essentials of WISC-III and WPPSI-R Assessment.* New York: Wiley.

Kennerknecht, I., Grueter, T., Welling, B., Wentzek, S., Horst, J., Edwards, S., & Grueter, M. (2006). First report of prevalence of non-syndromic hereditary prosopagnosia (HPA). *American Journal of Medical Genetics Part A, 140,* 1617–1622.

Kiernan, R. J., Mueller, J., Langston, J. W., & Van Dyke, C. (1987). The Neurobehavioral Cognitive Status Examination: A brief but differentiated approach to cognitive assessment. *Annals of Internal Medicine, 107,* 481–485.

Kongs, S. K., Thompson, L. L., Iverson, G. L., & Heaton, R. K. (2000). *Wisconsin Card Sorting Test—64 Card Version.* Lutz, FL: Psychological Assessment Resources.

Korkman, M., Kirk, U., & Kemp, S. (2007). *NEPSY—Second Edition.* San Antonio, TX: Harcourt Assessment.

Kraemer, H. C. (1992). *Evaluating medical tests: Objective and quantitative guidelines.* Newbury Park, CA: Sage.

Kuo, H-K., Jones, R.N., Milberg, W. P., Tennstedt, S., Talbot, L., Morris, J. N., & Lipsitz, L. A. (2005). Effect of blood pressure and diabetes mellitus on cognitive and physical function in older adults: A longitudinal analysis of the advanced cognitive training for independent and vital elderly cohort. *Journal of American Geriatric Society, 53,* 1154–1161.

Kuo, H-K., Jones, R.N., Milberg, W. P., Tennstedt, S., Talbot, L., Morris, J. N., & Lipsitz, L. A. (2006). Cognitive function in normal-weight, overweight, and obese older adults: An analysis of the advanced cognitive training for independent and vital elderly cohort. *Journal of American Geriatric Society, 54,* 97–103.

Lashley, K. S. (1929). *Brain mechanisms and intelligence.* Chicago: University of Chicago Press.

Leach, L., Kaplan, E., Rewilak, D., Richards, B., & Proulx, G. B. (2000). *Kaplan Baycrest Neurocognitive Assessment manual.* San Antonio, TX: Harcourt Assessments.

Leark, R. A., Greenberg, L. K., Kindschi, C. L., Dupuy, T. R., & Hughes, S. J. (2007). *Test of Variables of Attention professional manual.* Los Alamitos, CA: The TOVA Company.

Lee, G. P., Loring, D. W., & Martin, R. C. (1992). Rey's 15-Item Visual Memory Test for the detection of malingering: Normative observations on patients with neurological disorders. *Psychological Assessment, 4,* 43–46.

Leritz, E. C., McGlinchey, R. E., Lundgren, K., Grande, L. J., & Milberg, W. P. (2008). Using lexical familiarity judgments to assess verbally mediated intelligence in aphasia. *Neuropsychology, 22,* 687–696.

Lewis, R. F. (1995). *Professional user's guide for the Digit Vigilance Test.* Odessa, FL: Professional Assessment Resources.

Lezak, M. D. (1983). *Neuropsychological assessment.* New York: Oxford University Press.

Lezak, M. D., Howieson, D. B., & Loring, D. W. With Hannay, J. & Fischer, J. S. (2004). *Neuropsychological Assessment* (4th ed.). New York: Oxford University Press.

Libon, D. J., Mattson, R. E., Glosser, G., Kaplan, E., Malamut, B. M., Sands, L. P., Swenson, R., & Cloud, B. (1996). A nine-word dementia version of the California Verbal Learning Test. *The Clinical Neuropsychologist, 10,* 237–244.

Llorente, A. M., Williams, J., Satz, P., & D'Elia, L. F. (2003). *Children's Color Trails Test (CCTT).* Odessa, FL: Psychological Assessment Resources, Inc.

Luria, A. R. (1966). *Higher cortical functions in man.* New York: Basic Books.

Luria, A. R. (1973). *The working brain: An introduction to neuropsychology.* New York: Basic Books.

Malmgren, R. (2000). Epidemiology of aging. In C. E. Coffey & J. L. Cummings (Eds.), *Textbook of geriatric neuropsychiatry* (2nd ed., 17–31). Washington, DC: APA Press.

Manly, T., Robertson, I. H., Anderson, V., & Nimmo-Smith, I. (1998). *TEA-Ch: The Test of Everyday Attention for Children.* Bury St. Edmunds, England: Thames Valley Test Company.

Martin, N. A. (2006). *Test of Visual Perceptual Skills, 3rd ed.* Novato, CA: Academic Therapy.

Matarazzo, J. D. (1972). *Wechsler's measurement and appraisal of adult intelligence* (5th ed.). Baltimore: Williams & Wilkins.

McCaffrey, R. J., Fisher, J. M., Gold, B. A., & Lynch, J. K. (1996). Presence of third parties during neuropsychological evaluations: Who is evaluating whom? *The Clinical Neuropsychologist, 10,* 435–449.

McCaffrey, R. J., Lynch, J. K., & Yantz, C. L. (2005). Third party observers: Why all the fuss? *Journal of Forensic Neuropsychology, 4,* 1–15.

McCaffrey, R. J., Williams, A. D., Fisher, J. M., & Laing, L. C. (1997). *The practice of forensic neuropsychology: Meeting challenges in the courtroom.* New York: Plenum Press.

McGlinchey-Berroth, R., Bullis, D. P., Milberg, W. P., Verfaellie, M., Alexander, M., & D'Esposito, M. (1996). Assessment of neglect reveals dissociable behavioral but not neuroanatomical subtypes. *Journal of the International Neuropsychological Society, 2,* 441–451.

McKhann, G. (1984). Criteria for the clinical diagnosis of Alzheimer's disease: Excerpts from the NINCDS-ADRDA work group report. *Neurology, 34,* 939.

Meehl, P. E., & Rosen, A. (1955). Antecedent probability and the efficiency of psychometric signs, patterns, or cutting scores. In D. N. Jackson & S. Messick (Eds.), *Problems in human assessment* (pp. 392–412). New York: McGraw-Hill.

Meier, M. J. (1997). The establishment of clinical neuropsychology as a psychological specialty. In M. E. Maruish & J. A. Moses, Jr. (Eds.), *Clinical neuropsychology: Theoretical foundations for practitioners* (pp. 1–31). Mahwah, NJ: Lawrence Erlbaum Associates.Meier, M. J. (1998). On the emergence of clinical neuropsychology as a specialty. *Division 40 Newsletter 4* (Spring), 7–8.

Mesulam, M. M. (1985). *Principles of behavioral neurology.* Philadelphia: Davis.

Meyers, J. E., & Meyers, K. R. (1995). *Rey Complex Figure Test and Recognition Trial.* Odessa, FL: Psychological Assessment Resources.

Meyers, J. E., & Meyers, K. R. (1996). *Rey Complex Figure Test and Recognition Trial. Manual Supplement.* Odessa, FL: Psychological Assessment Resources.

Milberg, W. P. (1996). Issues in the assessment of cognitive function in dementia. *Brain and Cognition, 31,* 114–132.

Milberg, W. P., Hebben, N., & Kaplan, E. (2009). The Boston process approach to neuropsychological assessment. In I. Grant & K. M. Adams (Eds.), *Neuropsychological assessment of neuropsychiatric and neuromedical disorders* (3rd ed., pp. —42–65). New York: Oxford University Press.

Milner, B. (1963). Effects of different brain regions on card sorting. *Archives of Neurology, 9,* 90–100.

Morey, L. C. (1991). *Personality Assessment Inventory: Professional manual.* Odessa, FL: Psychological Assessment Resources.

Naglieri, J. A. (2000). *Naglieri Nonverbal Ability Test—Individual Administration.* San Antonio, TX: Psychological Corporation.

National Academy of Neuropsychology. (2000a). Presence of third party observers during neuropsychological testing: Official statement of the National Academy of Neuropsychology. *Archives of Clinical Neuropsychology, 15,* 379–380.

National Academy of Neuropsychology. (2000b). Test Security: Official position statement of the National Academy of Neuropsychology. *Archives of Clinical Neuropsychology, 15,* 383–386.

National Academy of Neuropsychology. (2001). Definition of a neuropsychologist. Retrieved December 23, 2008, from http://www.nanonline.org/PositionPageLinks/Pages/DefinitionofaNeuropsychologist.aspx.

Navarrette, M. G. (1999). Verbal and nonverbal memory differences in bilingual children. *Dissertation Abstracts International 60,* 1013A.

Nelson, H. E. (1982). *National Adult Reading Test (NART): Test manual.* Windsor, England: NFER Nelson.

Nelson, H. E., & McKenna, P. (1975). The use of current reading ability in the assessment of dementia. *British Journal of Social and Clinical Psychology, 14,* 259–267.

Nezu, C. M., Finch, A. J., & Simon, N. P. (Eds.). (2009). *Becoming board certified by the American Board of Professional Psychology.* New York: Oxford University Press.

O'Carroll, R. E., Baikie, E. M., & Whittick, J. E. (1987). Does the National Adult Reading Test hold in dementia? *British Journal of Clinical Psychology, 26,* 315–316.

Ownby, R. L. (1990). A study of the expository process model in mental health settings. *Journal of Clinical Psychology, 46,* 366–371.

Paolo, A. M., Ryan, J. J., & Troster, A. I. (1996). Demographically based regression equations to estimate WAIS-R subtest scaled scores. *The Clinical Neuropsychologist, 10,* 130–140.

Parsons, O. A., Vega, A., & Burn, J. (1969). Different psychological effects of lateralized brain-damage. *Journal of Clinical and Consulting Psychology, 33,* 551–557.

Pascal-Leone, A., Davie, N. J., Rothwell, J., Wasserman, E. M., & Puri, B. K. (2002). *Handbook of transcranial magnetic stimulation.* London: Arnold.

Penrose, R. (1997). *The large, the small and the human mind.* Cambridge, England: Cambridge University Press.

Poeck, K. (1986). The clinical examination for motor apraxia. *Neuropsychologia, 24,* 129–134.

Poreh, A. M. (2000). The quantified process approach: An emerging methodology to neuropsychological assessment. *The Clinical Neuropsychologist, 14,* 212–222.

Poreh, A. M. (Ed.). (2006). *The quantified process approach.* Lisse, Holland: Swets & Zeitlinger.

Pugh, K. G., Milberg, W. P., & Lipsitz, L. A. (2001). Frontal executive dysfunction in community dwelling elderly persons with preserved memory [*abstract*]. *Journal of the American Geriatrics Society, 49,* 77–78.

Randolph, C. (1998). *Manual for the Repeatable Battery for the Assessment of Neuropsychological Status.* San Antonio, TX: The Psychological Corporation.

Raven, J. C. (1994). *Advanced Progressive Matrices Sets I and II.* Oxford: Oxford Psychologists Press. (Original work published 1965)

Raven, J. C. (1995). *Coloured Progressive Matrices Sets A, Ab, B.* Oxford: Oxford Psychologists Press. (Original work published 1947)

Raven, J. C. (1996). *Progressive Matrices: A Perceptual Test of Intelligence.* Oxford: Oxford Psychologists Press. (Original work published 1938)

Raven, J., Raven, J. C., & Court, J. H. (1998). *Raven manual: Section 4. Advanced Progressive Matrices.* Oxford: Oxford Psychologists Press.

Reitan, R. M. (1955). The distribution according to age of a psychological measure dependent upon organic brain functions. *Journal of Gerontology, 10,* 338.

Reitan, R. M., & Davison, L. A. (Eds.). (1974). *Clinical neuropsychology: Current status and applications.* New York: Wiley.

Reitan, R. M., & Wolfson, D. (1993). *The Halstead–Reitan Neuropsychological Test Battery: Theory and clinical interpretation.* Tucson, AZ: Neuropsychology Press.

Reitan, R. M., & Wolfson, D. (1996). Theoretical, methodological and validated bases of the Halstead–Reitan neuropsychological test battery. In I. Grant & K. M. Adams (Eds.), *Neuropsychological assessment of neuropsychiatric disorders* (2nd ed., pp. 3–42). New York: Oxford University Press.

Rey, A. (1941). L'examen psychologie dans les cas d'encephalopathie traumatique. *Archives de Psychologie, 28,* 286–340.

Rey, A. (1958). *L'examen clinque en psychologie.* Paris: Presse Universitaire de France.

Reynolds, C. R. (2002). *Comprehensive Trail-Making Test.* Austin, TX: PRO-Ed.

Reynolds, C. R., & Horton, A. M., Jr. (2006). *Test of Verbal Conceptualization and Fluency examiner's manual.* Austin, TX: PRO-ED.

Reynolds, C. R., & Kamphaus, R. W. (2004). *Behavior Assessment System for Children, Second Edition: Manual.* Circle Pines, MN: American Guidance Service.

Reynolds, C. R., & Kamphaus, R. W. (2003). *Reynolds Intellectual Assessment Scales professional manual.* Lutz, FL: Psychological Assessment Resources, Inc.

Reynolds, C. R., & Voress, J. K. (2007). *Test of Memory and Learning—Second Edition.* Austin, TX: PRO-ED.

Robertson, L. C. (1995). Hemispheric specialization and cooperation in processing complex visual patterns. In F. L. Kitterle (Ed.), *Hemispheric communication: Mechanisms and models* (pp. 301–318). Hillsdale, NJ: Erlbaum.

Robertson, I. H., Ward, T., Ridgeway, V., & Nimmo-Smith, I. (1994). *The Test of Everyday Attention.* Bury St. Edmunds, England: Thames Valley Test Company.

Roid, G. H. (2003). *Stanford–Binet Intelligence Scales, Fifth Edition,* Itasca, IL: Riverside Publishing.

Roth, R. M., Isquith, P. K., & Gioia, G. A. (2005). *Behavior Rating Inventory of Executive Function—Adult Version professional manual.* Lutz, FL: Psychological Assessment Resources.

Rourke, B. P., & Murji, S. (2000). A history of the International Neuropsychological Society: The early years (1965–1985). *Journal of the International Neuropsychological Society, 6,* 491–509.

Ruff, R. M. (1998). *Ruff Figural Fluency Test professional manual.* Odessa, FL: Psychological Assessment Resources.

Ruff, R. M., & Allen, C. C. (1996). *The Ruff 2 & 7 Selective Attention Test professional manual.* Odessa, FL: Psychological Assessment Resources, Inc.

Russell, E., Neuringer, C., & Goldstein, G. (1970). *Assessment of brain damage: A neuropsychological key approach.* New York: Wiley.

Saetveit, J. G., Lewis, D., & Seashore, C. E. (1940). *Revision of the Seashore Measure of Musical Talents* (University of Iowa No. 5). Iowa City: University of Iowa Press.

Sattler, J. M. (1992). *Assessment of children* (3rd ed.). San Diego: Sattler.

Sbordone, R. J. (1996). Ecological validity: Some critical issues for the neuropsychologist. In R. J. Sbordone & C. J. Long (Eds.), *Ecological validity of neuropsychological testing* (pp. 15–41). Orlando, FL: St. Lucie Press.

Sbordone, R. J., & Guilmette, T. J. (1999). Ecological validity: Prediction of everyday and vocational functioning from neuropsychological test data. In J. J. Sweet (Ed.), *Forensic neuropsychology: Fundamentals and practice* (pp. 227–254). Lisse, Netherlands: Swets & Zeitlinger.

Sbordone, R. J., & Saul, R. E. (2000). *Neuropsychology for health care professionals and attorneys* (2nd ed.). Boca Raton, FL: CRC Press.

Sbordone, R. J., Saul, R. E., & Purisch, A. D. (2007). *Neuropsychology for psychologists, health care professionals, and attorneys* (3rd ed.). Boca Raton, FL: CRC Press.

Schmidt, M. (1996). *Rey Auditory Verbal Learning Test: A handbook.* Los Angeles: Western Psychological Services.

Schoenberg, M. R., Duff, K., Scott, J. G., & Adams, R. L. (2003). An evaluation of the clinical utility of the OPIE-3 as an estimate of premorbid WAIS-III FSIQ. *The Clinical Neuropsychologist, 17,* 308–321.

Schoenberg, M. R., Scott, J. G., Duff, K., & Adams, R. L. (2002). Estimation of WAIS-III Intelligence from combined performance and demographic variables: Development of the OPIE-3. *The Clinical Neuropsychologist, 16,* 426–438.

Schretlen, D. (1997). *Professional manual for the Brief Test of Attention.* Odessa, FL: Professional Assessment Resources.

Schretlen, D. J., Munro, C. A., Anthony, J. C., & Pearlson, G. D. (2003). Examining the range of normal intraindividual variability in neuropsychological test performance. *Journal of the International Neuropsychological Society, 9,* 864–870.

Seashore, C. E., Lewis, D., & Saetveit, D. L. (1960). *Seashore Measures of Musical Talents* (rev. ed.). New York: Psychological Corporation.

Seguin, E. (1907). *Idiocy: Its treatment by the physiological method.* New York: Bureau of Publications, Teachers College, Columbia University. (Original work published 1866)

Sharland, M. J., & Gfeller, J. D. (2007). A survey of neuropsychologists' beliefs and practices with respect to the assessment of effort. *Archives of Clinical Neuropsychology, 22,* 213–223.

Sheslow, D., & Adams, W. (2003). *Wide Range Assessment of Memory and Learning, Second Edition administration and technical manual.* Lutz, FL: Psychological Assessment Resources.

Shipley, W. C. (2008). *Shipley Institute of Living Scale—2.* Los Angeles, CA: Western Psychological Services.

Sivan, A. B. (1992). *Benton Visual Retention Test* (5th ed.). San Antonio, TX: Psychological Corporation.

Slick, D., Hopp, G., Strauss, E., & Thompson, G. B. (1999). *Victoria Symptom Validity Test (VSVT) for Windows.* Odessa, FL: Psychological Assessment Resources.

Sliwinski, M., Lipton, R. B., Buschke, H., & Stewart, W. (1996). The effects of preclinical dementia on estimates of normal cognitive functioning in aging. *Journal of Gerontology: Psychological Sciences and Social Sciences, 51,* 217–225.

Smith, A. (1991). *Symbol Digit Modalities Test.* Los Angeles: Western Psychological Services.

Sparrow, S. S., Cicchetti, D. V., & Balla, D. A. (2005). *Vineland Adaptive Behavior Scales Second Edition.* Circle Pines, MN: American Guidance Service.

Stern, R. A., & White, T. (2003). *Neuropsychological Assessment Battery. Administration, scoring, and interpretation manual.* Lutz, FL: Psychological Assessment Resources.

Strauss, E., Sherman, E.M.S., & Spreen, O. (2006). *A compendium of neuropsychological tests: Administration, norms, and commentary* (3rd ed.). New York: Oxford University Press.

Sweet, J. J., Nelson, N. W., & Moberg, P. J. (2006). The TCN/AACN 2005 "Salary Survey": Professional practices, beliefs, and incomes of U.S. neuropsychologists. *The Clinical Neuropsychologist, 20,* 325–364.

Tombaugh, T. N. (1996). *Test of Memory Malingering*. North Tonawanda, NY: Multi-Health Systems.

Tombaugh, T. N., & Rees, L. M. (2008). *Computerized Test of Information Processing technical manual*. North Tonawanda, NY: Multi-Health Systems.

Tulsky, D. S., & Zhu, J. (2000). Could test length or order affect scores on Letter Number Sequencing of the WAIS-III and WMS-III? Ruling out effects of fatigue. *The Clinical Neuropsychologist, 14,* 474–478.

Tuokko, H., Hadjistavropoulos, T., Miller, J. A., Horton, A., & Beattle, B. L. (1995). *The Clock Test*. Toronto, Canada: Multi-Health Systems.

Vanderploeg, R. D. (2000). *Clinician's guide to neuropsychological assessment* (2nd ed.). Mahwah, NJ: Erlbaum.

Vigil Continuous Performance Test: User's guide. (1996). San Antonio, TX: Psychological Corporation.

Wechsler, D. (1955). *Manual for the Wechsler Adult Intelligence Scale*. New York: Psychological Corporation.

Wechsler, D. (1997). Manual for the Wechsler Adult Intelligence Scale—*Third Edition*. San Antonio, TX: Psychological Corporation.

Wechsler, D. (1999). *Manual for the Wechsler Abbreviated Scale of Intelligence*. San Antonio, TX: Harcourt Brace.

Wechsler, D. (2001a). *Wechsler Individual Achievement Test—Second Edition*. San Antonio, TX: Psychological Corporation.

Wechsler, D. (2001b). *Wechsler Test of Adult Reading*. San Antonio, TX: Psychological Corporation.

Wechsler, D. (2002). *Manual for the Wechsler Preschool and Primary Scale of Intelligence—Third Edition*. San Antonio, TX: Psychological Corporation.

Wechsler, D. (2003). *Manual for the Wechsler Intelligence Scale for Children—Fourth Edition*. San Antonio, TX: Psychological Corporation.

Wechsler, D. (2008a). *Wechsler Adult Intelligence Scale—Fourth Edition*. San Antonio, TX: Pearson.

Wechsler, D. (2008b). *Wechsler Fundamentals: Academic Skills*. San Antonio, TX: Psychological Corporation.

Wechsler, D. (2009). *Wechsler Memory Scale—Fourth Edition*. San Antonio, TX: Pearson.

Wechsler, D., Kaplan, E., Delis, D., Fein, D., Maerlander, A., Morris, R., & Kramer, J. (2004). *Wechsler Intelligence Scale for Children, Fourth Edition, Integrated technical and interpretive manual*. San Antonio, TX: NCS: Pearson.

Wechsler, D. & Naglieri, J. A. (2006). *Wechsler Nonverbal Scale of Ability*. San Antonio, TX: Psychological Corporation.

Wecker, N. S., Kramer, J. H., Wisniewski, A., Delis, D. C., & Kaplan, E. (2000). Age effects on executive ability. *Neuropsychology, 14,* 409–414.

Weigl, E. (1927). Zur Psychologie sogenannter Abstraktionsprozesse. *Zeitschrift fur Psychologie, 103,* 2–45 [Translated by M. Rioch and reprinted as "On the psychology of so-called processes of abstraction"]. *Journal of Abnormal and Social Psychology, 36,* 3–33, 1948.

Weinstein, C. (2001). For your information: Definition of a clinical neuropsychologist—Official position of the National Academy of Neuropsychology (Draft). *Massachusetts Neuropsychological Society Newsletter, 11,* 9.

Welsh, K. A., Butters, N., Mohs, R. C., Beekly, D., Edlands, S., Fillenbaum, G., and Heyman, A. (1994). The Consortium to Establish a Registry for Alzheimer's Disease (CERAD) Part V: A normative study of the neuropsychological battery. *Neurology, 44,* 609–614.

Wetzel, L., & Boll, T. J. (1987). *Short Category Test, Booklet Format*. Los Angeles: Western Psychological Services.

Widows, M. R., & Smith, G. P. (2005). *Structured Inventory of Malingered Symptomatology professional manual*. Lutz, FL: Psychological Assessment Resources.

Wiederholt, J. L., & Bryant, B. R. (2001). *Gray Oral Reading Test—Fourth Edition*. Austin, TX: PRO-ED.

Wilkinson, G. S., & Robertson, G. J. (2006). *Wide Range Achievement Test 4 professional manual*. Lutz, FL: Psychological Assessment Resources.

Williams, K. T. (2006). *Expressive Vocabulary Test, Second Edition*. Minneapolis, MN: Pearson Assessments.

Wilson, B. A., Ivani-Chalian, R., & Aldrich, F. (1991). *Rivermead Behavioural Memory Test for Children*. Bury St. Edmunds: Thames Valley Test Company.

Wilson, B. A., Alderman, N., Burgess, P. W., Emslie, H., & Evans, J. J. (1996). *Behavioral Assessment of the Dysexecutive Syndrome*. Bury St. Edmunds, England: Thames Valley Test Company.

Wilson, B. A., Greenfield, E., Clare, L., Baddeley, A., Cockburn, J, Watson, P., Tate, R., Sopena, S., & Nannery, R. (2008). *The Rivermead Behavioural Memory Test, Third Edition*. London: Pearson Assessment.

Wilson, R. S., Rosenbaum, G., Brown, G., Rourke, D., Whitman, D., & Grisell, J. (1978). An index of premorbid intelligence. *Journal of Consulting and Clinical Psychology, 46,* 1554–1555.

Wilson, R. S., Rosenbaum, G., & Brown, G. (1979). The problem of premorbid intelligence in neuropsychological assessment. *Journal of Clinical Neuropsychology, 1,* 49–53.

Woodcock, R. W., McGrew, K. S., & Mather, N. (2001a). *Woodcock Johnson III NU Tests of Cognitive Abilities*. Itasca, IL: Riverside.

Woodcock, R. W., McGrew, K. S., & Mather, N. (2001b). *Woodcock Johnson III NU Tests of Achievement*. Itasca, IL: Riverside.

Woodcock, R. W., McGrew, K. S., & Mather, N. (2007). *Woodcock Johnson III NU*. Itasca, IL: Riverside.

Yeates, K. O. & Bieliauskas, L. A. (2004). The American Board of Clinical Neuropsychology and American Academy of Clinical Neuropsychology: Milestones past and present. *The Clinical Neuropsychologist, 18,* 489–493.

Yesavage, J. A., Brink, T. L., Rose, T. L., Lum, O., Huang, V., Adey, M. B., & Leirer, V. O. (1983). Development and validation of a geriatric depression rating scale: A preliminary report. *Journal of Psychiatric Research, 17,* 37–49.

Annotated Bibliography

BOOKS

Artiola, I., Fortuny, L., Hermosillo, D. H., Heaton, R. K., & Pardee, R. E. (1999). *Manual de normas y procedimientos para la Batería Neuropsicológica en Español*. Brookfield, VT: Swets & Zeitlinger Publishers.

> *This book describes a comprehensive system of assessment procedures designed to assist in the neuropsychological evaluation of the Spanish-speaking individual. It presents the normative data for multiple standard neuropsychological tests collected in Madrid, Spain, and the USA–Mexico border region over a 4-year period.*

Baron, I. S. (2004). *Neuropsychological evaluation of the child*. New York: Oxford University Press.

> *This book is a useful guide for the neuropsychological evaluation of the child client. It combines a collection of normative data for the neuropsychological tests most commonly used with children; it covers issues, considerations, and concepts crucial to the neuropsychological assessment of children. A central part of the book is a review of the tests available for the neuropsychological evaluation of the child.*

Boone, K. B. (Ed.). (2007). *Assessment of feigned cognitive impairment: A neuropsychological perspective*. New York: The Guilford Press.

> *This text synthesizes the expanding literature on symptom simulation in neuropsychological assessment and then provides evidence-based recommendations for clinical and forensic practice. The book contains a comprehensive discussion of symptom fabrication, the available cognitive effort assessment techniques, and the use of these techniques in specific clinical and forensic populations.*

Bush, S. S. (2007). *Ethical decision making in clinical neuropsychology*. New York: Oxford University Press.

> *This book is part of the American Academy of Clinical Neuropsychology and Oxford Workshop Series and as such is an easy-to-read and well-organized guide to the practical application of ethical decision making in the neuropsychological setting. It begins with a discussion of ethical resources, introduces an ethical decision-making model and then applies the APA ethical standards to daily clinical practice,*

Bush, S. S., & Martin, T. A. (1999). *Geriatric neuropsychology: Practice essentials*. New York: Taylor & Francis.

> *This book is a useful guide for the neuropsychological evaluation of the elderly client. It is written with the clinician in mind, but is an evidence-based approach. It covers the pragmatics of the neuropsychological evaluation of the geriatric patient, as well as assessment issues and the selection and use of neurocognitive and psychodiagnostic measures specific for diagnosis in the elderly. There are chapters concerning the more common neurological disorders in the geriatric patient, the relationship of test results and neuroimaging findings, and clinical considerations, such as decision-making capacity and ethical considerations in the assessment of the older patient.*

Clark, D. L., & Boutros, N. N. (1999). *The brain and behavior: An introduction to behavioral neuroanatomy*. Oxford, England: Blackwell Science.

> *This behavioral neuroanatomy book was written with the clinician in mind. It is helpful in understanding functional neuroanatomy, or the neuroanatomy that underlies certain behavior.*

Denney, R. L., & Sullivan, J. P. (Eds.). (2008). *Clinical neuropsychology in the criminal forensic setting.* New York: The Guilford Press.

> *This book focuses on the legal and clinical bases for neuropsychological practice in the criminal forensic setting. It presents clinical suggestions and guidelines in the context of critical legal issues and judicial reasoning, as well as specifically addressing how to conduct criminal neuropsychological evaluations and present neuropsychological findings, opinions, and testimony to the criminal court.*

Grant, I. G., & Adams, K. M. (2009). *Neuropsychological assessment of neuropsychiatric and neuromedical disorders.* New York: Oxford University Press.

> *This book, like its previous editions, is a classic text on the neuropsychological aspects of diseases affecting brain and behavior. It contains chapters describing major test systems (e.g., Halstead–Reitan Battery, Boston Process Approach) and reviews of the application of neuropsychological techniques to a variety of clinical populations and problems. New to this edition is a consideration of common sources of comorbidity such as multiple sclerosis and diabetes, psychiatric and behavioral disorders associated with traumatic brain injury, the effects of cognitive impairment on driving skills, and neuropsychology in relation to everyday living.*

Heaton, R. K., Miller, S. W., Taylor, M. J., & Grant, I. (2004). *Revised comprehensive norms for an expanded Halstead–Reitan Battery: Demographically adjusted neuropsychological norms for African American and Caucasian adults.* Odessa, FL: Psychological Assessment Resources.

> *This book comprises up-to-date normative data for the basic tests from the Halstead–Reitan Battery and many tests not part of the original battery (e.g., Thurstone Fluency). The norms are demographically corrected for gender, age, and education for African American and Caucasian adults.*

Heilman, K. M. (2003). *Clinical neuropsychology* (4th ed.). New York: Oxford University Press.

> *This is a definitive compilation of chapters reviewing the classic neurobehavioral syndromes (e.g., aphasia, apraxia, amnesia, and neglect).*

Jarvis, P. E., & Barth J. T. (1994). *The Halstead–Reitan Neuropsychological Battery: A guide to interpretation and clinical applications.* Odessa, FL: Psychological Assessment Resources.

> *This text was developed to instruct readers how to systematically interpret and apply in a clinical setting the test results from administration of the Halstead–Reitan Battery.*

Lamberty, G. J. (2008). *Understanding somatization in the practice of clinical neuropsychology.* New York: Oxford University Press.

> *This text is part of the American Academy of Clinical Neuropsychology and Oxford Workshop Series designed to educate the clinician about the role somatization can play in neuropsychological assessments. It covers definitional, historical, epidemiological, and other considerations, as well as the current state of knowledge about neuropsychological assessment, comorbid disorders, and treatment approaches in patients with somatization.*

Larrabee, G. J. (Ed.). (2005). *Forensic neuropsychology: A scientific approach.* New York: Oxford University Press.

> *This book represents a comprehensive approach to the application of neuropsychology to legal issues in criminal and civil litigation. Its chapters comprise discussions about general principles, ethics, malingering, neuroimaging, and issues related to particular applications, such as mild traumatic brain injury, assessing civil competencies and criminal responsibility, and medically unexplained symptoms.*

Larrabee, G. J. (Ed.). (2007). *Assessment of malingered neuropsychological deficits.* New York: Oxford University Press.

> *This text was written specifically for the clinical forensic neuropsychologist and is a comprehensive review of the procedures and methods available to evaluate malingered neuropsychological deficits. It presents information on defining malingering and identifying it in neuropsychological evaluations through pattern analysis, specific tests, and standard neuropsychological measures. It focuses on malingered cognitive and*

psychiatric symptoms, but also considers noncredible findings in neurological examination and addresses the topic of coaching.

Lezak, M. D., Howieson, D. B., & Loring, D. W., with Hannay, H. J., & Fischer, J. S. (2004). *Neuropsychological assessment (4th ed.).* New York: Oxford University Press.

This book is a comprehensive general text that includes such topics as neuroanatomy, neuropathology, the procedures involved in neuropsychological evaluation, and an encyclopedic description of neuropsychological tests. This 4th expanded edition includes an increasing number of tests developed in many parts of the world. Although the book has grown considerably in size since the first edition years ago, it maintains the same organization and focus as previous editions.

Loring, D. W. (1999). *INS dictionary of neuropsychology.* New York: Oxford University Press.

The International Neuropsychological Society sponsored this topic dictionary to standardize terminology in the field of neuropsychology. This comprehensive work contains entries from adult and developmental neuropsychology and from neurology, clinical psychology, cognitive psychology, neurosurgery, neuroimaging, neuroanatomy, psychiatry, rehabilitation, and multiple other areas relevant to neuropsychology. This book is also useful because it contains the many abbreviations and acronyms that are found in medical records.

McCaffrey, R. J., Williams, A. D., Fisher, J. M., & Laing, L. C. (1997). *The practice of forensic neuropsychology: Meeting challenges in the courtroom.* New York: Plenum Press.

This book addresses the particular issues confronting the neuropsychologist who enters into the forensic arena and who uses neuropsychology in legal matters. The book includes chapters discussing the history of forensic neuropsychology and special problems associated with it. It also contains chapters that address forensic evaluations in traumatic brain injury, including the special issues pertaining to mild traumatic brain injury. Also discussed are general clinical issues such as fixed versus flexible batteries, determination of premorbid functioning, and special issues relating to testimony.

McCrea, M. A. (2008). *Mild traumatic brain injury and postconcussion syndrome: The new evidence base for diagnosis and treatment.* New York: Oxford University Press.

This text is part of the American Academy of Clinical Neuropsychology and Oxford Workshop Series and summarizes the current evidence base for diagnosing, managing, and treating mild traumatic brain injury (MTBI) and postconcussion syndrome. It covers the definitions of MTBI, the basic and clinical science of MTBI, the natural history of MTBI, and various issues pertaining to postconcussion syndrome.

Mitrushina, M., Boone, K. B., Razani, J., & D'Elia, L. F. (2005). *Handbook of normative data for neuropsychological assessment (2nd ed.).* New York: Oxford University Press.

This book discusses the issues of norms in neuropsychological assessment and then presents a comprehensive review of the normative data for 26 commonly used tests. For each test, the authors include a brief history of the measure, its relationship with demographic factors, a method for evaluating the normative data, a summary of the status of the norms, and summaries of the normative studies. It also provides meta-analysis tables of predicted values for nine of the tests discussed.

Ponton, M. O., & Leon-Carrion, J. (Eds.). (2001). *Neuropsychology and the Hispanic patient: A clinical handbook.* New York: Psychology Press.

This book contains discussion of the cultural, methodological, research, and forensic issues affecting the administration and interpretation of neuropsychological tests to Hispanic individuals. The editors have tried to cover a life-span developmental spectrum from pediatric to geriatric, and they include assessment decision trees and summaries of relevant normative data.

Reitan, R. M., & Wolfson, D. (1993). *The Halstead–Reitan Neuropsychological Test Battery: Theory and clinical interpretation (2nd ed.).* S. Tucson, AZ: Neuropsychology Press.

This text guides the clinician in use of the Halstead–Reitan Neuropsychological Test Battery. The chapters cover the theory and rationale behind the battery and a description of the tests and their administration and scoring, along with the normative guidelines for interpretation of the test results in various adult patient populations.

Reynolds, C. R. (1998). *Detection of malingering during head injury litigation.* New York: Plenum Press.

The book contains chapters describing a variety of current approaches to the assessment of malingering. The chapters cover base rates and test sensitivity and specificity, forced-choice techniques for detecting malingering, detecting malingering through clinical techniques, various fixed test batteries and the MMPI-2, as well as the detection of malingered memory disorders and commonsense approaches to the evaluation of malingering.

Reynolds, C. R., & Fletcher-Janzen, E. (Eds.). (2009). *Handbook of clinical child neuropsychology* (3rd ed.). New York: Springer.

This text covers a comprehensive range of topics in pediatric neuropsychology, including neurodevelopment, assessment and diagnosis, and intervention techniques from a developmental perspective. It emphasizes current best practice, up-to-date science, and emerging theoretical trends in the field.

Rogers, R. (Ed.). (2008). *Clinical assessment of malingering and deception* (3rd ed.). New York: The Guilford Press.

Although not specific to neuropsychological assessment, this book is invaluable in exploring the issues of detection of malingering in various clinical disorders. It explores the issue of malingering in relation to posttraumatic disorders, psychosis, amnesia, and substance abuse. The book also includes chapters on children and deception as well as assessment techniques for the detection of malingering.

Spreen, O., Risser, A. H., & Edgell, D. (1995). *Developmental neuropsychology.* New York: Oxford University Press.

This text is a comprehensive overview of pediatric neuropsychology. It covers early neural and cognitive development, issues in developmental neuropsychology, developmental disorders, and functional disturbances in various areas such as attention, language, and learning.

Strauss, E., Sherman, E. M. S., & Spreen, O. (2006). *A compendium of neuropsychological tests: Administration, norms, and commentary* (3rd ed.). New York: Oxford University Press.

This book is a comprehensive compilation of the most commonly used measures in neuropsychological assessment. The authors discuss general assessment issues such as history taking and report writing and then present a description of each neuropsychological measure, its source, and its purpose, as well as administration, scoring, normative data, and comments on reliability and validity. This book is a must for every clinical neuropsychologist's library.

Yeates, K. O., Ris, M. D., & Taylor, H. G. (1999). *Pediatric neuropsychology: Research, theory and practice.* New York: The Guilford Press.

This book contains review chapters focused on the major medical disorders of childhood with neuropsychological consequences. It includes discussions of assessment and neuroradiology.

JOURNALS

Applied Neuropsychology. Publisher: Psychology Press.

> *This journal is oriented toward clinical neuropsychology and clinically relevant topics. It publishes articles and case studies dealing with assessment, brain functioning, neuroimaging, neuropsychological treatment, and rehabilitation.*

Archives of Clinical Neuropsychology. Publisher: Elsevier.

> *This journal contains articles concerning the psychological aspects of the etiology, diagnosis, and treatment of disorders of the central nervous system. It also publishes articles dealing with delivery and evaluation of services, ethical and legal issues, and approaches to education and training. The Archives of Clinical Neuropsychology is sponsored by the National Academy of Neuropsychologists.*

Archives of Neurology. Publisher: American Medical Association.

> *This journal contains articles relevant to clinical neurology with an emphasis on diagnostic and treatment issues. It contains many articles on the clinical presentation and clinical–pathological correlates of neurological diseases with neuropsychological consequences.*

The Behavioral and Brain Sciences. Publisher: Cambridge University Press.

> *This journal publishes interdisciplinary articles in psychology, neuroscience, behavioral biology, cognitive science, artificial intelligence, linguistics, and philosophy. Articles are circulated to a large number of potential commentators who provide open peer commentary. It is a great source of theoretical ideas in neuropsychology and neuroscience.*

Brain. Publisher: Oxford Journals.

> *This journal publishes articles on a wide range of topics in neurology with many on the neural basis of cognition and behavior. It is one of the most cited journals in neuropsychology and neurology, with many classic papers covering both basic and clinical research.*

Brain and Cognition. Publisher: Elsevier.

> *This journal publishes research articles, theoretical papers, critical reviews, case histories, historical articles, and scholarly notes relevant to cognitive processes and the brain. It contains articles relevant to clinical description of patients but mainly focuses on experimental studies.*

Brain and Language. Publisher: Elsevier.

> *This journal focuses on the neurobiological mechanisms underlying human language. Articles represent both lesion-based approaches as well as functional and structural brain imaging, electrophysiology, and other experimental approaches to the understanding of language representation and processing.*

Child Neuropsychology. Publisher: Psychology Press.

> *This journal presents research on the neuropsychological effects of disorders affecting brain function in children and adolescents. The primary emphasis is on original empirical research, integrating theory, method, and research findings in child and developmental neuropsychology.*

The Clinical Neuropsychologist. Publisher: Psychology Press.

> *This journal publishes in-depth discussions of matters related to educational, clinical, and professional issues important to the neuropsychologist engaged in clinical practice. TCN is the official journal of the American Academy of Clinical Neuropsychology.*

Cognitive and Behavioral Neurology. Publisher: Lippincott Williams & Wilkins.

> *This multidisciplinary journal presents articles containing original data on theoretical concepts, basic brain processes, and major clinical issues in the areas of neuropsychiatry, neuropsychology, and behavioral neurology. It is the official journal of the Society for Behavioral and Cognitive Neurology.*

Cognitive Neuropsychology. Publisher: Psychology Press.

> *This journal publishes research related to the study of cognitive processes from a neuropsychological perspective, including perception, attention, object recognition, planning, language, thinking, memory, and action. It includes research on both normal and pathological processes, as well as neuroimaging and computational modeling.*

Cortex. Publisher: Masson.

> *This international journal presents articles concerning the study of interrelations of the nervous system and behavior with a particular focus on the effects of brain lesions on cognitive functions.*

Developmental Neuropsychology. Publisher: Psychology Press.

> *This international journal presents scholarly research concerning the study of brain and behavior relationships across the lifespan. It publishes articles on the appearance and development of behavioral functions as they relate to brain functions and structures ranging from children to the elderly.*

Journal of Clinical and Experimental Neuropsychology. Publisher: Psychology Press.

> *JCEN publishes scholarly research concerned with behavioral impairment associated with neurological disorders and neurological dysfunction. It includes articles focused on the etiology, course, and prognosis of brain diseases, scientific issues related to psychological assessment in brain disease, and the biological bases of cognitive functions.*

Journal of Cognitive Neuroscience. Publisher: The MIT Press.

> *Contributions in this journal address both descriptions of function and underlying brain events and reflect the interdisciplinary nature of the field covering developments in neuroscience, neuropsychology, and cognitive areas of neuropsychology. Topics covered include development of cognitive psychology, neurobiology, linguistics, computer science, and philosophy.*

Journal of International Neuropsychological Society. Publisher: Cambridge University Press.

> *JINS publishes research articles in both the experimental and clinical or applied areas of neuropsychology. Topics covered include development of cognitive processes, brain–behavior relationships, adult and child neuropsychology, developmental neuropsychology, speech and language disorders, and issues related to behavioral neurology, neuropsychiatry, neuroimaging, and electrophysiology. JINS is the official publication of the International Neuropsychological Society.*

The Journal of Neuropsychiatry and Clinical Neurosciences. Publisher: American Psychiatric Publishing.

> *This is the official journal of the American Neuropsychiatric Association. It publishes articles concerning clinical, educational, and research links between neuroscience and behavior in the broad field of neuropsychiatry.*

Neurocase. Publisher: Psychology Press.

> *This journal publishes single case studies that bear on theoretical issues in brain–behavior relationships, group studies of participants with brain dysfunction that address issues related to the understanding of cognition, as well as reviews of topics in neuropsychology, neuropsychiatry, and neurology.*

Neuropsychologia. Publisher: Elsevier.

> *This journal is an international journal of the neurological, behavioral, and cognitive sciences. Neuropsychologia presents articles promoting the study and understanding of human and animal behavior and cognition and papers integrating experimental, clinical, and theoretical neuropsychological contributions. In addition, the journal publishes articles focusing on the analysis of cognitive disorders resulting from injury or disease of the central nervous system.*

Neuropsychological Rehabilitation. Publisher: Psychology Press.

> *This journal publishes research on human experimental and clinical research related to rehabilitation, recovery of function, and brain plasticity.*

Neuropsychology. Publisher: American Psychological Association.

This journal publishes original, empirical research investigating the relationship between the brain and cognitive, emotional, and behavioral functioning across the life span. Applied clinical research with relevance to experimental investigations is encouraged.

Neuropsychology Review. Publisher: Springerlink.

This publication presents original evaluative review articles concerning significant topics in neuropsychological assessment, neurobehavioral aspects of neurological disorders, and theoretical analyses of human brain function.

Psychological Assessment. Publisher: American Psychological Association.

This journal publishes primarily empirical articles on the research, development, validation, application, and evaluation of clinical psychological assessment instruments, as well as articles on clinical judgment and decision making, methods of measurement of treatment process and outcome, and dimensions of individual differences as they relate to clinical assessment.

Index

Nancy Hebben is an Assistant Clinical Professor of Psychology in the Department of Psychiatry at Harvard Medical School. She holds a doctorate in clinical psychology with a specialty in neuropsychology from Wayne State University in Detroit, Michigan, a degree she earned in 1979. She was licensed as a psychologist provider in Massachusetts in 1980 and in Oklahoma in 2005. She was an intern with Edith Kaplan at the Boston Veterans Administration Medical Center from 1978 to 1979. Then as part of a National Research Service Award, Dr. Hebben did a 3-year postdoctoral fellowship in neuropsychology at the Massachusetts Institute of Technology, where with Suzanne Corkin she studied pain perception in patients undergoing cingulotomy for chronic pain and intractable psychiatric disorders and was fortunate enough to work with Henry Molaison, better known throughout his lifetime as H. M. In 1982 she began at the McLean Hospital as the Chief Consultant in Neuropsychology, a position she held until 1998 when she modified her position to Clinical Associate and began to focus primarily on her private practice. As a clinical neuropsychologist Dr. Hebben has provided neuropsychological assessments of more than 4,000 children, adults, and geriatric patients, and she has supervised more than 4,000 neuropsychological assessments by numerous predoctoral and postdoctoral fellows specializing in neuropsychology. Dr. Hebben is board certified in Clinical Neuropsychology by the American Board of Professional Psychology. She has taught a course in Clinical Psychology each fall for over twenty years at Harvard University Extension School, and she has published numerous papers on topics in clinical neuropsychology and pain perception. Dr. Hebben is a coauthor with Dr. Milberg and Dr. Kaplan of the chapter "The Boston Process Approach to Neuropsychological Assessment" in *Neuropsychological Assessment of Neuropsychiatric & Neuromedical Disorders,* edited by Kenneth Adams and Igor Grant. She has also contributed to both editions of *Essentials of WISC-IV Assessment,* authored by Dawn P. Flanagan and Alan S. Kaufman. Dr. Hebben has consulted with attorneys in Massachusetts, California, Connecticut, Florida, Georgia, Illinois, Kentucky, Maine, Maryland, Michigan,

Missouri, Montana, New Hampshire, New York, Ohio, Oklahoma, Rhode Island, South Carolina, Vermont, Washington, D. C., and Wisconsin in both civil and criminal cases on issues of brain damage, traumatic brain injury, competence, carbon monoxide exposure, electrical injury, and elevated blood lead levels.

William Milberg is an Associate Professor of Psychology in the Department of Psychiatry at Harvard Medical School. He is also the Associate Director for Research of the Boston Division of the New England GRECC (Geriatric Research, Education, and Clinical Center). He holds a doctorate in clinical psychology with a specialty in Neuropsychology from Wayne State University in Detroit, Michigan, a degree he earned in 1978. He was an intern with Edith Kaplan at the Boston Veterans Administration Medical Center from 1978 to 1979 and a postdoctoral fellow at Harvard University in the Department of Psychology from 1979 to 1980. In 1981 he joined the GRECC, where he conducts basic and clinical research on the neuropsychology of cognition. He has taught formal courses in neuroanatomy and neuropsychological assessment at Harvard University for more than 20 years and directs a pre- and postdoctoral clinical training program in Neuropsychology in conjunction with the Psychology Service of the VA Boston Healthcare System. Dr. Milberg is a frequent lecturer on topics related to cognitive assessment in older adults. Dr. Milberg has published almost 100 papers and chapters on various topics in the neuropsychology of higher mental functions. He is a coauthor with Dr. Hebben and Dr. Kaplan of the chapter "The Boston Process Approach to Neuropsychological Assessment" in *Neuropsychological Assessment of Neuropsychiatric & Neuromedical Disorders,* edited by Kenneth Adams and Igor Grant. He is also board certified in clinical neuropsychology by the American Board of Professional Psychology.